UNCERTAIN JUSTICE

This book is dedicated to our son, Chris Greenwood,
and our literary agent, Michele Becker

Uncertain Justice

Canadian Women
and Capital Punishment
1754–1953

F. Murray Greenwood and
Beverley Boissery

DUNDURN PRESS
TORONTO · OXFORD

Editor: Marc Côté
Proofreader: Julian Walker
Design: Jennifer Scott
Printer: Webcom Limited

Canadian Cataloguing in Publication Data

Greenwood, F. Murray (Frank Murray), 1935–
    Uncertain justice: Canadian women and capital punishment, 1754-1953

Includes bibliographical references and index.

ISBN 1-55002-344-6

1. Women prisoners — Canada — History. 2. Death row inmates — Canada — History.
3. Capital punishment — Canada — History. I. Boissery, Beverley, 1939– . II. Title.

HV8699.C2G73 2000   364.66'082'092271   C00-931877-1

1 2 3 4 5   04 03 02 01 00

THE CANADA COUNCIL | LE CONSEIL DES ARTS
FOR THE ARTS | DU CANADA
SINCE 1957 | DEPUIS 1957

Canadä

ONTARIO ARTS COUNCIL
CONSEIL DES ARTS DE L'ONTARIO

We acknowledge the support of the *Canada Council for the Arts* and the *Ontario Arts Council* for our publishing program. We also acknowledge the financial support of the *Government of Canada* through the *Book Publishing Industry Development Program, The Association for the Export of Canadian Books,* and the *Government of Ontario* through the *Ontario Book Publishers Tax Credit* program.

Printed and bound in Canada.
Printed on recycled paper. ♻

www.dundurn.com

Dundurn Press	Dundurn Press	Dundurn Press
8 Market Street	73 Lime Walk	2250 Military Road
Suite 200	Headington, Oxford,	Tonawanda NY
Toronto, Ontario, Canada	England	U.S.A. 14150
M5E 1M6	OX3 7AD	

Table of Contents

Foreword

The purpose of The Osgoode Society for Canadian Legal History is to encourage research and writing in the history of Canadian law. The Society, which was incorporated in 1979 and is registered as a charity, was founded at the initiative of the Honourable R. Roy McMurtry, a former attorney general for Ontario, now Chief Justice of Ontario, and officials of the Law Society of Upper Canada. Its efforts to stimulate the study of legal history in Canada include a research support program, a graduate student research assistance program, and work in the fields of oral history and legal archives. The Society publishes volumes of interest to the Society's members that contribute to legal-historical scholarship in Canada, including studies of the courts, the judiciary and the legal profession, biographies, collections of documents, studies in criminology and penology, accounts of significant trials, and work in the social and economic history of the law.

Current directors of The Osgoode Society for Canadian Legal History are Robert Armstrong, Jane Banfield, Tom Bastedo, Brian Bucknall, Archie Campbell, J. Douglas Ewart, James Flaherty, Martin Friedland, John Honsberger, Kenneth Jarvis, Allen Linden, Virginia MacLean, Wendy Matheson, Colin McKinnon, Roy McMurtry, Brendan O'Brien, Peter Oliver, Paul Reinhardt, Joel Richler, James Spence, and Richard Tinsley.

The annual report and information about membership may be obtained by writing: The Osgoode Society for Canadian Legal History, Osgoode Hall, 130 Queen Street West, Toronto, Ontario. M5H 2N6. Telephone: 416-947-3321. E-Mail: mmacfarl@lsuc.on.ca.

In recent years, scholars in all disciplines, feminists and traditionalists, have increasingly recognized how significant issues of gender are in understanding most aspects of the human condition. Indeed gender as a category of analysis has assumed a place at least as central as class and race in the very best historical work.

In *Uncertain Justice,* the husband and wife author team of Beverley Boissery and Murray Greenwood apply gender analysis to the study of the trial and execution of female criminals in colonial and modern Canada.

Through eight major case studies and many minor ones *Uncertain Justice* reveals the evolution of this aspect of capital punishment across the course of Canadian history. An analytical introduction and conclusion bracket the case studies and together with two thematic chapters engage critical gender issues. Most notably these include the execution of those who may have been innocent, the long exclusion of women from criminal juries, the emergence of the "battered woman syndrome," and jury nullification of many laws, including infanticide and abortion. Two themes which loom particularly large are the use of paternalistic 'sham chivalry' to protect individual women at the expense of stereotyping them generally as weak-minded and the relentlessly political nature of much of the criminal law process, particularly with regard to the exercise of mercy. *Uncertain Justice* is an engagingly written book which offers numerous insights into one of the darker sides of Canadian criminal justice history.

R. Roy McMurtry
President

Peter N. Oliver
Editor-in-Chief

Acknowledgments

Friends helped in many ways. Douglas Hay of York University gave us an important research lead on the trial of Marie Corriveau. Patricia Kennedy of the National Archives of Canada put us on to the "murder" committed by Newfoundland's Eleanor Power. Historian Gary Bannister generously shared his notes and sent us a processed copy of the trial transcript, thus saving us much money and many hours of work. Jim Phillips of the University of Toronto informed us of the piracy proceedings against Margaret Jordan and Barry Cahill of the Public Archives of Nova Scotia supplied all relevant records. Our family physician, Dr. Melodie Herbert, assisted greatly by explaining some of the intricacies of various autopsy reports.

Only fellow authors can understand the debt we owe Drs. Carla Paterson of U.B.C. and Barry Wright of Carleton for reading and critiquing the manuscript. We are also greatly indebted to University of Toronto's Professor Carolyn Strange for aid and advice and to The Osgoode Society for Canadian Legal History for its generous research grant and the four critiques it organized. Editor-in-Chief Peter Oliver gave important continued support, as did our friend George Tuttle. Osgoode's indomitable Marilyn MacFarlane was her usual efficient, friendly self and Marilyn's husband Bill, of the Toronto Metropolitan Police, generously shared his knowledge of ballistics. Kirk Howard, publisher of Dundurn Press, gave us enthusiastic acceptance and editor Marc Côté helped us integrate the legal and narrative sections and polish the final manuscript.

Last but not least, we thank our agent Michele Becker for her "chivying" and encouragement and our son Chris for countless hours of reading, research and critiquing, especially with regard to women on Canadian criminal juries.

Thank you all again.

Introduction

Nineteen passengers and a crew of four died instantly on September 9, 1949 when their Quebec Airways plane fell out of the sky. After crashing against a rocky bluff near the St. Lawrence, about seventy kilometres north-east of Quebec City, the DC-3 plunged into dense brush below. Parts of it littered the ground and hung from trees. Most of the bodies jammed the front end in a tragic, "mangled disorder."[1]

Oscar Tremblay, an eyewitness to the crash, was one of the first on the scene. In a sidebar to the main story in the *Montreal Gazette* the next day, he described the plane falling from the sky, the horrific sight of the mangled bodies and his feelings: "We thought we would find the plane in flames but we didn't. There was no fire at all, just a mass of wreckage and all those bodies. There was nothing we could do so we came out of the bush and reported [the accident] ... but I'll never forget that sight as long as I live." As grieving relatives hurried to Quebec City, two independent teams began investigating the crash.

The passengers on the ill-fated Montreal-Baie Comeau flight had been a typical cross-section of the travelling public: families with small children; important executives such as E.T. Stannard of New York, president of Kennecott Copper Company; and Mrs. J.A. Guay, wife of a Quebec City jeweller. Within two days most of the bodies had been identified and a few details of the tragedy became general knowledge. Evidence pointed to a violent explosion before the crash and on September 14 the *Montreal Gazette* reported that a metal box, recovered from the crash site, would be featured in the coroner's inquest.

Shortly before the end of September 1949, investigators revealed the metal box to have been a time bomb. J. Albert Guay was subsequently charged with his wife's murder and police continued to investigate two dupes: Marguerite Pitre, a friend of Guay's, and her paralysed brother, Généreux Ruest. For the grieving relatives and friends of the victims as well as the general public, the horror was complete. The third-worst plane crash in Canadian history to that point had been a murder plot. Twenty-three innocent people had died so that J. Albert Guay might marry his teenage mistress.

The prosecution against Guay moved quickly and resulted in his hanging, January 12, 1951. Before his death, however, he made a statement, raising Marguerite Pitre and Ruest from the level of dupes to accomplices. As a result, they were charged with murder. At her trial Mrs. Pitre confidently cracked jokes. Invariably dressed in black, she became known in the French-language newspapers as Madame le Corbeau, or The Crow. English-language wits responded with a slogan, based on one that advertised the popular band leader, Sammy Kaye; listeners were advised to Swing and Sway with Sammy Kaye. Pitilessly, members of the public mocked Pitre and Ruest. "Swing and Sway," they taunted, "with J. Albert Guay."

Was Mrs. Pitre a dupe? Did she check the package containing the bomb onto the plane knowing full well that its detonation would lead to the deaths of twenty-three people? Although a case can be made for her possible innocence, which two judges of appeal accepted, Marguerite Pitre's association with J. Albert Guay led to the scaffold in 1953. She was the last woman executed in Canada.

Uncertain Justice: Canadian Women and Capital Punishment, 1754-1953 tells the stories of many women charged with various offences, all carrying the death penalty. In 1754, capital crimes were more than two hundred. By the time of Marguerite Pitre's execution, that number had dwindled to two — treason and murder — and in 1976 the death penalty was abolished altogether in Canada.

Mrs. Pitre was one of approximately one hundred women to die on the gallows in Canadian history.[2] Hundreds more faced the prospect, but were either found not guilty or had their sentences commuted. Through studies of some of these cases, *Uncertain Justice* shows how deeply English and Canadian criminal law has been governed by male patriarchal attitudes, which many times can be called a 'sham' form of chivalry. This observation is not necessarilly new, but sham chivalric attitudes, their interplay with criminal law, and its patriarchal administration are a major theme of this book.

While the fates of women are, of course, the book's focus, the second theme highlights, mainly through profiles and biographical vignettes, the evolution of Canadian criminal law. This study extends to all those tried on capital charges, men as well as women. Given the recent reversals in many convictions, it is fascinating to study the history of the convictions and executions of innocent people and the nullification of the law by juries. When the first trials were held in the British colonies that would later become Canada, there were no defence attornies. Later, the lack of a first-rate lawyer played a part in the execution of Elizabeth Workman in 1873. Many, many Canadian men shared her fate for the same reason. Therefore by including males in this study of capital punishment in Canada, *Uncertain Justice* shows something about the lot of all citizens in our country — past, present, and potentially future.

In late eighteenth century Britain, pickpockets frequently plied the crowd while one of their kin dangled from the hangman's rope. These spectacles, and the derisive scoff-law involved, were part of the "bloody code," which in 1800 included more than the previously-mentioned two-hundred capital offences. These ranged from servants stealing forty shillings (£2) or more from a dwelling house (at a time when a senior male servant might earn £12 annually, excluding room and board);[3] shoplifting over £5; burglary; horse or cattle stealing; highway robbery; to rape, murder and treason. The idea was simple, yet it resounds today in many debates on our justice system: punitive laws and punishment would terrify the populace into obedience. Regular evidence of this judicial harshness would gain points from the law and order segment. Frequent commutations demonstrated the reasonableness and compassion of government. Thus, the bloody code was a central part of royal and aristocratic rule. But as the business class gained influence, especially following the Great Reform Act of 1832, it attacked this kind of justice, advocating the more sure sanction of the penitentiary and, by the 1840s, it had succeeded.[4] Naturally enough these developments in Britain found their way to what we now call Canada. By 1877 Canadian capital crimes were limited to treason, murder and piracy, with rape after 1873 being punished either by death or imprisonment between seven years and life. Piracy eventually became an optional capital crime as well.

Several factors played a part in mitigating such a rigorous capital code. Private citizens were often unwilling to prosecute property crimes if they thought the accused might be singled out for execution. Juries frequently condoned "pious perjury" — ignoring facts no matter how strong the evidence — frequently, undervaluing stolen goods, effectively commuting the punishment.[5] In one instance, despite absolute proof that the pilfered property was worth £3. 10s., the jurors valued it as two pence below the two shillings capital limit. In other cases they recommended mercy — pleas which were, however, by no means always allowed. Presiding judges commonly indulged in restrictive legal interpretations, such as deciding in 1774 that a charge of stealing a cow could not be sustained since the animal, two and a half years old, had not calved. Clearly, then, it was not a cow but a heifer. The use of force to enter or even break open a desk inside a store negated the capital nature of shoplifting in other cases (1711, 1726, 1787).[6]

The benefit of clergy was an antiquated exemption that was first used in the early middle ages to remove ordained clerics from the jurisdiction of the royal courts. By 1350, it had been extended to all male accused who could read. By the turn of the eighteenth century, females could claim it and the necessity to exhibit literacy by reciting Psalm 51:1 was abolished. In general it could not be pled a second time for the same offence. In the later middle ages, certain crimes began to be excluded from the benefit (usually by statute): forgery, murder, treason, rape, burglary, larceny in a dwelling house or a shop, sexual intercourse with a girl under ten years, highway robbery, buggery and so on. These remained the true capital offences. Except for recidivists, benefit of clergy was retained until its abolition in 1827 (later in what became Canada) for grand larceny (stealing more than a shilling) and manslaughter — to give two examples.

By far, the most important mitigator of capital punishment was the royal prerogative of mercy. Death sentences by hanging were regularly commuted to lesser punishments, usually transportation from England, with jail sentences becoming important in the early nineteenth century. In the Canadas, banishment was the common substitute until the opening of the Kingston Penitentiary in the 1830s. During the period covered in this book, 1754-1953, a softening of public opinion greatly increased the commutation rate. For instance, in London and Middlesex in the 1750s, that rate was only about 32%; by the 1790s it had risen above 72%.[7] Commutations from the beginning had been influenced by judges' reports and socially respectable intervenors, for the bloody code was part and parcel of governance by the landed classes, especially outside the big cities. At times governments heightened the drama by insuring that prisoners were saved from hanging while actually on the gallows with the noose in place!

Pregnant women convicted of a capital crime could have their execution deferred through a procedure known as "pleading the belly." In such a case, after the convicted woman said she was pregnant, the sheriff engaged in a slapdash roundup of a "jury of matrons," twelve supposedly married and discreet women familiar with childbirth. This group questioned and physically examined the prisoner to determine whether she was "quick with child," that is, the fetus had begun to move and was therefore alive. Studies of the process during the reigns of Elizabeth I and James I show that fully 20% of capitally convicted women successfully "pled their bellies."[8] In the Old Bailey Sessions Papers, 1677-1800, James C. Oldham found a 47% success rate.[9] There were of course abuses. Matrons hanging around the court house were often found to be friends of the convict. In 1698, a Frenchman named Misson observed a common and understandable practice in the jails: frequently, the women declared "that they are with Child, and often too the poor Criminals are ... for they came never so good Virgins into the Prison, there are a sett of Wags that take Care of these Matters ... [so they might] save their Lives."[10]

Most scholars of this practice in England equate a successful pleading with the likelihood of commutation.[11] This is not to say that after being delivered of the child the women were never executed. Indeed, sometimes their babies suckled until the very last moment.[12] In St. John's Newfoundland, 1834, Catherine Snow was hanged following a successful examination by matrons.[13] The general tendency in belly cases was but one of the many aspects of leniency afforded capitally-convicted women. By the 1880s in England and Canada, medical practitioners had replaced the jury of matrons.

It is well known that throughout Europe and North America, since the eighteenth century, the crime rate for women, especially for violent offences, has been much lower than that for men. In Halifax, between 1750 and 1800, for example, charges against females for all offences constituted less than 15% of the total. The difference was even more pronounced in capital cases, where charges against women accounted for 10% of the total.[14] In the District of Montreal during the half-century after 1812, female convictions in the Court of King's/Queen's Bench (which dealt with capital and other serious offences) ran at approximately 5.4% of all convictions.[15] Carolyn Strange finds that in post-Confederation Canada men were convicted of capital crimes at a rate of more than twenty-five times that of women.[16] The relative lack of violence by women in England, from 1650 to 1850, has been attributed to female socialization, less use of potentially lethal tools, and less alcoholic consumption, among other factors.[17]

The nature of female crime differed enormously in other ways from the masculine variety. Overwhelmingly domestic or private, it occurred primarily within the family household grouping. Juries and officials thought much of it relatively excusable, such as most dwelling house larcenies by servants and infanticide. Other cases, such as murders by domestics of their employers, were considered heinous. Occasionally women were not only involved in public crimes, but took the leadership role usually reserved for men. Margaret Whippy, the leader of a burglary gang which stole several barrels of gunpowder was hanged in Halifax, 1768, probably for acting beyond her prescribed gender role as docile subject or at worst a duped and lowly assistant to a male criminal. In sentencing Whippy's gang members to death, Chief Justice Jonathan Belcher stressed that "Tho' the Offence committed by you all is of the same Species, yet it is differently heightened in the Sex, the Malice & Deliberation of One."[18]

Mary Campbell of Montreal had already suffered embarrassment in the pillory for petty larceny when she was convicted of highway robbery in 1794. By assaulting a certain Pierre Bourdon, she had put him "in bodily fear and danger of his life" when she stole a purse of money totalling thirty shillings. Governor Lord Dorchester obviously considered this violent recidivist a serious threat to society, ordering her banished from the entire British Empire, not just Lower Canada as sometimes occurred, and to be escorted to the United States frontier by a civil official or if necessary by a military guard. Although extremely reluctant to use capital punishment, Dorchester had his secretary inform the Montreal sheriff that "you will clearly explain to her the Terms upon which she is pardoned, & that if she returns to the Province she will as surely be executed as convicted."[19]

Female murderers overwhelmingly committed private and not public acts of violence, often killing close family members (including common law) or those persons living in the household, that is, grandchildren, stepchildren, companions, employers and husbands. Not included as victims for the purposes of these statistics are landlords/landladies, neighbours or co-workers. Given the definition, forty-five of fifty-five murders by women after Confederation were private.[20]

Of the ten public murders committed during this time, none assumed a manly or leadership role. Elizabeth Popovich ended on the gallows in 1946 for helping her husband, also executed, rob an Ontario store owner.[21] Marguerite Pitre seems to have been enthralled by and definitely beholden to her creditor-friend, J. Albert Guay.[22] Thrill-seeking Florence Lassandro, of Fernie, British Columbia, liked to drive with rum-runners, carrying a pistol of her own. Driving with Emilio Picariello, "emperor" of the runners in 1922, Lassandro fatally shot a constable in Alberta before an eye-witness.[23] Her pathetic plea on the gallows — "Why do you hang me when I didn't do anything? Is there no one here who has any pity?" — is a reminder that insistence on innocence can sometimes be misleading.[24]

Private murders can be divided into those punished severely and others for which leniency was predictable. Husband killers often ended on the gallows. The four such pre-Confederation convicts recounted by Frank Anderson in his *A Dance with Death: Canadian Women and the Gallows 1754-1953* were hanged. The English courts and public treated female servants who murdered or attempted to murder their employers quite harshly.[25] While the sample for Canada is very small, it suggests the British pattern would have been followed had there been many more cases. Julia Murdock was hanged in Toronto, 1837, for murdering her employer with rat-poison, despite her youth, beauty and a strong recommendation for mercy from the jury. Notwithstanding many interventions in her favour, disturbed immigrant orphan Hilda Blake was executed, 1899, in Brandon, Manitoba for a similar crime.[26] Grace Marks (made famous by the Margaret Atwood novel, *Alias Grace*) was convicted of murdering her master and served almost thirty years in prison. Teenie Maloney, who killed her mistress, probably escaped the noose only because her crime in retrospect seemed to point to manslaughter, not the murder for which she was convicted.

Other private murders were dealt with leniently. From the second half of the nineteenth century, it appears that executions for infanticide were very rare, if any existed at all.[27] In Canada, where convictions were obtained (and these, as in England, were very difficult to come by from the eighteenth century on) there seems to be no evidence of an execution. The secondary sources dealing with pre-Confederation cases give us examples only of pardons or nothing at all.[28] In each of the seven known cases after Confederation, the death penalty was commuted.[29] Surprisingly, child killing (a year or older) by mothers was also treated leniently, probably because of male assumptions about female mental imbalance.[30] In Lower Canada, in 1829, Judith Couture, who killed her five children, escaped the gallows.[31] So did Minnie McGee of Prince Edward Island who, in 1912, murdered her ten year old son and five other children. Strongly recommended for mercy by the jury (but not the judge), officials in the Justice Department deemed her medically, if not legally, insane and commuted her sentence to life imprisonment.[32]

Accused people in the eighteenth and early nineteenth centuries faced a heavily stacked deck. There was no legal aid, no genuine right of appeal in Canada before 1892 and no power to testify in one's own behalf until 1893. It was only in 1836, in Britain and both Canadas, that defendants were entitled to legal counsel in felony (capital) cases, as opposed to high treason and, illogically, non-capital misdemeanours such as assault or perjury. Before this, courts from the 1730s almost always allowed accused felons to employ counsel, but did not allow those professionals to address the jury. This led to pathetic spectacles, such as an illiterate man in 1801, in Quebec City, offering what the newspaper report of the trial described as a one sentence defence of his life.[33]

For non-capital crimes there were numerous penalties enforced during the period 1754-1953: branding, whipping, the pillory, transportation (first to the American colonies, then to Australia), banishment and jail terms (usually of two years or less, until the creation of penitentiaries). For high treason committed by males, in practice, the convict was drawn to the place of execution on a sledge or hurdle, hanged until dead, eviscerated, beheaded and, at least symbolically, quartered. The heads, after treatment with preservatives, were usually displayed in public places. Much of this gruesome practice lasted until 1814. The mandatory sentence for murder was death by hanging, followed by dissection of the body (until 1832 in England). Particularly atrocious murders by males (until 1834) could result in an order that the corpse be hung in chains ("gibbeted"). By 1783, the use of a drop or trap door to break the prisoner's neck and bring about instantaneous death was becoming standard practice. It replaced lingering strangulation, during which the victim might have to have his or her legs pulled on, and which allowed a corrupt sheriff and friends to occasionally cut down the prisoner alive.

Females who failed in their duty of obedience by murdering their employers or husbands were guilty of what was known as petit or petty treason. The penalty for this crime was to be drawn to the gallows on a sledge, rather than riding in a cart, and to be burned alive at the stake. By the eighteenth century, hangmen had adopted the practice of trying to strangle the prisoner before the flames reached her. This punishment was altered in 1790 and somewhat later in British North America.[34] Such convicts thereafter were drawn to the place of execution, hanged and dissected. Men who murdered their wives were not deemed guilty of any treason and were treated as murderers. Likewise, male servants who killed their masters, though petty traitors, were hanged. Petit treason was abolished in Britain in 1828 and shortly afterwards in Canada.[35]

Until 1868 in Britain and a year later in Canada, executions were public, often attracting thousands of spectators. Everywhere in the North Atlantic triangle, except perhaps Puritan New England, the atmosphere was that of a carnival, complete with drunkenness, betting, swearing, stealing, brawling and screams of pity or vituperation.[36]

One hanging in London in 1807 drew the incredible number of 40,000 spectators and ironically left almost a hundred dead or dying on the street when this "death-deterring" scene was over.[37] The carnival-like atmosphere prevailed also in British North America. John Ross Robertson, a journalist and local historian wrote in his *Landmarks of Toronto* (six volumes 1894-1914) of an execution in 1816 that had "a great crowd of people surrounding the yard and when [the condemned farmer Elijah] Dexter was led out a great cheer went up. Farmers had driven their families for miles to witness the sight and business, for the time was entirely suspended." According to Robertson, an 1828 York hanging attracted more than "ten thousand people and the greatest excitement prevailed."

As mentioned earlier, we have built on the pioneering work of many fine scholars: Carolyn Strange, Constance Backhouse, Franca Iocovetta and Jim Phillips, to name just a few. But many gross errors abound in some previous studies of Canadian women and capital punishment. Two shocking examples, from a sloppy professional and a populariser highlight this. D. Owen Carrigan, then a professional historian, wrote that in early Halifax a servant girl was executed after some household silver went missing: "The following spring, when the snow thawed, the cutlery was found in the yard ... She obviously had taken the silver outside to clean it and then forgotten it."[38] Jim Phillips's many careful searches in the Nova Scotia archives failed to turn up any reference to such a case.[39]

Anderson in his recent book, *A Dance with Death*, outdoes even this by claiming Marie-Anne Crispin (Bélisle), involved in a love triangle, was executed in Montreal for murdering her husband in 1858.[40] Anderson has this woman beat up the hangman who came to her cell and claims "she managed to shove several guards off the [gallows] platform before she was finally overpowered." Three newspaper accounts of the execution and one pamphlet on it make no mention of this incident and all reports have her spending her last hours in pious devotions.[41]

We would like to explain the format of the book. It is written mainly for the non-specialist — that is, for anyone who would like to know more about Canadian women and capital punishment. *Uncertain Justice* has four case studies from the pre-Confederation period in jurisdictions where English criminal law was applied (1754-1866), and four following Confederation (1867-1953). The first comes from 1754 Newfoundland; the second from Quebec, or Canada as it was called in 1763. The last chapter tells of two women facing the gallows in the 1940s and 1950s for killing their newly born children.

In Chapters 5, 6, and 10, and in the Conclusion, the book's themes are more fully explored. The horrifying possibilities of the executions of innocent people are raised, as are other topics — such as the battered-woman syndrome and jury nullification of the law. Chapter 6 reveals two surprising features from our study. The first concerns the evolution of women's "equality" with men as applied to the criminal jury panel. As hard as it may seem to understand, women were not equal with men in this across the country until the 1970s. The second concerns the effect a recommendation to mercy might have on an accused's fate. Both these are original and exploratory and written for the specialists as well as the general public.

Chapter One
The Eleanor Power Story

The summer solstice of 1754 had passed and, for a few blissful days, the near-constant rain, fog and drizzle of Newfoundland's weather were the things of memory. Soldiers and workers alike spent many of the long twilight hours in the pubs and taverns of St. John's and its surrounding villages. Ale and talk were cheap; so, too, were dreams. One sailor might brag that if only he had the money of one of the fishing admirals, he'd buy the finest mansion in the city of Dublin.[1] A servant might dream of being free from another's beck and call. But one night in Freshwater Bay, Eleanor Power stopped all such talk among friends by claiming that she knew how to make herself and these dreamers richer by one thousand pounds.[2]

From her work— either as a washerwoman or a maid-of-all-work — in the house of William Keen Sr., a merchant and one of Newfoundland's first justices of the peace, Eleanor had been afforded the opportunity to watch the elderly magistrate surreptitiously visit one of his trunks. The care that he took not to be observed convinced her that she had discovered the place where he kept his valuables. With his wealth an open secret, talk soon turned to robbing the prominent citizen.

Not only was Keen rich, he was deeply detested. After emigrating from Massachusetts in 1704, he had become a trader — the first to exploit the salmon fishery north of Cape Bonavista — and by 1740 he had created a thriving business.[3] A law-and-order man, he campaigned vigourously for a permanent, year-round justice system, with his attempts resulting in his appointment as a magistrate in 1729-30. Rising quickly through the judicial ranks, Keen became a commissary of the vice-admiralty court in 1736, Naval Officer for the port of St. John's in 1742, and Newfoundland Prize Officer in 1744. This legal power, his wealth, and the fact that the governors of the colony were in residence only during the fishing season, made Keen tremendously influential in Newfoundland.

Keen's judicial decisions were harsh and unpopular. In particular, he seemed to enjoy a running battle with the military stationed in St. John's, often placing soldiers in custody without notifying their commander, an uncommon practice contributing to his unpopularity.[4] On one such occasion, he sentenced a soldier to twenty days in jail and twenty-one lashes for allegedly stealing three potatoes — even though no one testified against him.[5]

By 1754, protests about Keen's judicial high-handedness reached far-off London. On May 28, the Board of Trade — the institution responsible for advising on colonies — considered a letter from a Colonel Hopson who had forwarded complaints against Keen from one of his officers. A Captain Aldridge had accused Keen of "unjust and illegal proceedings." The Board took the complaint seriously enough to order Governor Hugh Bonfoy, on his return to Newfoundland, to investigate the "outrages."[6]

Keen's son William Jr. — himself a justice — was also hated for his decisions. In 1754, he presided over the trial of a John Batt, accused of stealing a pair of shoes and their buckles. Finding Batt guilty, Keen Jr. sentenced him to fifteen lashes on his bare back as well as several hours in the stocks. It was not a popular verdict. After hearing rumours that a mob would interfere, the younger Keen decided to ensure that the sentence would be carried out. Before he could be tied to the whipping post, the convicted Batt escaped into a crowd of bystanders. After Keen intervened and the sentence was carried out, someone pointed to Batt's accuser, a John Vincent, yelling, "Now gentlemen, if you would be all of my mind, we will take that fellow and tie him to the post, and serve him in the same way." The gentlemen needed no further persuasion and enthusiastically began to assault Vincent. Once again, the intrepid younger Keen was forced into action as he later recalled. It was "with difficulty," he wrote in his report on the incident, that "I got him out of their hands; and it is my opinion, that had the man been left to their mercy, he would have been in danger of his life." The mob — deprived of its sport — grudgingly dispersed, only to return a couple of days later to the whipping post. Fuelled by a large quantity of *flip* (a potent drink of equal parts dark rum and spruce beer) they pulled out the irons that held the prisoner's hands to the stocks. Exhilarated by their success, the disenchanted group marched over to Keen's estate "in a riotous manner, and with hatchets, ... did there and then cut a broad flake [a long platform for drying and curing fish], being six beams in length, belonging to the said William Keen."[7]

Given the harshness of both father and son in executing their judicial responsibilities, it was no wonder Eleanor Power's friends felt little compunction about stealing from such a powerful but unpopular family. As they conspired, considering and rejecting various plans during the summer of 1754, their goal became something of an open secret in Freshwater Bay. By the last week of August a group of eight — including a number of soldiers — had coalesced around Eleanor and her husband Robert, under the leadership of soldier Edmund McGuire. Their strategy was simple. Eleanor and Robert Powers, Matthew Halluran, Paul MacDonald and Lawrence Lumley would sail a skiff to Keen's wharf in Quidi Vidi, a small fishing village near the mouth of the St. John's harbour where Keen had a summer house. There, they would meet up with Edmund McGuire and his soldiers and, after reconnoitring, break into the house at midnight.

The plot went awry from the beginning. On the way, Eleanor asked the boatman, Nicholas Tobin, if he knew "what was going on," then proceeded to blurt out the entire plot. Maybe to save the day, Lumley asked Tobin if he wanted to be a partner, promising "that he would get as much money as would last him, as long as he should live."[8] The boatman succumbed to the lure of easy wealth and later would be as easily persuaded to inform on the group once things had gone disastrously amiss.

The augmented party landed at King's Wharf, met up with one of the soldiers, Dennis Hawkins, and walked to Keen's summer house. As night fell, they waited, promising to be true and not betray each other; they each sealed their oaths by kissing a prayer book. Then, Halluran, McGuire and Lumley reconnoitred the grounds and came back disgusted. The place was crowded with people gutting and filleting fish and there was little chance they'd be able to enter Keen's house unobserved. Dismayed but not disheartened, the group went home. They would try again.

The second time, the main group walked to Keen's house before meeting the soldiers. Again, Matthew Halluran, armed with a scythe, investigated the house. Again, he returned disgruntled. Keen Jr. had arrived, his sloop and another moored at the wharf. The conspirators left, reassuring each other that the third time would be the charm.

That opportunity came on September 9, 1754. Deciding the time was right, Halluran sent Tobin to inform Eleanor and Robert Powers about 3:00 p.m. of his decision. Seven hours later, they — with Eleanor dressed in men's clothes[9] — met Tobin and MacDonald at the lower part of Keen's estate. Time passed; an hour, then two. Finally, Halluran arrived with four soldiers (McGuire, Hawkins, John Munhall and a new recruit, John Moody). The military men brought arms — two muskets and two bayonets.

Once again, the conspirators crept towards Keen's house, then split up. Tobin, chosen to act as a watchman, was given a musket by one of the soldiers and told to fire if anyone challenged him. Robert Power, also armed with a musket, stood guard at the nearby house of Edward Whealand. Hawkins guarded Whealand's door; MacDonald, Keen's. The other group, led by Halluran, broke into the house. Once Eleanor pointed out the precious chest, they grabbed it and ran. Lumley and Halluran took some silver spoons with them.

Reunited in the woods of the estate, the conspirators seemed flushed with success. No one had seen them, no hue and cry had been raised. Edmund McGuire broke open the chest, then gasped. The others crowded forward and startled, they too viewed the magistrate's "treasure" — liquor.

Their hopes of wealth shattered, Eleanor Power and Lawrence Lumley left the scene.[10] Tobin and Hawkins, also bitterly disappointed, tried to leave as well, but John Munhall grabbed them. It wasn't over, he told them. They'd come for Keen's riches and that's what they'd get. Edmund McGuire concurred, looking at the terrified men and swearing he'd shoot anyone who left. Furthermore, he told them, he was only sorry he hadn't shot Eleanor Power when he'd had the chance. After all her boasting, what had they got? Not the old man's gold and silver. After listening to her blarney and taking the risks, what had they found? Bottles of booze.

Munhall told Tobin he might as well take one of the bottles and "drink a dram." The rest of them followed suit and while they drank McGuire brooded on the fiasco. He had unfinished business with Justice Keen. Just weeks before, the magistrate had sentenced him to trans-portation after he had assaulted a constable.[11] The more he thought about the matter, the more he wanted revenge. If he could not get money, if Keen would not tell them where his riches were, he would "punish" the magistrate.

Bolstered thus by threats and alcohol, a more pugnacious group returned to the house. Again, Tobin and Hawkins watched Whealand's door with guns in their hands. Robert Power, musket in hand, defended the path between the houses and Paul MacDonald guarded the kitchen door. Entering the house, Halluran and McGuire climbed the stairs from the kitchen to Keen's bedroom. As they stealthily reached for a chest under his bed, the magistrate woke. Pitilessly, McGuire put a quilt over his head. But the old man had spunk and fought the intruders, managing to put out the candle carried by McGuire before catching Halluran by the leg, "all the time yelling, murder." Halluran struck Keen twice with the scythe he carried, while McGuire chopped at him with the musket's butt head. Just before they left, Halluran grabbed a pair of knee breeches and a single silver buckle to be added to the spoons he'd taken earlier.[12] With nothing more to show for their bloody night's work, the men disbanded and gloomily went home.

Keen lingered for ten days before dying, September 29, 1754.

The crime was a sensation and the authorities were quick to act. Tobin, smelling the wind, quickly turned King's evidence, implicating his associates. Their subsequent trial in the court of oyer and terminer would be the first for murder in Newfoundland's judicial history. It may even have been illegal.

Since the founding of Newfoundland, England had oscillated over the question of whether or not the colony should have permanent settlers. Newfoundland's main benefit was the cod fishing industry, exploited by merchants from England's western counties — Hampshire, Devon, Somerset and Dorset. The benefit was twofold: the sheer value of the cod fishery and it was a training ground for seamen who could then be recruited into the royal navy as the need arose.[13]

Britain needed the industry to be migratory, with men sailing to Newfoundland for the fishing season. From 1637, the government constantly discouraged permanent settlement on the island as, otherwise, settlers would be able to compete directly for the cod with the English fishing fleets. They would be difficult to press and if pressed into naval service, would not make themselves into able seamen. Furthermore, such settlers might trade with the other British colonies in America — a policy running counter to the prevailing mercantilist economic philosophy of the time. But despite official opposition, people arrived on the island and stayed to the extent that estimates of Newfoundland's population for the late 1750s ran from 6,000 to 10,308.[14]

Once the population began to grow, England faced the problem of governing it. In the beginning, Newfoundland had what came to be called a "floating government," as Britain had not envisioned Newfoundland as a colony. It set the island up as something akin to a warehouse, or a "mothership" to supply the fishing fleets. Rules and regulations, therefore, were concerned primarily with the smooth running of the cod industry. King William's Act of 1699, replacing royal charters given previously to merchants,[15] authorised the captain of the first ship to reach a harbour to become the "admiral" of it. The second one to sail in would then be vice-admiral and the third, rear-admiral. Not only could these "admirals" choose prime locations for their fishing operation, they resolved disputes among later arrivals concerning fishing areas. In particular, they had seasonal jurisdiction over ships' captains and Newfoundland's inhabitants concerning "the right and property" to fishing areas and places to treat the catch.

During the winter months, though, when the fishing admirals and the fleets returned to Britain, disorder ruled the island. By 1711, an island-made solution appeared and:

> several laws and orders made in St. John's for the better discipline and good order of the people, and for correcting irregularities committed contrary to good laws, and Acts of Parliaments, *all of which were debated at several courts held*, wherein were present the commanders of merchant ships, merchants, and chief inhabitants... These assemblies were somewhat anomalous, a kind of legislative, judicial, and executive, all blended together; and yet, perhaps, not more mixed than the proceedings of Parliament in Europe in very early times.[16]

This somewhat optimistic situation did not continue; frustration grew. The Board of Trade received a plethora of complaints and suggestions.

In 1729, these letters bore fruit and Britain began the practice of appointing governors, but only for the fishing season. They had various duties, such as sending persons suspected of having committed capital crimes to England, ensuring military personnel did not interfere with the fishing industry, and seeing to the prosecution of any who offended against church law. This covered a range of crimes from incest to blasphemy.[17] The first governor, Henry Osborn, authorized to "Appoint Justices of the Peace and Quiet of the said Island,"[18] appointed sixteen magistrates, including William Keen.[19]

Although their jurisdiction was supposedly limited to the winter months and confined to minor non-capital offences, these justices greatly exceeded their mandates, sitting all year round and hearing a variety of criminal and civil cases. British legal authorities questioned this almost immediately, deciding, in 1730, that the "admirals" had jurisdiction over everything directly related to the fishery with the magistrates' power limited to minor criminal cases involving breach of the peace. Furthermore, they had no power to levy taxes.[20] These decisions and limitations would not hinder the newly appointed magistrates though, as they grappled with their sense of Newfoundland's lawlessness.

Shortly after 1730, the governors began to appoint their junior officers as surrogates who toured the island's harbours, administering civil and criminal justice, again seemingly in opposition to King William's Act.[21] In 1744, the governor established a court of vice-admiralty (appointing Keen as one of the judges) without authorization from London. This court was supposed to limit itself to maritime legal questions, but it soon exceeded these limits, hearing cases involving debt and landed property.[22]

Criminal justice on the island continued to be a problem. Section 13 of King William's Act, 1699 stated that:

> all robberies, murders and felonies, and all other capital crimes whatsoever, which ... shall be done and committed in or upon the land in *Newfoundland* ... shall and may be enquired of tried, heard, determined and adjudged in any shire or county of this kingdom of *England*, by virtue of the King's commission or commissions of *oyer* and *terminer*, and gaol delivery, or any of them, according to the laws of this land used for the punishment of such robberies, murders, felonies, and other capital crimes done and committed within this realm.

Arguably, this section prohibited capital punishment. Nor was any authority delegated to handle misdemeanours or other non-capital offences or any provision for the administration of justice in the non-fishing months of the year. Such would be done on an *ad hoc* basis of dubious legality. The problems could have and should have been predicted. Witnesses to crimes could and did vanish during the winter months. If offenders were held in security, friends frequently released them. In 1750, an order-in-council established a court of oyer and terminer to try all criminal cases except treason; the following year, the governor's powers were augmented so that he could order the execution of those sentenced to death without waiting for London's approval. But, importantly, an executive order-in-council could not override a provision in a parliamentary statute and may have been invalid as far as capital offences were concerned.

This new court was to sit only once a year, during the fishing season. As taxes could not be levied on the fishing industry, there was little money to pay for courts, jails and the like; consequently, fines became the preferred sentences in non-capital cases. This may explain the crowd's outrage of the sentence rendered by Keen Jr. To a people accustomed to fines, whippings must have seemed vindictively cruel and unusual.

The Court of Oyer and Terminer in Newfoundland was very primitive indeed compared to other senior criminal courts in the American colonies during the 1750s and 1760s. There was no chief justice and none of the commissioners was legally trained, except as magistrates in St. John's. The first commissioner ever appointed would become the victim of the Eleanor Power-inspired theft, William Keen Sr., an import-export merchant. The commissioners had no security of tenure whatever. In other colonies, a judge suspended or dismissed by a governor was guaranteed a hearing by the London authorities. In Newfoundland, a commissioner who offended the governor was liable simply to be left off the next annual commission or to be dismissed, without appeal, as a magistrate. Until the 1790s, no lawyer appeared before the senior criminal court, either prosecuting or defending.[23] Questions were asked of witnesses by the judges, jurors and sometimes the accused. Not surprisingly, legal niceties such as benefit of clergy were ignored.

This situation lasted in significant part until well after professionalization with the establishment of a permanent Supreme Court in St. John's in 1791-2.[24] It is not surprising then, that alone of all the provinces that became Canada, Newfoundland's legislature abandoned control over its future criminal law to the imperial Parliament in 1837.[25]

The primitiveness of Newfoundland justice in 1754 helped doom Eleanor Power to the gallows. The ten days between the assault on Keen and his death gave the authorities plenty of time to decide how they would proceed against the offenders. Nicholas Tobin, forgetting his solemn oath not to "discover" his fellow conspirators, having turned king's evidence, freely divulged information. His nine fellow-offenders were brought before a grand jury, which found a true bill — an indication that there was a case to be met — thus clearing the way for the trial. That Governor Hugh Bonfoy had pre-determined the sentences became dreadfully obvious. On October 7, the day before the trial, he sent an order to the sheriff, William Thomas, directing him to "cause a gallows to be erected at the end of Mr. Keen's wharf, for the execution of sundry persons, now in custody for the murder."[26]

At the trial the following day, Edmund McGuire, Mathew Halluran, Robert Power, Eleanor Power, Lawrence Lumley, Paul MacDonald, John Moody, John Munhall and Dennis Hawkins were formally charged:

> that [they did] ... feloniously, willfully, and of malice, fourthought [sic], break into the house of the said Wlm Keen esq and robbed the said house of sundry valuable things and assaulted the body of the said Wlm Keen esq and wounded, bruised, and cutt the body...[27]

The nine accused entered a plea of not guilty.

The only crown witness, the accomplice Tobin, told the story leading up to the brutal attack on Keen. He explicitly testified that Eleanor Power and Lawrence Lumley had left the group before Munhall and McGuire decided to rob the judge the second time; that only Munhall and McGuire entered Keen's house; and that they alone made the fatal attack. The prosecutor read a deposition from Thomas Allan and John Burton, surgeons, into the record, verifying that "in their opinions, the wounds that were given Mr. Keen on Monday night, the 9th September, occasioned his death." That completed the case against the prisoners.

With no defence lawyers, the accused now faced the near-impossible task of defending themselves against a sentence of death. When asked if they had anything to say, Edmund McGuire bravely led off. He knew his own case was beyond hope but he did try to save his friends by pointing out that only he and Halluran had committed the attack on Keen. He had had the gun and Halluran "a piece of an old scythe with a sharp point." But he also implicated Robert Power by stating that Power had proposed murdering Keen which he, McGuire, had refused.

Part of this was immediately contradicted by John Munhall. According to him, Robert Power "said he would not go into the house if they thought he intended to kill Mr. Keen." He swore he was not guilty of murder and begged to be transported. Halluran had nothing to say in his own defence. The Powers, Lumley, and MacDonald also had tried to point out that they were not guilty of murder, which (although guilty of burglary) might save them from the gallows. Moody added a few details to what had gone on. He had been a sentinel at the fort's magazine when approached by McGuire. When he joined the others, he'd noticed Eleanor Power "in mans cloaths" and Halluran with a hatchet as well as his scythe. He also said that he had known nothing of the intended robbery until that night and begged for transportation rather than death. As did Dennis Hawkins.

After these statements the judge charged the jury, which withdrew for a mere half hour before declaring all nine "guilty of the felony and murder charged in the indictment." When asked if they had "any reasons to offer that sentence should not be pronounced against them, the defendants answered they had not, and threw themselves on the mercy of the Court." Mercy, of course, could not be extended at that stage so Judge Michael Gill intoned the only possible sentence given the guilty verdict: that the defendants "be sent back to the place from whence you came, and from thence to the place of execution, and there be hanged by the necks until you are dead, and the Lord have mercy upon your souls." He forgot, or maybe didn't know, to order dissection as directed by a British statute passed two years before.[28]

There was one more ignominy for the two ringleaders. Edmund McGuire and Mathew Halluran "after being dead" were to be "taken down ... to be hanged in chains on some publick place, when and where the Governor" should be "pleased" to appoint.

After sentencing, the presiding judge was empowered by an imperial statute of 1752 to order the body of an executed murderer to be treated like this. This authority without statutory sanction had been exercised at least as early as Chaucer's era in the fourteenth century.[29] From time to time this added indignity was meted out to traitors, pirates and highway robbers, but in the eighteenth and the early nineteenth centuries the treatment was confined to those committing murders the Bench thought atrocious. Examples include a man slaying his employer or the latter's children, a magistrate, or in one case a mother and her son run through with a hedge-stake.[30] The purpose behind hanging in chains was threefold: retribution; appeasing the victim's family, who often appealed for the order; and, above all, deterrence.

In cases where hanging in chains was ordered, the body was encased in a suit of irons, previously made by an ironmonger, and set upon a gibbet, which was usually placed near the crime site or on a prominent hill. Efforts were made to preserve the body. It was normally tarred and in one instance where the head had rotted away, a wooden one replaced it. It is difficult to estimate the deterrent effect, except to say the "lower orders" felt great horror at the prospect of improper burial and travellers strove desperately to avoid gibbets at night. But in crowds, even after dusk, it was otherwise. After a Lewis Avershaw was gibbeted in 1795 on Wimbledon Common outside London, "for several months, thousands of the populace passed their Sundays near the spot, as if consecrated by the remains of a hero." In another case, over 100,000 people came to view the hanging in chains "and a kind of wake continued for some weeks . . . [with] ale and gingerbread."[31]

Women's bodies were supposedly never to be hung in chains. An early specialist in the field, Albert Hartshorne wrote in his book, *Hanging in Chains,* that it was "to the credit of humanity [among those who administered English law] that the bodies of women were not publicly exposed on gibbets in irons and chains." The diligent modern historian of British criminal law, Leon Radzinowicz, simply wrote "the bodies of women were not so exposed [in chains]," presumably because such exposure was unseemly.[32] The punishment was abolished in 1834.[33]

While hanging in chains was not a common punishment in Canadian history, it was far from unknown. In the first three chapters of this book, four victims suffered such a fate: two in Newfoundland (1754), one in Quebec (1763) and one in Nova Scotia (1809). In 1803, the Upper Canadian King's Bench ordered two convicts to be gibbeted.[34] One of the Canadian victims was, despite constant British practice, a woman, but nineteenth century Newfoundland historian Charles Pedley notwithstanding, that victim was not Eleanor Power.[35] In the mid 1830s three Newfoundland men were hanged in chains. One was Peter Downing convicted in early January 1834 of murdering a man, his child and servant girl during a burglary at Harbour Grace.[36] The corpse was gibbeted near the site of the killings, but the gibbeting seems to have been unpopular with some, for the dead man was soon cut down and placed on the doorstep of Dr. W. Stirling who had examined the murder victims. With the corpse came a note: "Dr. S. This is your man you were the cause of bringing him here take and bury him or Lookout should you be the cause of allowing him to be put up again we will mark you for it."[37]

Justice was swift in the eighteenth century, particularly in Newfoundland with its rudimentary legal system. On October 8, 1754, the date of the trial, Governor Bonfoy sent a second order to Sheriff Thomas, directing him to build a gibbet "capable of containing two men in chains." While they waited the governor's "pleasure," the prisoners were housed on the ship, H.M.S. *Penzance*, probably as a safety measure in case their friends should try to rescue them from the St. John's jail. Thomas, armed with another order from Bonfoy, went to the *Penzance* two days later for McGuire and Halluran. The sad party wended its way to Keen's wharf, where the two men were "hanged by their necks on the gibbet [gallows] erected" for that purpose.[38] Then, after death, they were cut down and taken to the gibbet to be hung in chains.

Bonfoy sent Thomas the following day, October 11, for Robert and Eleanor Power. They were executed at midday, back to back, "and then their bodys ... were taken down and buried near the said gallows." Thus Eleanor Power became the first English Canadian woman to be hanged, and with her husband, the first married couple to hang together.[39]

The governor's will done, he could now exercise his pleasure. Tobin, as part of his king's evidence deal, received a free pardon. The five remaining men, under sentence of death, remained in temporary custody on the *Penzance*; these worried Governor Bonfoy, as he felt they couldn't be transferred to the "town gaol." It simply could not offer "sufficient security for so many." Therefore, on October 12, Sheriff Thomas, armed with yet another order, took Lumley and MacDonald from the *Penzance* to the prison before delivering the three soldiers (Moody, Munhall and Hawkins) into the custody of their commanding officer, Captain Aldridge.

But the crime, together with the fact that many had known it would take place, shook Newfoundland's establishment. Bonfoy sent a letter to justices of the peace throughout the island, October 12 1754:

> Whereas I think it for the good of this Island in General, that gallows should be erected in the several districts in order to deter frequent robberys that are committed by a parcel of villains *who think they can do what they please with impunity.*
>
> You are therefore hereby required and directed to cause gallows to be erected in the most publick places in your several districts, and cause all such persons as are guilty of robbery, felony or the like crimes, to be sent round to this place, in order to take their tryals at the annual assizes held here, as I am determined to proceed against all such, with the utmost severity of the law.[40]

One can speculate whether Eleanor Power might have escaped execution had she been represented by a qualified lawyer before a proper court. In her trial she faced a court constituted by untrained personnel. Moreover the court had a pro-prosecution stance stemming from their activity as justices of the peace and with the difficulty non-professionals frequently had to put aside political or religious bias. In addition, there was no protection against intervention or interference by the governor. In Eleanor Power's case, that governor, Hugh Bonfoy, had implemented a rigorous anti-Irish policy.[41] Shortly after the conviction of the nine accused and the resulting four executions, presiding commissioner Michael Gill, writing to Bonfoy, exulted that "many of the enemies of our Religion and Liberty are quitting the place."[42]

Two defences might have been advanced in Eleanor Power's case. First, that the court was illegal under section 13 of King William's Act, 1699. It is true that in 1750 British Attorney General Dudley Ryder advised, without however offering justification, that King William's Act, section 13, did not prohibit the exercise of the royal prerogative to establish courts on the Island, this despite s. 13 using the mandatory word "shall."[43] It must also be noted that serious doubts had been entertained on this same point by the Board of Trade in 1738 and 1750 and yet later by Newfoundland's first Chief Justice, John Reeves.[44] A persuasive argument by counsel would likely have resulted in a reprieve and been reviewed by the new Attorney General, William Murray (later Lord Chief Justice Mansfield), and Solicitor General Sir Richard Lloyd. The result might have saved Eleanor Power. Although a favourable decision was not at all certain, the long delay may have worked in her favour.[45] The second possible argument was more potent: that while Power could legitimately be convicted of burglary, she was not guilty of murder. The first contention would be that she and Lumley had left the conspirators after the first break-in and did not rejoin them prior to or during the follow-up. In other words, they had dissociated themselves from any further felonious activity. The second contention would be that, for accomplices to be guilty of murder, there had to be a common understanding that deadly force was to be used to oppose any interference with the burglary.

In a late seventeenth century case, three soldiers set out to rob an orchard. One was assigned to guard the gate with a sword while the others climbed the trees. The sentry stabbed to death the owner's son who had come to investigate. Chief Justice Holt held the tree climbers were not guilty of murder, as there had been no agreement to resist opposition by using deadly force. Such an agreement was presumed in fact but the presumption was rebuttable.[46] This agreement among the conspirators could have been shown to have existed before the second break-in, but not before or during the first.

A verdict of not guilty on the murder charge might have had major repercussions. Although then considered a very serious offence punishable by death, burglary was not treated nearly as severely as murder. In London and Middlesex in the years 1749-71, 678 persons were executed. The highest ratio of hangings to convictions was for murder, with burglary ranking behind forgery and coinage offences, robbery, returning from transportation and defrauding creditors.[47] In nearby Nova Scotia, 1749-1815, the execution rate for burglary (45 cases) was 38% while that for murder (39 cases) was 59%.[48] Thus with seven guilty of murder and two not, counsel could have argued in a mercy petition that the persons to be hanged should be chosen from the former group, particularly those most active: Halluran, McGuire and Munhall. Eleanor Power's life might thus have been saved.[49]

After the Powers had been buried, and McGuire's and Halluran's decomposing bodies swung from their gibbets, what particularly incensed the governor and other officials was the fact that all ten of those implicated in the Keen burglary were Irish. Furthermore, the plot had been an open secret — and not just among lowly servants and soldiers. That no "respectable" person had thought fit to inform them of the plot gnawed at their sense of superiority and played into their prejudices. The murder of William Keen would have far-reaching consequences, important because by 1754 the Irish outnumbered other Newfoundland settlers in all large communities.[50]

Before Hugh Bonfoy had left England for his first tour as governor, the Board of Trade asked him to find out the status of the Irish on the Island. According to him, those who stayed throughout the winter had no way to support themselves and therefore stole to survive. They were a rowdy bunch and caused many of the disorders on the island. Even though no Irish persons before the Keen case had been tried in oyer and terminer, the governor now ordered magistrates to restrict their activities. He forbade them to set up in trade. Priests could not celebrate the mass or "officiate in any Church or Chapel." Furthermore, in Bonfoy's opinion, "Liberty of conscience is allowed to all Persons except Papists." Motivated by the crime and these orders, the magistrates vigorously enforced Bonfoy's wishes.[51]

The persecution did not stop with him though. The next governor, Richard Dorrill (1755),[52] received instructions from the Board of Trade to investigate the Irish as well, and he intensified the campaign against them. A priest at Harbour Grace was arrested for celebrating mass. After an informant alleged that mass was being held in homes, owners of eighteen dwellings in Harbour Main were fined and had some of their buildings razed to the ground. Those who could be identified as attending were ordered to be transported. Terrence Kennedy, of Crocker's Cove, for example, who had lent his house for mass and his own marriage service, was both fined and ordered transported. Irishmen and those merchants employing them in St. John's were prohibited from selling alcohol. If found guilty, their houses were to be destroyed and their lands seized.

Governor Palliser (1764-8) continued the fight against Irish settlement. Regulations forbade Irish people to move away from the harbour where they had fished during the summer. No more than two Catholics were allowed in a household unless, as their saving grace, it had a Protestant master. Irish women needed someone to post a good behaviour bond before they could land. A decade later, children born to Irish parents were ordered to be baptized as Protestants (presumably into the Church of England).[53] By and large, the Irish ignored many of these regulations and prospered.

In hindsight, it was ironic that Newfoundland Papists should cause so much concern. At the time that Irish children were ordered to undergo baptism into the Protestant faith, the Quebec Act of 1774, substituted an oath of allegiance for the Oath of Supremacy for Canadien Papists.[54] Furthermore, in a colony where Catholics far outnumbered Protestants, the act removed all barriers to practising the Catholic faith. Would Newfoundland have undergone such a backlash against the Irish if William Keen had not been murdered? Maybe, given the facts that it was only a quasi-colony and that the Catholics came from Ireland.

What became of the five "murderers" who did not hang? They waited, in a kind of legal hiatus, in the St. John's prison and its garrison for years while officialdom made up its collective mind. Governors Bonfoy and Dorrill's reports on them were debated; extracts made of the case were presented to King George II. Eventually, the five men were released from their manacles and given a pardon, which was conditional on their never returning to Newfoundland.

Eleanor Power, who dreamed of being rich, dressed in men's clothing to rob, and had played an active role in planning the first burglary, was quite possibly hanged for not knowing her place in society.[55] Newfoundland's criminal justice system of 1754 was far from anyone's ideal of the "rule of law." She could not, and did not, receive any protection from it.

Chapter Two
The Many Trials of
Marie-Josephte Corriveau

The changes in his parish of St. Vallier worried Father Thomas Blondeau. Little more than three years earlier, the British had conquered the mighty citadel of Quebec, fifteen kilometres or so northwest of his village. It might seem to the unpractised eye that nothing had altered as a result of the conquest, but Father Blondeau sometimes wondered if the events of 1759 were the catalyst for all that ailed St. Vallier.

Outwardly, people went about their business normally. The new year of 1763 had been welcomed with the usual *joie de vivre*. Frequent British patrols through the village dampened spirits, for certainly the villagers were careful to put the best face on things when the redcoats were in sight. But, there was a nasty undercurrent in the village and when people gathered to gossip, the talk turned vicious. More and more, Blondeau was becoming convinced that the canker eating away at decency and tolerance in St. Vallier was centred in the powerful Corriveau family — or, more realistically, one branch of it. He knew the Corriveaus well. The leading member, Jacques, was the village's captain of militia and responsible for much of the internal peace of the community. A cousin, Joseph, like Jacques, was wealthy enough to provide his wife with a large house and servants and had ensured that the children made advantageous marriages. Except, that is, his daughter Marie.[1]

Marie's first marriage, to farmer Charles Bouchard in 1749, had apparently been happy[2] with problems, if any, kept within the family. But, after fathering three children, Charles died in late April 1760. Marie waited fifteen months before marrying Louis-Helene Dodier in July 1761. Soon, their acrimonious marriage fuelled much of the gossip in the village,[3] because immediately, Dodier entered into various contracts with his unloved father-in-law: one, for the rental of his house; another for the half-ownership of a horse to be kept in his stables; and so on. By the summer of 1762, the peculiarly hostile dynamics between the two men escalated into litigation and the commanding British officer in the area, Major James Abercrombie, had his hands full with their endless disputes. Joseph Corriveau would complain that the rent hadn't been paid, that Dodier kept him from riding the jointly-owned horse, while Dodier detailed his father-in-law's irrational demands.

Abercrombie would later say that he believed that "the Old Man was Generally in the Wrong." This belief may have influenced him when Marie, claiming constant physical abuse by Dodier, unsuccessfully petitioned for permission to leave her husband. By January 1763, the major had had enough. Angrily frustrated by the time-consuming, petty quarrels and sordid domestic disputes, he threatened to fine the next guilty man $20 — a very large sum for the time.

Chancing upon the major on January 26, 1763, Corriveau complained that Dodier had assaulted him and therefore should pay the twenty dollars. What was more, this time it was not his word against his son-in-law's. He had a witness to the attack. Not surprisingly, Abercrombie refused to do anything until he had a chance to question Dodier and Corriveau's witness. Outraged by the major's inaction, Corriveau repeated his charge and when Abercrombie would not change his mind, he stomped off in disgust, ominously muttering that "some Misfortune will happen."

It seemed an open and shut case to the villagers when Dodier's body was found in his stable the next morning. They — from Captain Corriveau to the lowliest servant — had either seen or heard of one of the altercations. Like Major Abercrombie, everyone believed Joseph Corriveau to be a violent man. As evidence, some proceeded to rewrite history, telling all and sundry in hushed tones that Charles Bouchard had died after Corriveau had hit him with a currycomb, a tool used to groom horses' hair.

But, there were the British to consider. No one in St. Vallier knew if their stay in Canada would be permanent or not. Major Abercrombie was a frequent visitor as were the patrols of the 78th Regiment. So, rather than expose Joseph Corriveau to their mercies, the village decided to cover up the crime. When asked for advice, Father Blondeau suggested that Jacques Corriveau, who, as captain of militia, was responsible for keeping the peace, enlist seven or eight men who weren't related to the family to act as a coroner's jury. He himself would write up the proceedings. With this report in hand, Captain Corriveau went to

Abercrombie's headquarters. Noticing that he looked "very sad," Abercrombie asked, "What is the matter?"

"Poor Dodier is dead," the captain replied. The unfortunate man had slipped in the stables and been trampled to death by his horses.

The sudden death seemed suspiciously providential. In fact, too much so for the major to swallow. "I fear Corriveaux [sic] has done the deed," he protested immediately, refusing to believe the story.

"No," Captain Corriveau responded, on "the honour of our Family, he has not." And, knowing Abercrombie needed further convincing he produced the official certificate that Blondeau had drawn up to confirm his story. He and his son then swore they had seen horseshoe marks on the corpse. With almost indecent haste, Dodier was buried in St. Vallier the next day, January 28, 1763. And there matters, and Dodier, might have rested except for the ever-present village gossip and a British soldier's curiosity.

Sergeant Alexander Fraser came into Abercrombie's office two days after the burial. He was no stranger to St. Vallier or the affairs of the Corriveaus. Hearing of Dodier's death, he had immediately visited the barn to see the corpse for himself. To Abercrombie's consternation, Fraser swore the wounds could not have been made by horses. For one thing, they were far too sharp. In fact, they looked as if one of the stable's dung forks had made them. Village gossip agreed with him. Various people had told him that Dodier's horses were unshod and therefore incapable of making the sharp wounds on the body.

Abercrombie found no difficulty believing Fraser and, subsequently, a regimental surgeon found four head wounds about three inches from each other on the frozen body. One, near Dodier's upper lip had "penetrated through the flesh and upper Jaw." Another, about four inches deep, was a little below an eye. Two other blows on the left side had broken the skull. The lower jaw was also fractured, although there were no visible wounds, and the doctor agreed with Sergeant Fraser: a horse's hoof, whether shod or unshod, could not have inflicted these particular injuries.

Obviously, Dodier had died as a result of foul play; he had been murdered. Once the news became public, everyone, from Abercrombie down, believed that Joseph Corriveau, in one of his many fits of rage, had killed Louis Dodier by striking him in the head with one of the dung forks. But Abercrombie also believed that Marie, the widow, had somehow been an accomplice to the murder. The Corriveaus were arrested, sent to Quebec, and then jailed.

But under what kind of criminal law would they be tried?

Though Britain had taken possession of Canada by right of conquest, no one in the colony knew for certain if it would receive title to the colony. The most sophisticated understood that Britain and France were in the process of negotiating an end to the Seven Years' War. A debate raged in both countries and some American colonies as to whether Britain should take France's vast "acres of snow" in North America or the sun-kissed sugar plantation island of Guadeloupe. And, although France signed the Treaty of Paris in February 1763, and did in fact cede what was known then as New France — Canada and Acadia — to Britain, news of the treaty would not reach the colony until May of that same year, 1763.[4]

Governor Murray began administering the city of Quebec and its environs in 1759. He believed that "Necessity has no law,"[5] and that, as conquerors, he and his army could govern and administer justice in any way they wanted. In the first harsh winter of occupation, when even the gathering of firewood took on life and death overtones, Murray hanged at least three people without trial of any kind and had men and women whipped through the town. Only after the surrender of the remainder of Canada by the governor general of New France, François-Pierre de Rigaud de Vaudreuil, was some type of order instituted.

Both criminal and civil matters came before military courts — rape, assault, extortion, abuse, contract disputes, civil responsibility and the like. Many harsh sentences followed. After convicting a young man of robbery, a court martial sentenced him to one thousand lashes. Impossible as it sounds today, the court considered itself lenient: "The youth of the Offender was the sole Cause of ... inflicting so mild a Punishment." Another man, convicted of extortion, also received one thousand lashes. Other punishments creatively involved restitution. For example, after seriously injuring a child, the court ordered the offenders to pay the surgeon's expenses, a sum of £30 to the father and receive a further punishment if the child died from his wounds.[6]

Although *ad hoc*, the legal system generally followed a pattern described by General Jeffery Amherst: "That with respect to Thefts & Murder, it is absolutely Necessary the Military Law should take place; but with regard to Differences between the Inhabitants, I would have them settled among themselves, agreeable to their own Laws and Customs."[7] Obviously, if Jacques Corriveau, the St. Vallier captain of militia, had been able to "terminate all ... Differences" between his cousin and Louis Dodier the whole sordid story of his family and the village might never have become known. It is certainly arguable that if Major Abercrombie had not been so personally involved, St. Vallier might have been able to cover up the Dodier murder and the Corriveaus would have escaped arrest. But that is speculation.

Joseph and Marie Corriveau would stand trial before the military in a general court martial. With a panel of thirteen officers, it resembled others of the time. One officer acted as president-judge; the others became both jury and judges. Prosecution of the Corriveaus would be undertaken by a deputy judge advocate — in this case General Murray's military secretary, Hector Theophilus Cramahé, who also advised the officers on matters of law. The defence, which laboured under severe restrictions, would be handled by the royal notary, Jean-Antoine Saillant.[8]

The trial began on March 29, 1763, with Major Abercrombie, Sergeant Fraser and the surgeon giving evidence to the wounds and the events which had made them believe a murder had taken place. Once that was established, the court turned its attention to the false coroner's report. Father Blondeau admitted he had never seen Dodier's body himself, but had merely assisted in drawing up the inaccurate document from "Motives of charity, to cover the disgrace of a Whole Family." Once he and Captain Corriveau had decided on this course, no one in the village had objected.

On the witness stand, Captain Corriveau explained his actions the day following Dodier's death. Told of the death by his son, he had done his best "to hide the Shame of his Family." Following Blondeau's advice, he had assembled a coroner's jury and accepted its false report. For example, the horses had not been in the stable, although he had certified otherwise. Making little effort now to spare his cousin, he regaled the court with village gossip, namely that Joseph "had told the Priest some Misfortune might Possibly happen" to his son-in-law. Rather than throw this hearsay evidence out, as a criminal court would be obliged to do, the court martial accepted it as an important building block in the case against the accused.

Charles Denis, the next witness, testified that he had seen the corpse with its face covered in blood, but denied having anything else to do with the coroner's inquest. When Cramahé read the relevant passages aloud in court, Denis swore they were false. He hadn't seen the body under the horses' feet and only some inchoate fear of the British had made him participate in the inquest at all. According to Denis' testimony, Captain Corriveau had said something to the effect that if the matter wasn't handled correctly by the village, Major Abercrombie "was coming to take up the body." He, as well, proffered hearsay evidence. According to "his own people," he told the court, Joseph Corriveau's maid had heard him get up in the night, then she had "heard a great Screech." After that, Corriveau had returned home. Other members of the impromptu coroner's jury repeated the same themes.

The most damaging testimony came from a labourer who lived with the Dodiers, Claude Dion. He was the mysterious witness Joseph Corriveau had promised Abercrombie in January. Now, under oath, he told another version of the so-called assault. The sequence of events that resulted in Dodier's murder, Dion told the court, actually began two nights earlier. Corriveau had gone to Dodier's stable to collect the jointly-owned horse, which apparently had not yet been fed. Dodier told Corriveau to wait until he had fed the animal. An enraged Corriveau then screamed "a great deal of ill Language" at his son-in-law, threatening that Dodier would "not be long Master of this Horse" and claiming he would rather die than maintain the current relationship. A scuffle broke out after these words. Corriveau tried to butt-end Dodier in the stomach with his whip. That, according to Dion, was the true version of the assault Corriveau had reported.

When Corriveau, armed with a summons, returned to the village after seeing Abercrombie, he didn't serve it on Dodier, instead merely laughing about the incident. But things turned ugly again that very night. This time, though, the hostilities weren't between Dodier and his father-in-law. They involved Marie. At supper time, Dodier demanded his meal as soon as he entered the house, asserting that he had worked long and hard for it.

"You eat well but don't Work much, and perhaps you will not eat very long," Marie reportedly replied.

Infuriated by her response and, supposedly, the lack of food, Dodier slapped Marie several times. An uneasy Dion wanted to leave as soon as he had eaten but Dodier objected. When Dion then said he didn't feel well, Marie, perhaps referring to her own abortive attempts to leave Dodier, took the opportunity to point out that "People are not to be kept by Force."

The loquacious Dion had learned of the murder from a soldier (presumably Sergeant Fraser) the next morning. After rushing to the stable he had, according to his self-serving testimony, immediately seen that Dodier "had been Murdered, and not killed by his Horses, which were not Shod." And when he went into the house, Marie had sobbed, "My poor Dodier is Dead, his Horses were Vicious, they killed him."

That's impossible, scoffed Dion. "I do not say the Horses did not help, but they did not put him in the Condition he is in. Go see him, he has holes in his Head. These cannot be caused by the Horses which are not Shod."

"Then who killed him?"

Unable, or unwilling, to answer, Dion remained in the stable to become part of the mendacious coroner's jury. But when testifying about the inquest, Dion suddenly became vague and his answers echoed the others. He didn't know what had been concluded, little was read to him and, in any case, he had loudly declared the report false. He could not remember the names of those to whom he had supposedly told his version of the Corriveau-Dodier assault and although he recalled telling someone that Corriveau had murdered Dodier, he couldn't remember the name.

Captain Corriveau's son also testified to events on the morning Dodier's body had been found. Joseph Corriveau himself had come to his father's house for help, he told the court. He said that Dodier's horses had trampled him to death and he asked the younger man to bring a servant with him to "take up the Corpse" in the same way a person would "pity a dog." The young Corriveau cautiously answered that he would have to speak "to the Principal People of the Parish" first.

What purpose would that serve Corriveau asked, then gloomily added: "Let them take me, hang me. I am no run away. I shall not Dishonour my Family." The unimpressed young man then went for his father. He, like so many others, believed that Corriveau had murdered Dodier.

The court next began to establish the precise series of events leading up to Dodier's death. Isabella Silvain, Joseph Corriveau's niece and servant would be the first called to testify. Torn between loyalty to the family, her fear of British officialdom and a hazy recollection of the fateful night, she became an impossible witness.

In the weeks between the murder and the trial, she had sworn to several contradictory statements. Now, in court, while she was again under oath, they were read back to her. In the first, she denied having heard Joseph Corriveau get up in the night. Nor had she heard "a great Screech." Marie Corriveau had visited her parents' home about nine in the evening when they were in bed. She had spoken with them in a soft voice for a few moments, warmed herself by the kitchen fire for about half an hour, then braved the cold darkness to return home. In her second deposition, Isabella declared she had nothing to add, except that when she got up the next morning, about two hours before daylight, she had heard the sound of horses fighting. The following day she had made a third deposition. In this, she swore that Joseph Corriveau had arisen in the early morning. As she needed to relieve her bladder, she had followed him outside. Then she had heard the horses fighting and the great screech. At the time she had thought someone was beating the horses. She returned to the house and Joseph Corriveau came back a half hour later.

Faced with these inconsistencies, Cramahé warned his witness of the consequences for perjury, reminding her that she had now taken a fourth oath to tell the truth. What exactly had happened? Her answer confused everyone, including the court reporter. She now denied that Corriveau had gone outside at all on the morning following the murder, confessing that she had felt pressured to say otherwise when she was making the third deposition. Only this fear had made her implicate her uncle. As for the screech, yes, she had heard one, but it was only a little one. But then, in the very next breath, she decided it had been a great one after all.

"Tell the whole truth from first to last," an exasperated Cramahé told her. Totally unnerved, thoroughly frightened, Isabella Silvain tried to comply. But as the frustrated court reporter wrote, "she delivered herself in so indistinct, incoherent, and Contradictory a manner there was no possibility to take down the same." In the hope that time might give Silvain some measure of poise, the court adjourned. But Cramahé probably destroyed any possibility of that when he warned that if she could not give a better account of what she knew, she would "be tried for her Life for the Crime of Perjury." Whether or not he knew that perjury wasn't a capital crime in English criminal law is unknown. In any case, his words were counter-productive. When Silvain returned the next day, she remained "Obstinate and inconsistent" much to the disgust of the court reporter, the officer-bench and Cramahé.

By this point, the prosecution had established that Louis Dodier had died in suspicious circumstances and been killed by puncture-wounds to his head made by a dung fork. Following the "great screech" lead, it believed death had probably occurred just before dawn on January 27, 1763. The coroner's report, attributing death to blows from horses' hooves, had been discredited, although the members of jury had escaped censure for their part in the cover-up. Indeed, the court had conveniently ignored the falsehoods in the report. Members of the jury gave evidence free from any threats of perjury. Furthermore, they had been given such latitude, that, second and third hand gossip was entered into the court record as evidence against the accused.

That Joseph Corriveau had used threats and menaces against the accused seemed certain. That he and Dodier engaged in myriad quarrels and litigation was equally so. But did that make him the murderer? So far, no witness had placed him in the stables — the supposed scene of the crime — in the early hours of January 27, nor had anyone seen him lift the dung fork against his son-in-law. To tie down Corriveau's movements, Cramahé called members of the Corriveau household to the stand.

Françoise Bouchard, Marie's daughter from her first marriage, gave evidence that her mother had come to Joseph's house at seven o'clock the night before Dodier's death. Both her grandparents were in bed and Marie had a very quiet conversation with them, before warming herself by the fire, preparatory to returning home. Isabella Silvain had talked with her at the door before she left. Françoise had only heard of her stepfather's death when one of the workers came at daybreak saying there had been "an unlucky Accident, poor Dodier is stretched out dead in his own Stable."

The evidence Françoise presented was immediately contradicted by her grandmother. Joseph's wife, Marie-Joseph [sic] Bolduc, testified that Marie had not come to the house the night of January 26. She had come in the morning. Cramahé inaccurately reminded Bolduc that two witnesses had already sworn that Marie had come at nine o'clock the previous night and had had a whispered conversation with her parents. Bolduc staunchly denied the fact, and rather than opt out with an excuse that she might have been asleep at the time, reiterated her previous testimony. When asked why her husband had not issued Abercrombie's summons to Dodier, she recalled that her son-in-law was at work. She didn't know why a surgeon had not been called to examine Dodier's body as she "did not meddle in the Affair at all."

Another daughter of Marie's, the only one who lived in the Dodier house, was next called to the witness stand. She testified that her stepfather had woken her up about three hours before daylight, put her into bed with her mother, saying he was going to the "Mill to bolt his Flour." He had taken his horse's harness. A couple of hours later, her mother had sent her to ask Exochoria Montigny to put the horses into the stable. Montigny then found Dodier's bloodied body. Her mother had warned her to tell the truth on the stand, which she had now done.

Another family witness was Dodier's brother Joseph and he provided, at long last, an immediate motive for the killing that morning. Several unnamed people had told him that his brother had told Marie, "I go to the Mill tomorrow."

"Are you taking my father's horse?" she replied.

"She is mine as well as his," Louis Dodier supposedly answered.

At this point, Marie jumped out of bed, and rushed to her father's. It was after that, Joseph Dodier declared, that Isabella Silvain had heard the great noise, such as horses being beaten in the stable.

So, finally, Cramahé had his motive. Joseph Corriveau's quarrels with his son-in-law had escalated to a point of simmering, uncontrollable rage. It had only taken the pretext of Dodier using the horse to go to the flour mill to push him over the edge. Then, in the early hours of January 27, he had risen from his bed, gone to the stable, confronted Dodier, then killed him with the dung fork.

During the presentation of his case against the accused, Cramahé had skilfully built upon second, third and even fourth-hand 'evidence.' He had no compunction about allowing his witnesses to recall vague stories they had heard from unnamed people. And to portray Joseph Corriveau and his daughter as evil, malicious people he manipulated his witnesses into what amounted to character assassination.

Claude Dion repeated village gossip, which had Charles Bouchard, Marie's first husband, "killed by Corriveaux Father with the blow of a Currycomb." He had allegedly heard from Dodier that Joseph Corriveau would "serve him the same way if he could ... that he mistrusted him." Other people had heard another story, one where Dodier had found

Corriveau in his stable about ten o'clock one night. Unaware of the intruder's identity, he had grabbed a big stick. Then, after Corriveau had revealed himself, Dodier had ordered him off the premises, saying, "Get you gone, you Old Rogue, you want to murder me."

Marie's reputation suffered even more than her father's. Sergeant Fraser told the court that, a year or so before the murder, Marie had approached several soldiers, including himself, asking them to beat up her husband. As a pretext she suggested Fraser find the price of some turkeys Dodier was selling so outrageous that he "knock him down." In return, "she would do anything to Oblige him." Alexander McDonald, also of the 78th Regiment, told a similar story.

When asked if Marie had made proposals to him, the talkative, but forgetful Claude Dion became even more voluble than usual. This time his memory was excellent. Marie was no better than her father when it came to arguing with Dodier. He remembered her saying several times that she liked Bouchard more than Dodier. In fact, she wished she "was fairly rid of him at any price." Dion left a clear impression in court that the price was her body. She had often caressed him, he testified under oath, "saying my little Claude," and that "she should like a little Claude." When he had protested that her husband was "a very good Man," she'd replied that she would "be well pleased to be rid of Dodier, as she liked the name of Claude." To top it off, Marie "was much adicted [sic] to Drunkenness" and to "such a degree he had seen her Spew in her Children's caps, and [she] sold everything to procure Liquor."

The Corriveaus' counsel, Governor Murray's royal notary, Jean-Antoine Saillant, fought admirably and subtly for his clients, but his defence would be limited by the rules governing general courts martial. He was unable to cross-examine witnesses and could only read a prepared statement to the court. Acting on the assumption that the bench had bought their commissions as officers, which was standard practice at the time, he spoke to them as gentleman to gentlemen.

Yes, he began, a murder had occurred. That fact was undeniable. But, he asked, where was the murderer? "The Prisoners are Suspected" but "thoughts and Suspicions offer no Proofs." Even though public opinion had already convicted Joseph Corriveau, there was no reason for intelligent officers to follow along. There was, conveniently, an alternative suspect. A labourer who had lived in Dodier's house until three weeks before the murder had left threatening that he "should pay" for some injustice, "or the Devil take him else."

Saillant attacked the veracity of the prosecution witnesses. Most of them had been part of a false coroner's report. Why should their testimony now be believed? "Where a witness deposes against the truth, his Deposition becomes suspicious and ought to be rejected," Saillant argued. Noting that the prosecution was relying solely on the convenient parts of Isabella Silvain's testimony, that is, that Marie Corriveau had come to her father's house at nine in the evening, he called for the entire testimony to be thrown out. And what attention should be paid to a man who was the sworn enemy of the accused? Captain Corriveau's son, who testified to Marie's low morality, had been involved in litigation with Joseph and during an altercation had broken two of the elder man's ribs.

In fact, according to Saillant, even Major Abercrombie's testimony should be discarded. Abercrombie had acted as a judge in several of the Dodier-Corriveau litigious quarrels. Saillant declared it was a widely accepted legal principle that "a Judge cannot be heard as a witness in the cause, which he has instructed."

Nor should the court heed village gossip: "If attention was paid to Publick Clamour, many innocent people would be found guilty of whatever crimes gossip convicted them of." Nor should it accept hearsay evidence, especially when the source was unnamed. And, as for the animosity between Dodier and his wife, Saillant shrugged, "well, disputes will happen between Man and wife, especially in the Peasantry."

But, conceding that the court would not dismiss the evidence he considered tainted, Saillant then proceeded to demonstrate its various flaws.

What weight should the court give to Corriveau's threats? If making threats was proof of guilt, hundreds, even thousands of people should then be considered murderers. He found little difficulty with Claude Dion's damaging "partly Tragical, and partly Comic" testimony. "This witness talked much better of what has not come under his own knowledge, than of what he really" knew. Dion had boasted under oath that if he had told the truth to Abercrombie when first questioned, Joseph Corriveau would have "been in a bad Situation." Didn't the officers realize that he had admitted lying to the major? And lied under oath as well?

Again, Saillant hammered away at the prosecution's mendacious witnesses, asking which oath was sacred to these men and when could they be considered truthful? Was it only when the lie might fit into the court's preconceived set of facts?

Saillant next tried to redeem his clients' reputation. If the court believed Joseph Corriveau to be an argumentative, aggressive fool, it should weigh that opinion against the facts of his life. Corriveau had lived in St. Vallier all his life, had been highly influential and respected in the village. All his eleven children resided there. He had held such important parish offices as church warden and school trustee, positions "entrusted" to none "but Men of Acknowledged Probity and good Morals."

To counter much of the character assassination, Saillant wished it were possible to produce Dodier himself as a defence witness. The court would then hear that the deceased had been as much an aggressor as the accused, that he had instigated quarrels about wood, had pushed Joseph Corriveau around, and had threatened to throw him into the oven. In fact, the court would learn that Dodier had "behaved worse to his Father in Law than the latter to the former."

As for Marie, about a month before Dodier's death, she had gone to Major Abercrombie to plead for permission to leave her husband on the grounds of assault. She had even taken refuge in a neighbouring house to avoid his beatings, telling Dodier she could no longer live with him unless the British major forced her to do so. The fact that Dodier beat her was well known. Even Dion had admitted that Dodier gave her "a few Slaps" several times.

The "little Claude" incident, which Dion had described for the court, was easily explained in class terms. Those of us "acquainted with the manner of speaking and thinking of the Country People," the sophisticated Saillant told the British officers, would "not be surprised at this kind of Language. Nothing [was] more innocent." Dion's avowed horror after seeing Marie vomit into her children's caps was also easily explained. His youthful ignorance attributed to drink that "which was often the Effect of the weakness and Infirmities of the [female] Sex." Surely the court knew that many "Women endeavour to conceal from their Husbands, the Infirmities to which they are Subject by nature, and with much more reason, from a Servant, a young Lad." In any case, if the officers chose to believe Dion, whose fault was it anyway that Marie was intoxicated? Was not the husband the master of the family? Was it not Dodier "to whom the Authority was given, by all Laws Human and Divine."

The fact that Dodier had married into the Corriveau family was probably the best available proof that the gossip about the currycomb was false. Bouchard had died from "a Putrid Fever." Dion must have believed that for: "In a country Parish, all know one another and could it be imagined two Men would have exposed themselves knowingly to the Risque of being unhappy, by connecting themselves with a Family against which there was the least Reproach?"

In his concluding remarks, Saillant reminded the court, as if it needed a reminder, that murder was a serious offence. Joseph and Marie Corriveau had been confined to jail since their arrest in February. They were not the first innocent people jailed by the British, nor would they be the last. Given the importance of the charge and the notoriety of the crime, there should have been a thoroughly convincing prosecution. But what had happened? Tainted evidence was allowed to stand, hearsay gossip accepted, and character assassination encouraged. In fact, the prosecution had failed to meet its mandate to produce "two Witnesses of a good Character, and declaring the same Circumstances" before it. Saillant understood the tremendous pressure to find and punish Dodier's murderer. The court of public opinion had already condemned Corriveau. British officers, accustomed to leadership and to weighting options, should strenuously resist confirming that opinion.

As for Marie, what evidence was there that she had been an accessory to Joseph's supposed murder? No witness had placed her at the scene at the time of the killing. Two witnesses said she had visited her parents the evening before the murder. But her own mother testified that the visit had been the following morning. If the evidence against her father was circumstantial, that against Marie was farcical. The court had heard stories about her wanting the soldiers to beat her husband up and to allegations that she was a drunkard. Did those things make her an accessory to murder?

Apparently they did. On Wednesday, April 6, 1763, after listening to Cramahé's summing up, the court found Joseph Corriveau guilty of murder and sentenced him to "be Hanged for the same" a week later on April 13. It found Marie "Guilty of knowing of the said Murder, and doth therefore adjudge her to Receive Sixty Lashes with a Cat and Nine Tails upon her bare back, at three different places, viz., under the gallows, in

Quebec's public market and in the parish of St. Vallier, twenty lashes at each place." Her left hand would be branded with the letter M. The unfortunate Isabella Silvain, who like so many inhabitants of St. Vallier had lied under oath, was quickly tried for perjury, found guilty and sentenced to receive thirty lashes, ten at the same time and place as Marie would receive hers. Her left hand would be branded with the letter P.

Thankful that the trial was finally over and that satisfactory verdicts had been returned, Governor Murray quickly ratified the proceedings. A carpenter was hired to build the gallows and preparations made for the floggings. The Corriveaus and Isabella Silvain remained in jail. The women's state of mind can only be guessed at. But Joseph must have mulled over and over again the injustice of his fate because he and a handful of others knew with absolute certainty that he was no murderer.

He finally cracked the night before his scheduled execution. It's been said that the prospect of hanging concentrates the mind wonderfully and he proved no exception. After consulting with his confessor, he offered a bargain to Governor Murray. In exchange for a pardon he declared "it was Marie Josephte [sic] Corriveaux who killed her Husband in his Bed, with a Blunted Hatchet. That the Night of the 26th of January about ten O'Clock, this Declarant being then in his Bed, his Daughter knocked at the Window, and said in a low voice, Father come." When Joseph "opened the Door, she came in and told him Dodier is Dead."

"How?" Joseph asked.

"I killed him."

Joseph then apparently whispered the news to his wife and then told Marie "to begone," that she was "a Vile Wretch." Marie obeyed her father at first, but later returned, begging that he help her put the body into a sleigh which they would then abandon on "the high Road." Later, he had helped her drag the body into the stable.

Stunned by this admission, Murray ordered Marie brought from jail the following day to hear her father's confession. Sadly, she acknowledged its truth. She had indeed killed Dodier. Her father had only helped her take the body to the stable, and even then he reproached her all the time. After the corpse had been strategically placed, she had returned home to burn the blood-soaked sheets and washed any other incriminating evidence away. Her daughter Angelique had woken up before all signs had been obliterated. No one else, particularly Isabella Silvain, had known anything.

On April 14, the court martial reconvened. In stark contrast to the proceedings against Joseph, there were no witnesses and Saillant could not present mitigating evidence. Marie pleaded guilty and within minutes the court sentenced her "to suffer Death for the same by being Hanged in Chains wherever the Governor shall think proper." As a final insult, Marie was ordered to pay an ironmonger's costs for making her cage.

What were the officers thinking? Nine of them had sat through days of detailed testimony. Convinced beyond a shadow of a doubt that Louis Dodier had met his death in the early hours of January 27, when struck in the face with a dung fork, they had condemned an innocent man to death. Saillant had correctly pointed out the problems with the prosecution's case. It relied on hearsay evidence, on witnesses who had previously lied under oath. Moreover, it was heavily circumstantial. No one had been able to place Joseph Corriveau at the murder scene because he hadn't been there. The charges against Marie had been equally unproven.

Without any doubt, the officers and the government were embarrassed. They had endorsed a sentence which condemned an innocent man and which would have allowed the guilty person to roam free eventually. Now, they reacted viciously. Marie was not only sentenced to hang but to be gibbeted as well. This degrading punishment was unknown in French law and the court martial's sentence was unique in English criminal law. Hanging in chains actually meant a rehanging and was a gender specific punishment. Until and except for Marie Corriveau, only male criminals suffered this fate.

Marie was probably hanged on or near the Plains of Abraham, across the river from her home in St. Vallier, on April 18, 1763. Shortly afterwards, her body was taken to Pointe Lévy about thirty kilometres from her home and gibbeted at a site frequently visited by travellers. Her decaying body was only exposed to public view for about five weeks — a very short time by English standards for male criminals. Maybe this "mercy" came from Governor Murray's well-known policy of conciliating the newly conquered Canadiens. But, nevertheless, the gibbeting of Marie Corriveau, besides revealing ignorance of British practice, showed everyone that the British were in Canada to govern, with extreme rigour if necessary.

Would Marie Corriveau's fate have been better if she had waited two more years before murdering Dodier? It probably would have been worse under the new civil government. By English criminal law she would have faced a charge of petit (or petty) treason. In a carryover from the feudal idea of allegiance in return for protection, petit treason meant murder aggravated by betrayal. The crime was limited to three situations: a) where a cleric murdered an ecclesiastical superior; b) where a servant murdered his or her employer; c) and where, as in Marie's case, a wife killed her husband.[9] After the Revolution, American women became "citizens." Whatever the equalizing logic of citizenship, they of course remained, under civil and criminal law, almost entirely subordinate to men. There was one single exception: male legislators considered the petit-treason of husband-murder to be too barbaric and feudal as well as too illogical to impose on American citizens. Repeal was widespread. But women living in the British Emire were subjects; repeal in Britain was almost a generation and a half away.[10]

If a husband murdered his wife, his punishment, after conviction, would have been strangulation by hanging, followed by dissection; women murderers, however, were punished differently. The sentence for petit treason specified that a woman be publicly burned alive at a stake.[11] By the eighteenth century, however, public morality (or squeamishness) had evolved sufficiently to permit executioners to strangle the unfortunate women to death before the flames reached their bodies. If Marie Corriveau had been so sentenced after a trial for petit treason, she might have died like Eleanor Elsom in 1722 before a crowd of thousands, with children sitting on their father's shoulders, all straining for the best view of the victim:

> clothed in a cloth, "made like a shift," saturated with tar, and her limbs were also smeared with the same inflammable substance, while a tarred bonnet had been placed on her head. She was brought out of the prison bare-foot, and being put on a hurdle, was drawn on a sledge to the place of execution near the gallows. Upon arrival, some time was passed in prayer, after which the executioner placed her on a tar [sic] barrel, a height of three feet against the stake. A rope ran through a pullet in the stake, and was placed around her neck, she herself fixing it with her hands. Three irons also held her body to the stake, and the rope being pulled tight, the tar

barrel was taken aside and the fire lighted ... She was probably dead before the fire reached her, as the executioner pulled upon the rope several times whilst the irons were being fixed.[12]

Although most women were "probably" dead before the burning began, accidents could and did happen. Catherine Hayes was convicted in 1726 of murdering her husband and while she was "being strangled in the accustomed manner ... the fire scorching the hands of the executioner [while] he relaxed the rope before she had become unconscious, and in spite of efforts at once made to hasten combustion, she suffered for a considerable time the greatest agonies."[13]

On the other hand, if Marie Corriveau had been tried under the English criminal law, she might have received greater protection. As an accused traitor, she would been entitled to a full trial — not a mere half hour's acceptance of her guilty plea. She would have had a defence by legally trained counsel and her lawyer could have examined and cross-examined witnesses, argued questions of law, addressed the jury and advised his client on her final statement. Thus, a clever advocate might well have exploited the problems in the case.

How could virtually every witness swear the wounds were consistent with punctures made by a dung fork when Marie confessed she had hit Dodier with a blunt hatchet? At least one credible witness would have had to link her to the act. Hearsay evidence and village gossip would not have been permitted. Most importantly, a lawyer with the right to multiple challenges might have found a jury sympathetic enough to the story of the Dodier marriage to recommend mercy. And given Murray's conciliatory policy, her life might then have been spared.

News of Joseph Corriveau's pardon, negotiated as part of his confession, infuriated the Deputy Judge Advocate General, Charles Gould in the War Office, London.[14] Murray and Amherst had regularly sent back copies of various courts martial involving civilians, but it was the Corriveau fiasco which caught and held Gould's eye. Probably Marie's unique sentence of gibbeting was responsible for the War Office's sudden, close attention to justice in Canada.

In any case, Gould wrote that as the military had no power to try civilians by courts martial, Murray's pardon for Joseph Corriveau was useless. His complicity in Dodier's murder could only be absolved by a royal pardon. And, while expediting that process, Gould chided Cramahé that he had "only to hint to you a doubt which is entertained with regard to the Trial of Persons not Military, by Courts Martial." Although he supposedly meant this "hint" for Cramahé's ears, Gould could not leave well enough alone. He hoped there would be as little official notice of the Corriveau pardon as possible because "the Court Martial appear to have exceeded their Jurisdiction in his trial as well as in those of Marie Josephte [sic] Corriveau ... and Isabella Silvain" as none were "military Persons." For good measure, he sent a letter with similar sentiments to the governor of Quebec.

These letters reached the city in November 1763 and, naturally enough, outraged Murray. How lucky it was, he wrote sarcastically in reply, that "we did not know, how limited our Jurisdiction has been here for four years past. His Majesty's new Subjects, already prejudiced against us by every popish Art, must have conceived a Strange Opinion of their new Masters, who had no Law to punish the most notorious Murder that perhaps has ever been committed." Besides, he pointed out in his reply, Secretary of State Lord Egremont had approved the legal jurisdiction the governors of Canada had set up in 1761. Why hadn't Gould responded in that year when a court martial had tried a civilian, convicted him of robbery and arson and sentenced him to death and gibbeting? Murray could only conclude that news of that court martial had not reached London.

He had a good point. In March 1761 an ex-soldier in the French army had been sentenced "to be hanged by the Neck, near the City of Montreal Until his Body be dead. After which his Body to be Carried from the place of Execution, to the most Convenient Place near the place where this Horrid Crime was Committed, and they to be Hung In Iron on a Jibbet, in the same manner as practiced in England, Until his Bones shall drop asunder, as a Terror to all evil minded People."[15]

Months after Murray's letter, Thomas Gage, who as governor of Montreal had approved the sentence passed on the soldier, wrote to the War Office explaining just how much havoc Gould's "hint" had caused. He, himself, had not the "smallest doubt" as to the legality of Canadian courts martial and he begged leave to tell Gould of the "Difficultys [sic] and Questions" he had raised. The basic premise that the deputy judge advocate general could not ignore was that "no Government can subsist without Law." In Canada, French law had ceased with the conquest. The army, therefore, had "constituted new Courts of Judicature, and Criminal Cases were ordered to be tried by Genl. Courts Martial." The controversy between Gould and the Canadian governors undoubtedly hastened the establishment of a civilian judicial system in 1764.[16]

Maybe, just maybe, the exemplary manner in which Marie Corriveau was dealt with explained her posthumous fate. Rarely has anyone been so vilified through legend. After her death, no one remembered Dodier's abusive behaviour. Village gossip, conspicuously unembarrassed that it had condemned an innocent man, now centred itself on Marie with a vengeance. There was no further talk of Joseph Corriveau battering Charles Bouchard to death with a currycomb. Instead, the unfortunate man had died after Marie poured molten lead into his ear while he slept. The number of husbands she purportedly murdered multiplied from one to seven. As a way of making her even more diabolical, the number of months between the two real marriages shrank from fifteen to three.[17]

Joseph Corriveau returned to St. Vallier where he lived until his death in 1795. By that time, Marie, now known simply as "la Corriveau" had become thoroughly dehumanized. Legend had her skeletal body begging a traveller to take her to a Satanic celebration as she surrounded the unfortunate man with her bony limbs. Travellers, afraid of her ghost, went far out of their way to avoid the site of her gibbet. Mothers used her spectre to scare their children into good behaviour in much the same way as their contemporaries in England used the bogeyman. Popular genealogy played games with her ancestry, now having her descended from a famous Parisienne poisoner. Her mother, who had so reluctantly testified, perjuring herself as she sought a way not to incriminate either husband or daughter, now also became a poisoner.

Marie Corriveau truly became a villain. Gossip generated legend, which tattooed itself into Quebec's consciousness, first through oral history, then in the mid-nineteenth century, by the works of popular historian Philippe Aubert de Gaspé. After that, other writers and artists took inspiration from her story, each embellishing it to suit themselves. In the end, little remained of the real woman and few, if any, knew that she had lived in a marriage so brutal that she had gone so far as to beg the commanding British officer in the area for permission to escape it. The bruises and dislocations inflicted on her by Louis Dodier conveniently escaped public memory.

In April 1763 Marie Corriveau had no chance for mercy from the officer-bench of her court martial. Days before these men had condemned an innocent man to death based on their acceptance of hearsay evidence and village gossip. Probably, in their minds, Marie did not deserve mercy. She had murdered her husband and seemed to have been prepared to let her father hang in her stead. This, too, was uncertain. Maybe, when the actual time had come, Marie would have confessed her guilt. We will never know. Nor will we know for sure why the village of St. Vallier turned on Joseph Corriveau. Did its distaste and distrust for him begin with Marie's marriage to Dodier? Were Dodier's attacks on Marie at the root of his problems with Joseph Corriveau? Was he so brutal that two of his three stepchildren lived with their grandparents rather than with him? And what exactly happened the night of January 26 to turn Marie into a murderer? Certainly, Claude Dion did not detect that frame of mind before he left the house that night. Did Marie suddenly become a battered woman who could take no more abuse? Was she protecting her daughter Angelique from Dodier? Again, we will never know.

Village gossip was dead wrong about Joseph Corriveau. The legends and myths that grew up around Marie Corriveau were equally rooted in fantasy. Marie, a woman wronged in life, did not deserve the full sum of her lasting infamy.

Chapter Three
"Beauty, Thou Pretty Plaything!": Margaret Jordan — Murderer? Pirate?

In Halifax, in 1810, few doubted that "a Superior Being" concerned himself "in the transactions of mortals."[1] After all, the sensational events of the previous year had provided just one more proof that He protected the righteous. Furthermore, He had shown the punishment a transgressor might expect if "impelled by lawless passion" he or she "wantonly shed the blood of a fellow creature."

For law students Charles Fairbanks and Andrew Cochran, the lesson from 1809 was crystal clear: "we should observe the conduct of those around us, whether it be good or bad ... we should treasure up the recollection of the former, as a lamp to light and cheer us on the journey of life, and the latter, as a beacon to warn us from approaching, too closely the rocks and shoals which have proved fatal to others."[2]

To those unable to reason, Nova Scotia's authorities offered a most graphic lesson. For months a body "blackened and shrunken, dangled from a chain on the bank, at Black-rock cove, now part of Point Pleasant Park."[3] In death, Edward Jordan, convicted murderer, pirate, served as Providence's example, reinforcing conformity to a society he had rebelled against.

Unfortunately, a decade earlier in far-off Ireland, Margaret Croke had no lamp, beacon or dangling corpse to guide her. She had married Edward, an attractive man with dark hair and eyes, a flashing grin and very white teeth in 1798.[4] But for all his handsomeness, Jordan was a man with a history of trouble and a self-asserting axe to grind.

He had begun life respectably. Raised by God-fearing parents, he had inherited the family farm "under ... [his] mother's direction" when only sixteen. His probity brought his landlord's attention, and he made the young man a deputy-receiver of rents on the estate. It was an unpopular job, as Jordan soon discovered when one of the tenants informed against him, alleging that he was secretly training rebels at night. His good reputation meant nothing. Appeals to the landlord were useless. The mere allegation of being a rebel was enough to taint him and, after eight days in jail, Jordan found himself scheduled for execution the next day, apparently without undergoing a trial.

He promptly leapt over the prison wall and escaped.

From that moment until April 1798 he kept his head low, working as a farm labourer. But eventually word reached him that Irish Dragoons had burned his house down and "thrown ... [his] mother into the fire."[5] Jordan immediately joined the rebels. Given a command, he soon found action, taking part in a battle against the British at Wexford where, according to his confession, he saved Protestant lives and never robbed or murdered.[6]

With the end of the rebellion in 1798 he took advantage of the Amnesty Act. Once again a free man without a price on his head, he married Margaret Croke, the couple living in her father's house until the following year. When it was discovered that his papers weren't in order, Jordan was arrested, jailed, and tried. The charges against him were flimsy and he was acquitted. Not eager for further trouble, he left the area, moving his family to New Ross where he worked in a merchant house for four years, until it failed.

At this point, Edward Jordan must have realised he'd used up his options in Ireland and struck out for the New World. After all, nothing he had done so far, with the possible exception of his marriage, had succeeded and he must have been sufficiently canny to realise that Ireland would rise again in rebellion. With his luck, it seemed inevitable he would find himself again in the hands of the British authorities unless he left the country.

So the Jordans with their four children emigrated first to the United States. According to Margaret, it was there "where my wretched husband became jealous of me, and commenced a course of severe treatment towards me, which continued to increase, until it arose to the most violent and cruel treatment, which could be offered by a husband to his wife." She would have left him, she later averred, except "for my little children, for whose sakes I have, for long years, submitted to every species of ill treatment."[7] Apparently more than his marriage fell apart, for Jordan next dragged his family to Lower Canada, trying Montreal first, then Quebec, and ending at Percé on the Gaspé peninsula where he once more tried farming.

Again he ran into trouble, dogged by an owner's debt, and it must have seemed fortuitous when he met the Tremaines of Halifax. They loaned Jordan £70 and in 1808 he sailed to Nova Scotia with four hundred quintals (48,000) of fish and some produce.[8] He told the Tremaines about a schooner that needed only rigging and workers to become seaworthy. He did not intend to run into debt to outfit it, but Jordan promised that if the brothers invested in the ship it would make money for all of them. The Tremaines sent him back to the Gaspé with men and the rigging, promising to take the ship into their fleet and run it between Halifax and the West Indies. At his trial, Jordan testified that he finished the work and sent the ship now named the *Three Sisters* to the Tremaines with a bill of sale and a general power of attorney so they could register it. He estimated its value at £500 and looked forward to his share of the profits from the Halifax-West Indies trade.

There was, of course, another side to the story.

When Jordan visited Halifax and insisted he had a thousand quintal of fish back in the Gaspé, which would take care of his debts to them, the Tremaine brothers became highly suspicious. The Halifax merchants put their own master on *Three Sisters*, Captain John Stairs, sent him to the Gaspé and sued Jordan for the outstanding monies. Back home, an increasingly desperate Jordan found his credit drying up as rumours reached the peninsula that he did not own the ship: "every one I owed demanded payment and those I could not satisfy sued me, and sold my property at one third of its value, which drove me to Despair." No matter what evidence Stairs or the Tremaines presented, Jordan believed that the brothers had cheated him; that they merely held the ship in trust for him and that he was the true owner.

This delusion would be fatal.

John Stairs had been unlucky enough to have been a press-gang victim and forced onto a British man-o-war several years earlier. Surprisingly, he had learned to love the sea and survived until obtaining an honourable discharge. Then, using this naval experience, he signed on to a merchant ship and soon earned his master's ticket. Returning to Halifax for a rest, he became embroiled in the Jordan affair.

When he went to take possession of Jordan's dried cod in the Gaspé, he found less than one hundred quintals — not the thousand that Jordan had claimed. In his version of the story, he repossessed the

Three Sisters, taking formal possession of it in the Tremaines' name. In consequence, Jordan got drunk and remained "intoxicated every day."

Margaret Jordan was also desperate. She had expected her husband to bring clothing and other necessities from Halifax. He, of course, had no money to purchase anything and with her "children naked and comfortless, [she] applied to Captain Stairs for some cotton to make clothes for them." He gave her some calico, presumably prompted by kindness. An inebriated Jordan saw a different motive for Stairs's generosity. Margaret later testified at the trial that "he conceived it had been given as a reward for improper conduct on my part, and beat me in a severe and cruel manner." Even by the time of the trial, four months later, Jordan's "resentment" had "not diminished."

According to the trial report, when the schooner left for Halifax, about September 10, 1809, it was manned by Stairs, his mate, John Kelly and two seamen, Thomas Heath and Benjamin Matthews. Edward and Margaret Jordan were on board with their son and three daughters — the *Three Sisters* for whom the ship had been named. Versions of the story differ. Stairs thought he was doing Jordan a favour by taking him back to Nova Scotia so he could clear his name. On the other hand, Jordan believed he and his family were being sent to a Halifax debtor's prison "which drove ... [him] to distraction." In Ireland he had escaped jail by jumping a fence. This time, his escape plan would be more sinister.

Shortly before noon, on September 13, Stairs went below decks for his quadrant in order "to take the sun." Standing in his cabin, idly flipping through a book, with Heath a little back from him, he happened to glance at the skylight and saw a pistol pointed at him in Jordan's hand.

As he jumped back almost bumping into Heath, Jordan fired. Nearly blinded by the discharge, a relieved Stairs discovered the bullet had only grazed his nose, taking some skin with it.

Mate Thomas Heath was not so lucky because, after grazing Stairs's nose, the bullet rocketed into his chest. Heath then "fell to his knees, crying out, 'Oh, my God! I am killed'" while Stairs, wiping the blood from his face, made an unsuccessful search for weapons as the injured Heath scrambled up to the deck. With his pistols and cutlass gone, Stairs also ran for the deck, meeting Jordan on the way with "one foot on the ladder, a pistol in his left hand, and an axe in his right."

Stairs, a survivor of impressment into the British navy, had faced worse situations. Without panic, he grabbed hold of Jordan's arm and shoved him backwards, pleading, "For God's sake, save my life." When Jordan answered by cocking the pistol, he grabbed hold of the muzzle, wrestled it from him, threw it overboard, and summoned seamen John Kelly and Benjamin Matthews to help him. Matthews responded, running from the aft, "apparently wounded."

After some desperate fighting, Stairs managed to also throw the axe Jordan had carried with him overboard. Puzzled by the other seaman's lack of assistance, he called repeatedly for Kelly, who ignored him. His calls were eventually answered — but in a totally unexpected way. Like an avenging Valkyrie and with the broken handle of a boat hook in hand, Margaret Jordan appeared. She hit Stairs several times while yelling, "Is it Kelly you want, I'll give you Kelly."

About this time, Stairs heard three or four shots and, when he freed himself from Margaret and was able to go on deck, he found a bloodied, dead Heath. Again he tried to find a weapon, racing to the forward part of the ship. Jordan ran the opposite way and found another axe. Then he made his way towards Stairs. Encountering Matthews on the way, he hit him repeatedly and after witnessing this savagery, Stairs knew he had no hope on the ship. Pulling a hatch door from its hinges, he threw it into the sea and jumped in after it. At the time, the *Three Sisters* was approximately three miles east of Cape Canso, well clear of land. Although the weather was relatively warm, the sea was not.

Margaret Jordan's account put a slightly more believable slant on the initial attack. She later testified that Stairs had visited her cabin and, fearing her husband's jealousy, she had sent her son for a seaman to act as a chaperone. Unfortunately the boy brought his father and "immediately a quarrel ensued." By the time she reached the deck, she'd heard the pistol's fire and as she made her way down the companionway, she saw Heath. At this point, the turmoil, brutal scenes and the fearful screaming of her children drove her into "a state of distraction" so that she could not "positively" state to the court that she did not strike Stairs:

> to the best of my knowledge I did not; but, if I did, it
> was in a state of distraction arising from the scene
> which then presented itself to my view: my husband
> distracted with rage, — Heath lying bleeding on the

deck; — the sound of pistols in my ears, — an axe and pistol in the hands of Captain Stairs, who appeared determined on destructions; added to all, my children were screaming with fright.

A convenient memory, totally at odds with Stairs's testimony of "I'll give you Kelly." But it did indeed portray an image of womanhood that the court might accept — a female helpless in the face of male aggression, driven to distraction by scenes of blood.

During the trial, Jordan corroborated his wife's story, saying it was only because he thought Stairs was assaulting his wife that he had attacked the captain. No matter which version of the mêlée was true, two men were dead and to all intents and purposes so was John Stairs. Kelly and the Jordans must have talked about what to do next. Obviously they had to dispose of the bodies of Heath and Matthews and clean the ship. But where would they sail it? How could they escape the Tremaines and the long reach of the British navy? The United States? The West Indies? Ireland?

A few days later, the *Three Sisters* entered Newfoundland waters, anchoring first in Fortune Bay. Jordan now called himself "either John or Edward Tremaine,"[9] and the schooner was now captained by Kelly, claiming to be John Stairs. Almost immediately, Jordan tried to recruit seamen. Two applied, William Crewe and John Pigot, who wanted to work his way to Halifax. But something about the ship and its set-up bothered Pigot and he soon had second thoughts, worrying that Jordan and Kelly would not be able to protect him from being press-ganged into the British navy once the schooner reached Halifax. Only after Jordan gave him a bill of lading for one hundred quintals of fish as payment for the voyage and a justice of the peace threatened to tie him "to the flag staff, and punish ... and give ... [him] a man of war" for his money did Pigot reluctantly agree. Again, he had second thoughts and only after being threatened with irons did he return on board.

After spending a week or so in St. Mary's harbour, they took on a pilot to guide them to St. John's and there Jordan found Patrick Power, a navigator who preferred his winters in Ireland.[10] Telling him that he had a ship laden with cargo and with four hands in Bay Bulls, Jordan hired Power as his master.[11] Although Jordan repeatedly told Power he was in a hurry to leave for Ireland, he kept to his lodging, giving Power the excuse that he owed debts in the city. But after a few days Jordan's business in the city was apparently complete and they set off for the *Three Sisters*. Even that was difficult, for Kelly had taken the schooner to Trepassey and only after searching in various harbours did the men find her. But once they had, further trouble erupted. Jordan found Kelly, his family and two seamen on board, but not Margaret. She was ashore and when Jordan said he'd fetch her, Kelly claimed that only he knew where she was and went back to the shore for her. With his wife safely back on ship, Jordan went to bed. The others, including visitors from the shore, stayed up drinking grog until Jordan got out of bed and stormed into the cabin, furiously shouting at his wife, "You whore, I hear you talk."

Margaret screamed at the inherent violence in her husband's voice. A cool-headed Power interceded, taking away the musket. Thwarted, Jordan began fighting with Kelly and his wife, with Power trying to limit the damage. When Jordan next thought of his pistols, he found that Kelly had hidden them. When Power confiscated these as well, Kelly told him he "did not know what kind of a man Jordan was." Margaret next interceded with Power, asking him to throw the pistols overboard because he did "not know what mischief they had caused." The two continued to implore Power not to let the pistols get into Jordan's hands. Eventually, the three men managed to pacify Jordan after Power took Margaret's advice to "Give him some rum and he will go to sleep."

While he slept, Margaret, convinced that he meant to kill her, begged Pigot to put her on "shore, and let her take some of her clothes with her, as she was afraid her husband would kill her."[12] Power "overheard her saying several times, 'Take me ashore or he will kill me.'" Her pleas went for naught and while the three argued, Jordan stumbled into the room. He grabbed Powers by the chest, demanding his weapons while Margaret "screeched ... 'Power, are you going to let him take my life.'" Jordan replied that he'd never hurt her and inexplicably, given her professed fear, "they both went into the cabin, and were on good terms for the remainder of the day."

Jordan's other troubles were not so easily remedied. A wiser man would have been well out of British North America by now. Even the most stupid would have guessed that the Tremaines would have begun looking for their overdue schooner. That it would be remembered should have crossed Jordan's mind.

The *Three Sisters*, a typical Gaspé schooner, was easily recognizable. In fact, when compared to other ships of the time it was downright ugly, resembling today's container ships in many ways. It had been built for maximum haulage rather than speed or elegance and boasted little, if any, ornamentation, with no figurehead or cabin windows. A widely circulated description called it "a remarkable high stern Schooner." Contributing to her distinctiveness was "a yellow streak running fore and aft from the break of the quarter deck to the stern." Although it had no mouldings, there were imitations in the same yellow paint.[13] She also had tattered, tanned sails. No mariner would forget seeing the *Three Sisters*.

But if bad luck dogged Jordan, it seemed fortune smiled on John Stairs. He had used the press-gang experience to his advantage to earn his master's ticket. Now, his luck would border on the fantastic. Jordan had assumed that when Stairs flung the hatch overboard and dived into the Atlantic after it, he would die. If he didn't drown, surely hypothermia should have finished him.

Stairs, though, belted himself to the hatch and floated, scanning the sea for any passing ship while buffeted by the icy waves. Three and a half hours later, the miracle arrived in the presence of an American fishing schooner, *Eliza* which, against all odds, had heard his weak cries for help. Once on board he received food, dry clothes, and rum. The *Eliza's* captain, Levi Stoddard, though, refused two requests. First, Stairs asked him to pursue the *Three Sisters*, but the captain knew that if he did, a fight would follow and he or his men might be injured or killed. Nor would Stoddard sail to Halifax. That was also understandable, given the British navy's penchant for impressing American seamen. And so, Stairs remained on board the *Eliza* until she reached Hingham, Massachusetts, and then made his way post-haste to the British consul in Boston.

By October 10, 1809, nine days before Jordan signed his contract with Power, news of Stairs's survival had reached Halifax. The *Nova Scotia Royal Gazette* trumpeted the story of the murders and the seizure of the *Three Sisters*, calling it "an act of the greatest piracy, attended with most horrid barbarities." It also hoped "Printers in the neighbouring Provinces, indeed in all parts of the World, will give publicity to Capt. Stairs' Report, and the following necessary particulars — They may lead to the apprehension of the perpetrators." A letter from Stairs to the Tremaines dated September 26, 1809, detailing his version of the events of September 13, followed. In this, Stairs wrote that Margaret Jordan "appeared to take as active a part as her husband: — She assisted in killing poor Heath, who, in his agony, had got upon the deck."

The authorities reacted swiftly. Nova Scotia's governor, Sir George Prevost, issued a proclamation detailing the heinous activities and that "in order to encourage all persons to exert themselves in bringing the said Murderers and Pirates to justice, I have thought fit ... to offer a reward of £100 sterling."[14] The date was October 20, 1809, the day after Power had signed on to captain the *Three Sisters*. And, if that sum should not prove sufficient, the Tremaine brothers offered an additional £100.

Sublimely ignorant, Power tried to ready the ship for the long voyage to Ireland. On finding the existing provisions insufficient, he put the ship on a course for Bay Bulls where Jordan claimed to have friends. He went ashore the next day, returning with wood and water and expressing his regret that they hadn't set sail for Ireland from Trepassey. After he had gone ashore the following day, Power was asked by Margaret Jordan if she could also disembark as she needed to wash the children's clothes and, after seeing his reluctance, promised that someone could watch her. This turned out to be Pigot. Power found Jordan and reported that Margaret was also on shore and "he then seemed much disturbed, and asked ... Power to take her on board again" which they did.

That night Jordan wanted to set sail immediately. Power refused, giving the lack of wind as an excuse. Jordan countered by bringing a number of men to tow the vessel out and soon confided the reason for his urgency. A naval cutter from Nova Scotia had reached St. John's and was expected in Bay Bulls the following morning at which point the *Three Sisters* would be seized, or so he claimed.

"Why?" asked Power.

A debt, Jordan answered. That couldn't be, Power responded. The governor "would not send a King's Schooner" for a mere debt.

"I wish I had met with some other person but you, as I would now have been half way to Ireland," an exasperated Jordan countered.

If Jordan wanted another captain, that was fine with Power and he offered to leave the ship the next day. But no one would take him ashore. Jordan had determined that saying he "might as well take his life as go on shore that evening, and that he would stay up all night" to make sure Power stayed on board. The farce then continued. Kelly took the schooner's rowboat and set out for shore, promising to send the boat back for Power, who was below decks gathering his belongings together when someone shouted that the cable was cut.

Jordan, the farmer, had taken matters into his own hands, cutting the cable and ordering up the jib. Power stormed after Jordan and, finding him aft with an axe in his hand, shouted, "I see you have her under weigh . . ."

"I have, and you shall go to sea or blood!"

Power shrugged. What could he do? It had taken a while, apparently, but he now suspected Jordan "to be a terrible kind of man." He directed Pigot to claim the axe from Jordan, and seeing a sail in the distance, took the helm and ordered all hands on deck. Jordan now wanted him to set a course for Nova Scotia in the hope that people in Bay Bulls would give a false direction if asked. Power refused. A half hour later, one of the sailors saw another sail and when a panicking Jordan asked what it was, Power identified it as a fishing vessel. Again, Jordan requested that a course be set for Halifax; in response, Power threatened to strike the helmsman with "a handpike" if he changed direction.

Shortly afterwards, Power told Jordan that the approaching ship was the navy schooner. Jordan "seemed in great confusion and trouble" saying, "Lord, have mercy on me — what will my poor children do." Again, idiotically, he begged Power to say they were bound for Halifax; again the captain refused. Then, according to Power:

> The cutter fired at us to bring us to, and then came up and spoke to us. I told them we were bound for Halifax; upon which they desired us to put out our boat, and come on board. I told them we had no boat [Kelly had taken it]... They then put out one from the cutter, and *Mr. Simpson* came on board the *Three Sisters*, took possession of her and brought her to Halifax.

The Jordan family, Power, William Crewe and seaman Nathaniel Ryder were taken on to the cutter. Kept in chains near Power's berth, Jordan couldn't keep his mouth shut, maintaining it was all Kelly's fault: "if he had killed that Stairs, while he was on the hatch, all would have been well; and that he wanted Kelly to let him load a pistol or musket, but that Kelly said there was no necessity, as Stairs would drown before he reached the shore."

Kelly was also captured. After rowing ashore in Bay Bulls he had fled into the forest. Shortly afterwards, the Nova Scotia Regiment hunted him down. Their commanding officer, a Lieutenant Cartwright received a prize of £20 from the merchants of St. John's for freeing the island of such a dangerous criminal.[15] He would soon be sent to Nova Scotia and tried shortly after the Jordans.[16]

The hijacking of the *Three Sisters*, the return of John Stairs from his supposed watery grave and the capture of those responsible had both scandalized and titillated Halifax. The governor, appreciating the widespread interest and publicity, determined that the trial of Edward and Margaret Jordan for murder, piracy, and robbery on the high seas would be a spectacular example of the long reach of His Majesty's law. Prevost convened "a special Court of Admiralty for the Trial of Piracies, Felonies, and Robberies committed on the High Seas."[17] No expense would be spared, resulting in a raft of bills eventually reaching the provincial treasury. The sundries alone totalled £132.19.1. Most items were ominous: £4.12.8 for carpentry in making gallows, gibbets and a coffin; £3.8.6 in provisions and liquor for the constables, carpenters and smiths. The calligraphy for the warrants etc. cost £37.8.4 and the courthouse needed alterations. Four men laboured for two and half days to make it worthy of the court of vice admiralty.[18]

Those who observed the Jordan trial must have been overwhelmed by the pomp and ceremony. The governor himself presided over the court which included such luminaries as the "Right Honorable Sir John Borlase Warren, K.B. and K.C., one of His Majesty's most honorable Privy Council for the Kingdom of Great Britain, Vice Admiral of the White, and Commander in Chief of all his Majesty's ships of War on the coast of North America" on the bench. Weighed down with titles and their medals, the fourteen member bench must have been a splash of scarlet, blue and gold and an awe-inspiring sight — as it was designed to be.

The three main witnesses against the Jordans were Stairs, Pigot, and Power. Edward and Margaret were each permitted to make a statement. Jordan stressed the fact that he had taken only what he thought was lawfully his. Margaret's defence appealed to the heart strings: "I stand before you ... being brought to trial, in a strange land, where my character and past conduct are unknown and where no person can be called in my defence ... I have for many long years, submitted to every species of ill treatment" at the hands of Jordan. She gave her version of the assaults, claiming no clear memory of what had happened, going on to state: "From that to the time of the schooner's being taken, I suffered all that I could bear, and was frequently almost tempted to cast myself into the sea, and would have done it, but for my children, who still chained me to misery."

Certainly, if the statements of Pigot and Power are to be believed, Margaret Jordan seemed a prisoner on the ship. Her requests to go ashore were either ignored or, if granted as at Trepassey, she was promptly brought back on board the *Three Sisters*. There was absolutely no corroboration during the trial of Stairs's statement in his letter to the Tremaines, as published by the *Nova Scotia Royal Gazette*, that Margaret Jordan actively assisted in the murder of Thomas Heath.

The prosecution had painted a horrific picture of Jordan, stating his life should be forfeited "for it is not in the power of the human mind to reject the force of such testimony [concerning] ... such circumstances of horror, as cannot but raise a blush in the face of human nature. The crime of this unhappy man has been committed under the diabolical influence of almost every bad passion, that could irritate and torment his disturbed soul, nor could the presence of his wife and his children rouse a sentiment in him to oppose the instigation of the devil." The court agreed, sentencing him to hang on the gallows until dead and then to be gibbeted.

Against the thrust of the evidence, Margaret Jordan was found not guilty.

Two statements highlight the judgment. First, the court claimed to have "been very indulgent" to Margaret, in adjudging her not guilty. The members clearly thought she might have been found guilty of some crime or crimes. Indulgence was extended because of "some favourable circumstances which have appeared in your case." This gives rise to several questions: Which crime or crimes? What circumstances? Why were they significant?

Mrs. Jordan was charged with helping her husband murder Heath and Mathews — that is, with being a principal in the second degree, a capital offence without benefit of clergy. The evidence at trial, however, indicates that Heath, certainly, and Mathews, probably, were shot by Edward before Margaret joined the fray, although whether they died because of the shootings is unclear. Stairs testified that Jordan later struck Mathews' head three or four times with an axe, but there was nothing in the record to show Margaret encouraged or assisted her husband in this situation.[19] Thus, the trial report offers no warrant for thinking that Mrs. Jordan had been guilty of murder and it will soon become apparent the court thought she had not been. Stairs' statement in his letter to the owners of the *Three Sisters* that Margaret had finished off Heath was not repeated at trial.

While Margaret had not been proved a murderer, the evidence does suggest she may have committed other crimes. For instance, she seems to have acted as an accessory after the fact to the murder of Heath or, perhaps, Heath and Mathews both. This was not a capital offence, but a misdemeanour at common law — as were having assaulted or even having attempted with her husband to kill Stairs, for either of which she may have been guilty. Finally, it is almost certain Margaret assisted her husband in his piracy and hence was a pirate herself, unless the law excused her.

Aside from the paucity of official proof that Mrs. Jordan had murdered, the contents of the trial report were favourable to her only in tending to show she had acted in fear of her husband. Margaret's statement claimed that Jordan had subjected her over several years "to the most violent and cruel treatment" imaginable. She claimed that at Percé he had beaten her over the calico incident, believing it had been given by Stairs in exchange for sexual favours and he remained convinced of her infidelity down to the day of the trial. More generally, Margaret asserted that "at all times she had laboured on the greatest fear of his resentment." Pigot and Power, witnesses to events on board the *Three Sisters* after it arrived in Newfoundland, swore that Jordan threatened to kill his wife, the "whore," and that she was terrified this would happen. Perhaps the best evidence favouring the accused was given in response to defence counsel's cross-examination of Pigot: "Did the Prisoner Margaret Jordan, at all times, from the first time you saw her, appear to be in great fear of her husband, and altogether under his authority?" Pigot's answer was to the point: "Yes she did."

The fear motif makes it almost certain that Margaret owed her acquittal, even her life, to the operation of a rule of law now archaic: the presumption that when a married woman committed almost any indictable crime in the presence of her husband, she did so under such a compulsion as to warrant a verdict of not guilty. In other words, the presumption of "spousal coercion." It could be rebutted by evidence that she had acted voluntarily, by assuming a leadership role among a group of burglars for instance. Mere proof of activity greater than her husband's — say, in hiding stolen goods — was not sufficient.[20] Nor was evidence of a previous conspiracy of the spouses to commit the offence.[21]

The defence of spousal coercion was carefully considered by the court. Both prosecuting lawyers brought it up, only to deny its relevance. Mr. Hutchinson claimed it did not apply to murder, treason or robbery, of which piracy was often an example. The Solicitor General made a similar claim with regard to murder and piracy and further asserted that:

> in point of fact, I do not conceive it will appear that any coercion of her husband existed in the part she took, for, on the contrary, her interference must have been voluntary, and her feelings could have been under no restraint from the scene of Blood presenting itself to her view, when she exclaimed, in reply to Stairs calling for Kelly, [sic] "Is it Kelly you want? I'll give you Kelly."

The court included at least three highly trained men of law: Councillors Edward Brabazon Brenton, former practitioner, then a judge in the Chancery Court and deputy judge advocate general for British North America; Attorney General Richard John Uniacke; and the exceedingly learned Chief Justice of the Province, Samuel Salter Blowers.

The standard explanation of the rule's origins and rationale point to the subordination of the married woman to her husband, both in law and in practice. An alternative sometimes put forward — most notably in 1883 by the eminent judge and jurist Sir James Fitzjames Stephen — stresses the unfair operation of the benefit of clergy plea which, until the late seventeenth century, was not extended to lay women. Thus, were a couple to be convicted jointly of committing a "clergyable" felony, the husband, if he could offer a semblance of reading, would be lightly punished, while his wife, even where less guilty, would be sentenced to and might suffer death. It was argued by Stephen and others that to balance this injustice roughly, medieval judges elaborated the doctrine of spousal coercion.[22]

This alternate explanation, unsupported by historical proof, is undermined by simple chronology. Benefit of clergy emerged only after the Norman conquest for the clergy and was not extended to lay males until the thirteenth century. The spousal coercion defence, by contrast, dates back to Anglo-Saxon times, probably to the reign of King Ina in the early eighth century and at the very least that of King Canute (1016-35) in the eleventh.[23] Benefit of clergy was extended to lay women by Parliament in 1692; yet spousal coercion remained the law until abolished by statute in 1925 and was subjected to no serious legal criticism until the late nineteenth century. Moreover, there is evidence that the medieval rule was based on the married woman's subordination and that the benefit of clergy explanation was a seventeenth century rationalization.[24]

The reason for the rule, from the beginning to end, then, lay in the subordination of the wife to her spouse. This subordination was often expressed in normative terms: a married woman should obey her husband, as was indeed laid down by law. The presumption was also justified by supposed empiricism: actual subordination in the overwhelming majority of cases and situations. A sixteenth and a twentieth century judge, for example, were agreed that "the law was founded on the assumption that a woman would never dare to contradict" her familial lord.[25] As late as 1922 a peer of the realm could favour the rule by these arguments presented in the House of Lords:

> It is my firm conviction that the bulk of women to-day act under the direction of their husbands ... That is most assuredly true as you get down into the poor and poorer conditions of life. Nor am I one of those people ... who is prepared to destroy what has been established by the wisdom of our ancestors as though it were of no value at all ... If a woman commits a crime in the presence of her husband, I think it shows the immense sagacity of the Common Law when it says you shall assume she was doing it under his direction.

Lord Chancellor Birkenhead, the highest and most powerful legal official in the British Empire (and, as such, not intimate with the poor and poorer conditions of life) agreed, noting that among "the humbler ranks of society, it is ... absolutely true that there is a very great degree of that kind of control which our ancestors had in their minds when they surrounded a woman with their protection."[26] Ironically, Scotland — land of the arch-criminal who guided her husband, Lady Macbeth — never had a similar rule.[27]

From the beginning, there must have been critics of this rule — not arguing what ought to be but what actually was. Charles Dickens put the most famous critique into the mouth of Mr. Bumble, the bumbling parish beadle married to a know-it-all in *Oliver Twist*:

> "It was all Mrs Bumble. She *would* do it," urged Mr Bumble; first looking round to ascertain that his partner had left the room.
>
> "That is no excuse," replied Mr Brownlow. "You were present on the occasion of the destruction of these trinkets, and indeed are the more guilty of the two, in the eye of the law; for the law supposes that your wife acts under your direction."
>
> "If the law supposes that," said Mr Bumble, squeezing his hat emphatically in both hands, "the law is a ass — a idiot. If that's the eyes of the law, the law is a bachelor ..."[28]

The first serious criticisms from men of law or politicians occurred only in the late nineteenth and early twentieth centuries — beginning with a Royal Commission on the criminal law, 1878-9, and quickly followed by jurist James Fitzjames Stephen who pointed to a gross absurdity. Stephen postulated a case of theft committed jointly by a man and his wife and fifteen-year-old daughter in his presence. No proof was offered for or against coercion by the husband, but it was established that the daughter acted in response to her father's threats. The law in such a case would require an acquittal of the mother but conviction of the daughter.[29]

More than one judge in the period referred to the presumption as that "melancholy rule."[30] In Canada abolition occurred, without generating the slightest controversy, when the criminal law was codified in 1892. During the Common's debate, Minister of Justice Sir John Thompson answered in this straightforward way to the single question on the topic:

> The presumption under the common law is in many
> cases a strained one. In many cases the wife commits an
> act of violence in spite of her husband, but under the
> common law it is presumed she is acting under the
> compulsion of her husband if she does that in his
> presence. We now leave that to be a matter of evidence,
> to be proved in court, whether she acted under the
> compulsion of her husband or in spite of her husband.[31]

Reform came a generation later in the United Kingdom. In 1912 a
judge repudiated the rule, but it was restored on appeal.[32] By the 1920s,
however, the presumption began to appear more and more
anachronistic and absurd. Women attended universities, practised the
established professions of law and medicine, voted in elections and sat
as lawmakers in the House of Commons. The Great War had seen
hundreds of thousands working outside the home and many remained
employed afterwards: female shorthand typists, for example.

The beginning of the end came with the case of *R* v. *Peel and Wife*
in 1922.[33] It involved a fast-posting horserace betting scam carried out
jointly by a married couple. The husband was sent to jail; Mrs. Peel
gained an acquittal. Judge Darling condemned the rule as "absolutely
inappropriate to modern life" and "absurd" what with females "now
serving on juries and becoming members of Parliament" and "when
every one sees women's names at the top of all [university] class lists."
He also made clear that the presumption forced him to acquit, though
satisfied that in fact Mrs. Peel had not acted under compulsion from
her husband.

Following *R* v. *Peel and Wife*, legal and political forces attacked the
rule in earnest. A recurrent repeal campaign in Parliament got underway
immediately after. The very first parliamentarian to speak was a Viscount
Ullswater who devoted his maiden speech in the House of Lords to the
subject. Ullswater had it correct when he characterized the doctrine of
spousal coercion as connoting "an inferior and degraded status — a
thing which the women of the present day never would accept."[34] Repeal
of the presumption — but not the possibility of proving marital
coercion in cases other than treason and murder — came in 1925.[35]

Of vital importance to the Jordans' case is the scope of the
presumption in 1809.

The number and identity of the exceptions were never settled by Parliament, judicial decisions or juristic agreement. By the second third of the nineteenth century, the presumption clearly applied to almost all misdemeanours, such as assault,[36] and most felonies, that is, capital offences, including forgery, shoplifting, arson, and burglary. Consensus did exist that at least the two most heinous felonies, murder and high treason, were exempted. The first supposedly ran so contrary to nature and God's law that it could not be excused even by the duress arising from credible, present threats of death. Treason was widely deemed the mother of crimes, responsible for spawning such atrocities as rape, robbery, murder, and of course civil war. Moreover, the traitorous husband, having broken his sacred obligation of obedience to the state, was no longer entitled to be obeyed by anyone, not even the wife he held in legal vassalage.[37] Beyond exempting treason and murder, consensus broke down — although it was never suggested that piracy should be included with them.

The master jurist of the late seventeenth century, Sir Mathew Hale, added manslaughter to the list of exemptions.[38] This addition seems illogical, since the offence was not considered by men of law, then or later, as exceedingly grave. Manslaughter was indeed a felony, but one subject to the benefit of clergy and hence not really capital. In any case Hale's suggestion was taken up neither by the courts nor the jurists, not even by Sir William Blackstone or William Oldnall Russell, the eminent nineteenth century criminal law specialist, both of whom interpreted the exceptions very broadly.[39] The next addition chronologically was of far greater relevance to the Jordans' case.

The early eighteenth century commentator, William Hawkins, without providing reasons, included among the exemptions the crime of robbery, that is, theft accomplished by violence or threats thereof.[40] Again, this does not seem very convincing since duress as described above was a defence and it is also unclear why robbery should have been considered more heinous than burglary or arson, both of which often put life at risk. Although robbery gained more adherents than manslaughter, including Hutchinson in the trial being analyzed, it was generally ignored or rejected by judges and jurists, including the influential Blackstone.[41]

Another addition potentially relevant to the Jordans' case was offered by Blackstone himself. This was not a single offence but an entire category of them, what he called crimes "*mala in se*" or inherently evil, "being prohibited by the law of nature, [such] as murder and the like." This elastic exception to the presumption of spousal coercion was justified "not only because these [crimes] are of a deeper dye, but also, since in a state of nature no one is in subjection to another, it would be unreasonable to screen an offender from the punishment due to natural crimes, by the refinements of civil society." Being almost impossible to define, Blackstone's concept was virtually stillborn.[42]

A strong argument, then, can be made that in 1809 all felonies, except treason and murder, were covered by the presumption of the weak-willed, dutiful wife. This was explicitly laid down a generation later by the able judge James Parke, a Baron of the Exchequer and dominant personality on that court. Parke's judgment foreshadowed the shape of the law on point in the early twentieth century.[43]

One can readily understand why the court acquitted Margaret Jordan. The rule on spousal coercion, although not crystal clear, could most reasonably be interpreted in her favour. She had not committed murder. Being an accessory after the fact, assaulting someone and attempting to kill were all offences covered by the presumption. No one had ever suggested that piracy should be exempted. A successful piracy, though, necessarily involved robbery and that crime was occasionally put forward as falling outside the rule. This was not a logical suggestion, however, and had not been mentioned by Hale or Blackstone, the most influential exponents of the common law in 1809 and for decades after. And crimes *mala in se* were impossible to define with any confidence.

Two further points must be made. First: the fact that Margaret had personally engaged in violence did not act to rebut the presumption.[44] Second: the crown introduced no rebuttal proof except for the accused's telling Stairs, while striking him with a boat hook handle: "Is it Kelly you want? I'll give you Kelly." Standing by itself, the statement is ambiguous. It might mean she enthusiastically joined in the piracy or that she was simply bolstering her spirits or again she was showing manifest loyalty to a dreaded husband. Not only did the crown offer no persuasive proof of voluntary participation, but the defence provided cogent evidence that Mrs. Jordan had acted in fear of her husband. The assertions of Pigot and Power and her statement may or may not have been accurate, but they were not contradicted by the prosecution. The impression all this made on the editor of *The Novator* is clear from his editorial note that "whatever part she may have taken in the unhappy transactions with her husband, [she] has been incited to, more from the fear of his sanguinary arm, than induced by ... malice."[45] Undoubtedly the court had a similar impression.

Chapter Four
Julia Murdock — From "Comparative Innocence to ... Blackest Guilt"?

Upper George Street, Toronto
Thursday, August 17, 1837

Harriet Henry lay dead.[1] Horribly and indubitably. Her body sprawled against the bed, the head twisted at a grotesque angle. Foam filled the grimacing mouth.

Summoned at about 6:00 a.m. by Harriet Henry's servant-companion, Julia Murdock, neighbour James Orr knew nothing he or anyone else could do would help. He had seen a similar corpse in the "old country" and, correctly deducing that she had been poisoned, left the Henry house in order to summon the coroner, Mr. Henderson. At that point he seemed to be the only person concerned with the whys and wherefores of Mrs. Henry's death.

Maybe it was understandable. At best, she had enjoyed a very ambivalent relationship with her husband, James Henry. They did not live "upon as good terms as man and wife should" and some in the neighbourhood believed that James beat his wife. Julia Murdock was only one who spread such rumours. In any case, James Henry seemed to be little affected by his wife's death and rather than immediately going with Orr for help he sat on the bed, calmly dressing himself properly.

Julia Murdock's actions were even more inexplicable. After waking Orr, she had gone to Mrs. Dunlop, a friend of Mrs. Henry's, arriving at her shop about 6:30 a.m. There, she baldly announced that her employer had sent her for six silver spoons. The request sent off alarm bells. Mrs. Dunlop stalled for a while, asking how her friend was. Julia replied she was well and only after Murdock repeated her request twice more did Mrs. Dunlop part with the spoons. Ominously, she did not learn that her friend had died until after Julia had left.

By that time, Orr had returned to the Henry house. Certain in his own mind that Mrs. Henry had been poisoned, he began assiduously searching for evidence. He didn't have far to look — in fact, provisions laced with arsenic seemed to be everywhere. At the foot of the bed, he found a "delf" bowl with dead flies littering the remaining water gruel. A locked bureau drawer yielded newly cooked floured fish and some potato cakes. In the kitchen, he discovered the utensils the food had been in. One pot looked as if it had been licked clean and, shortly afterwards, Orr stumbled across the body of a dead cat, which had been alive when he had first entered the house that morning.

At eight o'clock the suspicious Mrs. Dunlop arrived at the Henry house. Immediately she accosted Julia, reproaching "her for her duplicity" and threatening to send her to jail. The sullen girl merely repeated that she'd told the truth, that Mrs. Henry had sent her for the spoons. At Mr. Henry's request, Mrs. Dunlop went into the bedroom to ask the "laying out" woman for Mrs. Henry's rings. When told there weren't any, the redoubtable Mrs. Dunlop once more confronted Julia, this time virtually accusing her of theft. Julia denied the charge, telling Mrs. Dunlop she'd probably find the rings in the bedside area. Somewhat to her astonishment, Mrs. Dunlop did indeed discover one of the rings in the straw mattress and another in a bureau drawer.

She also found a veil of Mrs. Henry's in a box belonging to Julia. Telling Mr. Henry her discoveries, she also asked why he had not sent for a doctor when his wife was so ill. He had, the new widower told her. In fact, he had sent Julia Murdock three times for the doctor and one of those times she had left the house at eleven o'clock and didn't return until three p.m. Mrs. Dunlop did not ask if Henry had scolded his wife's servant, or if he sent someone in her stead, given the length of Julia's absence. She did not seek Henry's reactions to Julia's leave of absence. She knew who had murdered her friend and she would see justice done.

Justice came swiftly. James Orr, who had left for the coroner's house within minutes after discovering the body, returned to the house and began collecting evidence — the "delf" bowl, the "licked-clean" pot, a potato cake and newly-cooked fish — all of which had been hidden in a locked drawer. Then, turning detective, he helped to find witnesses for the coroner's inquest.

After being woken by Orr, the coroner, Mr. Henderson, immediately gathered twelve men for his jury. The inquest was held later that day.[2] "Suspicion was excited by the cat being found also dead" and significantly also by the behaviour of both Julia Murdock and James Henry. Not only was the basin of gruel given to the doctors for examination, but also a bottle of fluid that Mrs. Henry had drunk, which had been given to her by her husband. Much also was made of the fact that James Henry had altered his customary eating habits. The previous morning he had refused to eat fish and taken a piece of pork instead.

The coroner next called two witnesses to connect Murdock with the purchasing of poison. James W. Brent, of J. W. Brent & Company, "Apothecaries & Druggists, seedsmen, Oil & color-men," was called to the stand.[3] He recalled selling some arsenic to "a young woman somewhat about the size and make of Julia Murdock" at the beginning of the week; when asked what she wanted it for, the young purchaser had replied, "to poison rats, sir." Although he could remember the conversation, he could or would not positively identify Murdock as his customer.

His apprentice had no such qualms. Cornelius Webster vividly remembered Murdock entering the store the previous day. In fact, she had asked him for "two penny worth" of arsenic. But, as he was serving another customer, he had referred her to his employer. He also remembered seeing Brent label the package and believed it was poison. At that point the inquest adjourned in order for Mrs. Henry's stomach to be examined by Doctors John King and Charles Widmer.

When it reconvened a few hours later, the doctors certified that from the "appearance of the stomach and the bowels ... Harriet Henry came by her death from the effect of a corrosive mineral poison ... which [they had] ... reason to suspect ... was arsenic, from experiments made on the contents of the stomach." That was enough for the jury, which found "That the said Harriet Henry ... departed this life by means of metallic poison, administered to the said Harriet Henry by Jane [sic] Murdock: and they further find that James Henry aided and assisted in the administration thereof." Both Murdock and Henry were taken to the Toronto jail to wait for their trial in the next assizes "on suspicion of having committed this horrid deed."[4]

Brought back to the house the next day, Murdock seemed in a state of shock, asking Orr what was happening, why she was incarcerated. He sternly replied that the authorities considered Mrs. Henry's death suspicious, that they were treating it as a poisoning case and furthermore that she knew best whether or not she was guilty and thus deserved being returned to jail. Later, he would recall that she had answered she "wished to God she had told all the day before."

As can be gauged by the newspaper coverage the crime engendered, the murder of Mrs. Henry was a sensation. The subsequent trial would be equally so with almost the full transcript printed in the *Toronto Patriot*. A Grand Jury had returned a true bill against James Henry and Julia Murdock on November 10, 1837 and a week later the trial began with the Chief Justice of Upper Canada on the bench.[5] After the prisoners had pleaded "not guilty," their respective counsels successfully asked for separate trials, after which the case against Julia Murdock began.

Attorney General Christopher Hagerman led the prosecution and, as he told the jury in his opening address, Murdock was charged with two counts of murder: with having jointly poisoned Harriet Henry and "as having induced Henry to do it." If guilty on either count, Murdock's "own life should be forfeited for the life she had taken." The jury should "calmly and cautiously" weigh all the evidence and not be swayed from their "conscientious belief" by any "feeling of compassion for the youth of the prisoner." Hagerman then recounted the basic facts of his case that his witnesses would later testify to: that the Tuesday before Mrs. Henry's death, Murdock had bought arsenic from Mr. Brent's store; that Mrs. Henry became ill immediately afterwards, showed symptoms of having been poisoned, and died early the following Thursday in "the greatest agony;" and that neither of the accused had sent for medical help.

James Orr, the first witness, told of being woken by Julia, of going to the Henry house, of finding the body, and of taking his suspicions to the coroner twenty minutes later. He identified the various contaminated foods and containers he had found on August 17: the "delf" bowl, with about twenty dead flies still in it; the "licked-clean" pot; and even a piece of a potato cake. Orr had last seen Mrs. Henry alive the Monday before her death, when she had been in good health. He also testified to James Henry's state of mind that Thursday morning: "he was in very low circumstances and asked witness to get him a ... coffin for the burial of his wife." Julia Murdock had seemed also concerned with Mrs. Henry's burial saying "that she had better be buried to-day as the body would not keep."

Only in 1836 had persons accused of murder received the full right to counsel; Julia Murdock was extraordinarily fortunate in obtaining hers. Henry Sherwood was the eldest son of Mr. Justice Levius Peters Sherwood, a nephew to Justice Jonas Jones. He had been educated by the

Reverend John Strachan and thus had powerful connections to the governing elite. Originally from the Johnstown District, Sherwood had set up a Toronto practice in November 1835. In June 1836, he successfully ran as a Tory candidate in the provincial election where, according to his biographer, Donald Robert Beer, "he rapidly learned the basics of procedure and debate ... spoke effectively and often on general issues ... [and] showed great interest in improving the administration of justice and raising the standards of his profession." [6] He would mount a well-thought out defence.

His defence began with the cross-examination of Orr. After Sherwood elicited the fact that Orr had known the Henrys for twenty-one months and claimed to know them "well," he then asked if the relationship between Harriet Henry and Murdock seemed to be one of mother and daughter. Yes, Orr replied, "they seemed fond of each other." In fact, Julia had told him that "Henry abused the deceased, and seemed hurt that such treatment should be given her."

Mrs. Dunlop's testimony centred on the fact that Mrs. Henry had been looking forward to the future. She had planned to move to new and better lodgings and spoke of attending auction sales. Julia Murdock had often come to her shop with messages from her employer, but that Thursday morning, August 17, Mrs. Dunlop's antennae had been triggered by two things: Julia's dress "was not as neat as usual" and her insistence on getting the silver spoons. Mrs. Dunlop confirmed that Henry beat his wife but when she had talked about it with her friend, Harriet had told her she "couldn't live happily away from" him.

The Crown's third witness was Mary Henry, James Orr's sister. She added little to the case, other than she had become sick herself after visiting Mrs. Henry the Wednesday before she died; that illness had subsequently spread to her family. This was why Martha Kilgore, the "laying out lady," thought Mrs. Henry had died from cholera. Mary Henry was her niece and had told her of the illnesses.

When Kilgore had first seen the body it was cold, except for the stomach, and it was "very dark about the bosom." She asked questions why no doctor had been summoned and received inconclusive answers. Henry had picked up the dead cat and wondered why it had died. He also told her that his wife had been "very bad" throughout the night before her death and had said at one point, "James, I shall not trouble you long." She had also apparently screamed several times and asked Henry to lie closer to her as she was cold. Mrs. Kilgore had not seen any rings on the body when she examined it.

Cornelius Webster testified next; his memory had become sharper since the coroner's inquest. He said that he had called his employer to serve Murdock and that he now remembered Mr. Brent labelling the package "poison." At the inquest, two days after the incident, he had only "thought" it was poison. Unfortunately, Sherwood did not exploit this discrepancy. James Brent's testimony was otherwise consistent with that which he had given at the inquest. He couldn't identify Julia then and he didn't at the trial. With his evidence, the crown now turned to its medical experts.

In her 1998 book, *Twisting in the Wind*,[7] historian Judith Knelman writes about female murderers and the English press. In the section "Proof of Poisoning" she states that there was no requirement in England for purchasers of poison to identify themselves until 1851. Obviously, given the testimony of Brent and Webster, this lack of identification applied to Upper Canada as well. Arsenic was a favourite for poisoners:

> easy to acquire, cheap [Julia Murdock paid only twopence], colourless, odourless, soluble in water, and hard to detect. Since the symptoms were not unlike those of severe diarrhoea or cholera [Martha Kilgore's conclusion], it was not usually suspected as a cause of death. When it was suspected, the Marsh (1836) or Reinsch (1841) tests could sometimes confirm it, but these were often used ineptly, and sometimes produced conflicting results.

The evidence of Drs. King and Widmer was therefore crucial to proving that Mrs. Henry died of arsenic poisoning and the care they took to confirm this reveals the state of research and forensic knowledge in Upper Canada in 1837.

When Dr. King had first viewed the body on August 17, at 10:30 a.m., he had seen nothing unusual except for "a livid mark along the upper part of the chest, extending to the neck and around it." He thought the mark was justified by what he was told, particularly by Mrs. Kilgore — namely, that the victim had vomited violently and continuously throughout the night. Therefore, he had gone to the inquest thinking Harriet Henry a victim of cholera. It was only after hearing the evidence of Orr and Brent, in particular, that he became sufficiently suspicious to tell the coroner he wanted to do an autopsy with a friend.

That friend was Dr. Christopher Widmer, a physician, surgeon, army officer, medical educator and administrator, justice of the peace, office holder and politician.[8] Born in England, he had come to Upper Canada as a surgeon during the War of 1812, retired on half-pay in 1817 and moved to York (Toronto). From that point, he had risen quickly to become a dominant member of the profession and was as concerned with its progress as Sherwood was with the progress of the legal profession. He set up York's general hospital, 1829, becoming its senior medical officer. As a justice of the peace, from 1822, he was, according to Paul Romney his biographer, "one of the most assiduous members of the Home District Bench." This assiduity may have had fatal consequences for Julia Murdock as we will see.

When King and Widmer began the autopsy at 2 p.m., August 17, King immediately noticed great changes in the body. Huge quantities of a "dark brown or blackish looking fluid" flowed from the mouth and nostrils. When the cadaver's stomach was pressed, the flow accelerated. King made his first incision along the chest and abdomen, remarking at the time that Mrs. Henry had been in good health, given the relative lack of fat. The stomach, though, was "much inflamed." The peritoneal covering was "still smooth and shining," presenting "an appearance as if it was injected minutely with red wax injection; it had a beautiful arborescent appearance." Not so beautiful perhaps were the stomach's contents: "about a pint and a half of a dark brown coloured fluid, somewhat like coffee grounds, but darker, from which numerous bubbles of gas escaped and continued to escape even when the matter was poured into a basin." Numerous white particles permeated the stomach, particularly "towards the larger extremity" and he had no doubt that had Mrs. Henry lived a few hours more, the stomach would have been perforated.

At this point in the dissection, Doctors King and Widmer had satisfied themselves that Mrs. Henry had died from the "effects of an irritant mineral poison, perhaps arsenic." The next step was to prove it. To this end, King carefully placed some of the stomach's particles and the mucous on clear white paper; bottled the fluids and rolled the stomach itself into a paper parcel which he tied. He also collected the bottle of fluid from which Mrs. Henry allegedly drank during the night and the various food items which had been found by Orr. He even requested the cat's body, but it had disappeared. The High Bailiff was deputised to bring the collection to the hospital that evening.

The next day King began his forensic analysis in earnest, beginning with the white particles. After finding they broke down into a "fine white powder," he made a line with them on white paper, "wet it with a little distilled water, pencilled it with nitrate of silver, after which he applied a little liquid ammonia." A yellow colour appeared for some time before changing to a dirty one. He duplicated the same experiment with some arsenic taken from a bottle belonging to the hospital, achieving the same result.

Next, he took another portion of the particles, about one-sixth of a grain or less, mixed it with a little newly made charcoal in a glass tube, and heated it. Shortly afterwards, "a distinct unequivocal metallic film appeared, resembling polished steel, formed in the neck of the tube." This experiment was repeated by Dr. Widmer who achieved the same result. Satisfied with their findings so far, the medical men retired for the night, making sure their equipment and the various items from Mrs. Henry's body were under lock and key.

On Saturday morning, King returned to the hospital's laboratory. He cut the paper on which the particles had lain into three, then boiled them in distilled water. To the first, he added "a drop or two of solution of pure potassa, and then the same quantity of a solution of sulphate of copper (blue vitriol)" and "a precipitate was thrown down of an apple green colour." Then a drop of liquid ammonia was added to the second piece of paper, followed by a drop of nitrate of silver (lunar caustic). A yellow precipitate resulted, which changed to a dirty dark colour after some time. Finally, "he passed a stream of sulphuretted hydrogen gas through the 3rd portion" gaining a deep yellow precipitate. He strained this through a filter, dried it, mixed it with a black flux and then heated it. This resulted in a metallic film. Using great caution, he applied heat to the film he had previously acquired from the stomach, removing as much of the charcoal as possible with the result that "the metal disappeared, but was succeeded by numerous white brilliant crystals, which were easily seen in sunshine; this is oxyde of arsenic, the same sort of poison taken by the deceased."

King had by now established that the victim died from the "effects of an irritant mineral poison," namely arsenic. After much more experimentation, he proved to his own satisfaction how the poison had been administered, obtaining:

> a very beautiful metallic crust ... from the precipitate thrown down by sulphuretted hydrogen. He was positive that a large quantity of the poison was present in the fish, from the results of the liquid test; the muriate of soda was thrown down by the solution of nitrate of silver, a little of which being added in excess, and then a few drops of ammonia, a copious yellow precipitate was produced. A copious green precipitate (Scheeles green) was also produced by the addition of the ammoniaro-sulphate of copper. Pure oxyde of arsenic was also obtained from one of the metallic crusts, resulting from the experiments upon the fish.

The careful King repeated his experiments several times then tried a myriad of other tests. He offered to explain them all to the court, but everyone was satisfied with his forensic knowledge that he had described in detail. The only question asked by Chief Justice John Beverley Robinson was how much arsenic would have been needed. Again, the methodical King worked through to his answer of between four and ten grains, maybe less if ingested on an empty stomach. His research and conclusions were corroborated by Dr. Widmer. This testimony completed the crown's case against Julia Murdock.

While the jurors may not have been able to follow King's descriptions of his various experiments, he made sure he had their attention by producing the tube of crystals in the courtroom. There, in tangible form, was the evidence of Mrs. Henry's death by arsenic poisoning. Unfortunately, for Julia Murdock, her lawyer had to counter that testimony with intangibles.

Sherwood began his address to the jury with a call to empathy. He could "easily imagine how anxious and painful their feelings must be" and his feelings were much the same. He'd been chosen to represent Julia and he now acknowledged that he did not "possess the talent or the knowledge or experience necessary for her defence." But he was fortunate, he went on, to be addressing twelve intelligent men and "a Judge who was as distinguished for his humanity, as for talent, learning and impartiality; and whatever omissions, legal or otherwise, he might make in her defence, would be supplied by his Lordship in his address to them."

He centred his defence on three factors. He freely acknowledged that Julia had bought the arsenic — she'd been open with Mr. Brent, telling him her employer needed it to control rats. She had not attempted to stifle investigation; rather, she had readily made some of the utensils available. The prosecution had proved beyond all reasonable doubt that Mrs. Henry had been a victim of arsenic poisoning, but otherwise its evidence against the accused was purely circumstantial. Mrs. Henry had indeed "hurried to an untimely death" but Sherwood denied vehemently that his client caused that death.

What motive had there been? Robbery? Again, Sherwood freely acknowledged that Julia had stolen the six silver spoons. But did theft make her a murderer? Many people go to fires, he reminded the jurors. While some attempt to put them out, others try to loot as many valuables as possible. Did anyone imagine that the looters set the fires? No, they merely took advantage of unfortunate circumstances, as Julia had done. And, the very fact that she had behaved that way, spoke towards her innocence. Rather than remaining in the house and disposing of the arsenic-laced food and washing the various utensils, she had run to Mrs. Dunlop to try to get the spoons. Yes, she had taken the fast track in acquiring them, but by no stretch of imagination could that mean she had "compassed" Mrs. Henry's death.

Was sex a motive? No one had "dared to hint" of "any criminal intercourse" between James Henry and Julia Murdock. While Henry's absences from his wife were known, the fact remained that he slept in the conjugal bed when at home, not in Julia Murdock's. Had Harriet Henry been so depressed by her husband's absences from home, his abuse and indifference towards herself that she might have taken her own life? The facts spoke against that. Mrs. Dunlop had described a friend who was looking forward to the future. Although Mrs. Henry was in great agony and distress during the last night of her life, she never once asked for medical help. Did that augur self-destruction? If so, why would anyone choose the most painful possible way to die?

Julia Murdock was a young orphan. The relationship she had had with Mrs. Henry bordered on that of a mother and daughter.

Sherwood admitted "it was impossible for the prisoner at the bar to prove that she did not commit the murder." Therefore he appealed to the jury's sense of fairness. How would they feel, if at some later stage, evidence emerged that would convict someone else of Mrs. Henry's death? How would they react "when they were hereafter told that the unfortunate prisoner who stood at the bar, had suffered death, though innocent, and that the evidence on which they convicted her, although entirely undoubted, was perfectly consistent with her innocence." Sherwood then cited some cases of innocents being hanged.[9]

In his summary, Sherwood hammered home the point that the only hard evidence against his client was that she had bought poison, stolen six spoons, and that "it did not appear from the evidence that the prisoner had cooked anything but the gruel and it was just as possible as Mr. Henry put the poison in it as that the prisoner" had done so. After citing divine authority "Whomso sheddeth man's blood, by man shall his blood be shed," Sherwood urged the jurors to remember that it was "better that ninety-nine guilty men should escape, than that one innocent man should suffer."

After this emotional appeal, Attorney General Hagerman dryly summarized the factual case against Murdock and Chief Justice Robinson summed up, "remarking at length upon the evidence." Unfortunately those "lengthy" remarks have not survived. The jury debated for an hour and a half before reaching its verdict — "guilty, with a strong recommendation to mercy" and given the verdict, Robinson placed the black cap on his head and sentenced Julia to death.

The hanging was scheduled for December 19, 1837.

By that time, however, political events had overtaken the sensation of Julia's trial; many of the key people in her trial found they were devoting their energies to a political cause. Toronto was a city in turmoil. The rebellion, led by William Lyon Mackenzie, had failed. In the aftermath, neighbour turned against neighbour.

Henry Sherwood, a lieutenant in the West York militia, was immediately appointed as a provincial aide-de-camp to Lieutenant Governor Sir Francis Bond Head, together with Chief Justice Robinson. Sherwood was a leader of the forces that attacked and routed the rebels at Gallows Hill on December 7. Later in January, he was appointed Queen's

Counsel and prosecuted in various trials against those accused of rebellion. Later, he would act as a judge advocate in the London court martial (December 27, 1838 to January 19, 1839).

Chief Justice Robinson was of course intensely caught up with the rebellion and its aftermath. He would be called upon to give many legal opinions and to advise regarding mercy and to preside over numerous trials. He was also the draftsman of the much-used Lawless Aggressions Act, 1838 — an act that enabled invading American "patriots" to be tried for *capital treason-felony in Upper Canadian courts.*

There is no mention in the minutes of any discussion by the Upper Canadian Executive Council regarding Julia Murdock's fate. It is almost as if the rebellion had made her irrelevant. Certainly, her lawyer had bigger fish to fry than to try to get his client's sentence commuted. If it seemed that the legal "higher-ups" had forgotten Julia Murdock's execution, the ordinary people might have been forgiven if they had done so as well. Instead, rumours about it permeated the city, reaching as high as Government House.

On December 15, Miss F.L. Bridgman, governess to Sir Francis Bond Head's seventeen-year-old daughter, wrote about the situation to a friend. After expressing her own loyalty and fuming at Mackenzie's temerity, Miss Bridgman informed her friend that the rebels' "attack has been rather premature in consequence of the [initial] success of their party in the Lower Province — it is now well known that they intended to attack us on the 19th, as on that day a young girl is to be executed for poisoning her mistress." Inexplicably, to Miss Bridgman's mind, many people perversely sympathized with Julia Murdock's plight: "Her guilt is proved beyond doubt, yet she persists in her innocence and being very young and pretty, there is a great feeling of pity towards her." What was more, the rebels had planned to take advantage of that pity:

> Immediately after her execution, Mackenzie intended to harangue the mob and raise their indignation against the cruelty and oppression of those who condemned her. A rocket was to be thrown up at the Garrison as a signal for their party to advance on the town when those within were sufficiently excited to join them; such was their wicked scheme which has been happily frustrated ... It is very well known now that it was their intention ...

to hang the Governor and his princial officers, to burn
the town and put everyone to death.[10]

No shred of evidence has ever surfaced that this fascinating story
might be true, even in part. One wouldn't expect any, of course. Why
would the rebels risk their liberal-republican cause by indulging in
atrocities.[11] Mackenzie, moreover, had decided by early November that
the uprising in Toronto and vicinity would take place the first week of
December. That decision was made before Murdock's trial and before
the Lower Canadian *Patriotes* scored their one and only triumph at St-
Denis, on November 23.[12]

There were two distinct newspaper accounts of the execution. The
Toronto Palladium represented one strand of reporting in England,
which was to describe female killers as unfeeling monsters — with the
exception of those who killed their own children.[13] The *Palladium*
portrayed Murdock as what we would today call a psychopath by
claiming there was "an awful fatality" to these dreadful events "in that
her father was hanged for the murder of her own mother."[14] The
accused had become so "hardened to life" that she showed not one whit
of emotion between the opening of her trial and the final swing of the
gallows' rope. Somewhat in self-contradiction, the paper claimed she
had twice tried to burn down the jail, once succeeding in setting her
bedding ablaze. Walking to the gallows, according to the appalled
reporter, she bid "her friends 'good bye,' with as much indifference as
though ... about to undertake a short journey of pleasure." Besides this,
she denied gallows-watchers a favourite treat. Julia Murdock stoutly
proclaimed her innocence as long as she had breath — "persisting to
the last, in her perfect innocence." This protestation outraged the
Palladium, especially as Julia knew that James Henry had died in
hospital after supposedly "having taken too much of the same poison
which had killed his wife."[15]

The *Christian Guardian* of Toronto, a Methodist newspaper run by
the Ryerson brothers, published a much more sympathetic account,
grounded in that strand of reporting that drew a moral lesson from the
convict's contrite and Christian confession. One of the Ryersons had
visited the jail almost daily and wrote that Julia's few friends reacted to
repeated denials of guilt by unsuccessfully searching for evidence to clear
her or at least mitigate the sentence.[16] Ryerson praised the young prisoner

as she "expressed her entire satisfaction with the conduct of all who were connected with her trial and condemnation." The day before her execution, she stated that "Divine Providence" had happily arranged things so that she could repent for her "sinful misimprovement of early religious advantages." According to Ryerson, Murdock accepted her death philosophically, as it would ensure that she avoided the "utter ruin" which must have occurred "had she been permitted to live, an unprotected orphan in the midst of surrounding temptation."

These revelations fell far short of a confession, but they did impress the religious Ryerson. To him, Julia's statements were nothing short "of a work of divine grace" and her conduct on the gallows so "highly becoming" that it "did not fail deeply to affect all ..." But there was a lesson to be learned from everything and Ryerson could not abstain from making one more point. The "most perfect decorum marked the conduct of the vast assemblage of persons who witnessed the event." Nevertheless it was "exceedingly revolting to our feelings to see among the spectators a large number of *females*. Their presence at such a time, influenced by a vain curiosity to witness such a scene, speaks lamentably destitute of those feelings of delicacy and tender sensibilities which rank among the most amiable adorning of the sex." The female spectators also offended the *Palladium*'s sensibilities, its reporter writing that in the "large concourse of people" watching the execution "were *several ladies!*"[17] Probably their motives were as varied as their male counterparts — curiosity, entertainment, vindictiveness, and a sense that accounts had been settled. Of course, diversions for respectable women outside the home — especially of the rowdy kind — were rare compared to those available to men.

Women attending executions and male condemnations were common during the eighteenth and nineteenth centuries. At the age of nine, the writer Philippe-Joseph Aubert de Gaspé attended the gruesome execution of the American "traitor," David McLane, in Quebec City in 1797. In later life, he recalled that the victim was "tall and remarkably handsome." He had "heard women of the people cry out in compassion: 'If only it were the old days, this beautiful man wouldn't die. There were be no shortage of girls who would agree to marry to him to save his life.'"[18] This was already an old tradition in eighteenth century Paris, "whereby an appeal for clemency might be granted if a woman happened to shout out a proposal of marriage to the prisoner on the way to his death."[19]

Shortly before Confederation, a husband and wife, Mary and Richard Aylward, were jointly executed at Belleville, Upper Canada. The atmosphere was certainly carnivalesque among the December crowd estimated at up to 9,000. Drunks and minor fights were noted and a whole cross-section of the population, according to the local newspapers, attended: "There were old men with whitened locks and bent forms, and infants nursing on their mother's [sic] breasts, young men and maidens, boys and girls, of all sizes and ages,' according to the *Intelligencer* of Belleville.[20]

The *Hastings Chronicle* condemned the conduct of the crowd in general as extremely bold and was distressed by the female presence: "we cannot admire the taste of the fair daughters of Hastings who thronged to witness the scene. Many were there whose better sense should have kept them away, leaning on the arms of their young gallants and apparently regardless ... that two fellow beings were about to be issued into eternity."[21] Following the 1838 hanging of American patriot raider James Morreau, the *Niagara Reporter* expressed shock "to see so many well dressed and apparently respectable females so thoroughly unsexing themselves" by watching the execution.[22]

Despite Julia Murdock's protestations of innocence and the jury's recommendation to mercy, she was hanged. Why?

There is almost nothing in the secondary sources on the subject of recommendations in pre-Confederation Canada. This much can be stated. Recommendations go back almost as far as criminal juries. Reasons included previous good character, youth, family responsibility, mental deficiency, provocation, service to the state, doubts about the prosecution's case, distaste for laws deemed oppressive, sympathy for political idealists and, quite simply, female gender.

We don't know even the incidence before 1867 of jury interventions attempting to convince the Crown to be merciful.[23] There are some snapshots, but they are misleading ones. The newspaper reports of the Montreal and Quebec assizes in the first decade of Lower Canada (1792-1801) reveal only one in over twenty-five capital convictions. But there is no assurance that the two *Gazettes* were comprehensive. By stark contrast, there was the Niagara assize during the Rebellion period of 1838, where recommendations ran at 50%, but obviously reflected a special situation in which jurymen were acting against perceived government oppression. Of the fourteen Upper Canadian and three American raiders at Short Hills who underwent trial, fully nine Upper Canadians were acquitted — three of them clearly against the evidence! Of the remaining eight accused, four were recommended to mercy. In one case, when an exasperated Mr. Justice Jonas Jones asked why, the foreman, after much hesitation, responded, "On no particular grounds."[24]

More significantly, we understand almost nothing about the effect jury recommendations had on executive decisions to commute, although women with recommendations were certainly not exempted by "chivalry" from hanging in contemporary England, the model for all things legal in Upper Canada.[25] One Daniel George was sentenced to death at the Montreal Assizes 1797 for stealing effects worth forty shillings or more from a dwelling house. The jury asked for mercy because George was simple-minded; accordingly, he was banished from Lower Canada. This result is virtually meaningless. In the entire history of Lower Canada to 1841, when the "bloody code" was seriously restricted, only a handful of people were executed for petty property crimes — such as dwelling house larceny, shoplifting, pickpocketing — while hangings for serious property crimes like stealing cattle or horses, or burglary, were fairly common.[26]

Then there was the case of Ojibwa Angelique Pilote,[27] who was convicted of infanticide in Niagara, in 1817, under a statute thought grossly oppressive by most interested jurists, judges, lawyers and politicians in Britain, Nova Scotia, New Brunswick and Lower Canada — jurisdictions where it had been repealed. The statute, dating back to James I, created a very strong presumption of murder if it were proved the mother had concealed the birth of her child. It formed part of Upper Canada's criminal law. This perceived injustice played in Pilote's favour, as did the fact that native people often gave birth in secret. Merciful interventions were received from the Niagara Grand Jury, many magistrates and prominent local people, as well as several locally-stationed military officers. These interventions, more than the jury's recommendation, resulted in Pilote's sentence being reduced from death to a year in jail.

American "Colonel" James Morreau, military leader of the Short Hills raid, was hanged at Niagara in 1838. The Lieutenant-Governor of

Upper Canada, Sir George Arthur and his advisers dearly wished to make a similar extreme example of a leading Upper Canadian participant, the farmer and carpenter Jacob Beamer. This, despite the jury's recommendation for mercy. Their aim was thwarted by the Governor-in-Chief of British North America, Lord Durham, as running contrary to his policy of pacification through leniency. Arthur's complaint to Durham included a revealing sentence: "Recommendations of juries ... [are] not given great weight by his [Executive] Council."[28]

This statement perfectly represents the hostile attitude of the self-styled aristocratic British North American elites to "public opinion" in the era before responsible cabinet government, achieved in the late 1840s. Those with long memories or extensive legal knowledge could easily recall the case of Colonel E.M. Despard, leader of a plot to foment mutiny and a civilian uprising in London, 1802. Convicted of treason, Despard was drawn, hanged and quartered despite the jury having added these words to its verdict: "My Lord, we do most earnestly recommend the prisoner to mercy on account of the high testimonials to his former good character and eminent services."[29] In the Murdock case, Chief Justice John Beverley Robinson's comprehensive notes on the trial significantly did not even mention the jury's "strong" recommendation to clemency.[30] Despite another strong recommendation, the Aylwards were executed together at Belleville, Upper Canada in 1862.[31] As in the Murdock case we do not know why the authorities ignored the recommendations and in general we don't have any idea how such decisions were made.

As for Julia Murdock, though, we have some basis for reasoned speculation. The Upper Canadian governing elite probably thought that catering to popular attitudes, the jury recommendation, and the sympathy detected by Miss Bridgman would foster anarchy. Especially so, as it appeared to the Family Compact that patriot opinion on both sides of the border sympathized with Murdock's plight. In other words, the hanging was in all likelihood an exemplary act of governance. No doubt those in power justified this by the horrible death Mrs. Henry suffered, the absence of grounds for mitigation, and the betrayal of trust personified by Murdock as a servant-companion.

The legal and social establishment in England often portrayed female servants as immoral and dangerous. They were almost all portrayed as cunning thieves.[32] About a third of London's prostitutes in the 1850s were supposedly domestics.[33] Many were considered well-placed to use undetectable poison and poisoning was greatly feared by the landed and moneyed classes.[34] The law dealt with them harshly. Stealing from a dwelling house in the amount of forty shillings or more was capital and remained so (with the minimum amount raised in 1827 to £5) until 1832.[35] Murder of her master or mistress by a servant woman was traditionally considered as a form of treason (petty treason), the sentence for which was being burned alive at the stake.[36] This was the law, with the penalty changed, in England until 1828 and, with the penalty unchanged, in Upper Canada until 1833, only four years before Murdock's execution.[37]

But the real question raised by Murdock's defence counsel was her innocence, discussed, in a very general context, in the next chapter.

Chapter Five
The Capital Conviction of Innocent Persons

Julia Murdock was probably convicted on insufficient evidence. She may also have been innocent of the murder. There is a distinction between innocent persons capitally-convicted who met their fate because of a distorted application of the law and those who were in fact not guilty. The former did substantially what the prosecution alleged, but we think and/or numerous informed people living at or near the time thought, they should have been discharged, or in the peculiar case of Eleanor Power, at least spared the gallows, because the law was not properly applied. The possibility of innocent people, male and female, going to the gallows or the electric chair or being injected lethally is and always will be crucial to the debate over capital punishment and, as such, deserves analysis.

This is the theme of the chapter, but it should be first understood that guilty women have also been declared not so. Carolyn Strange in her article "Wounded Womanhood" presents two fascinating, but very different cases of this happening through sham chivalry.[1]

Clara Ford was tried for murdering unarmed Frank Westwood, of a good family, in 1895. Almost immediately after the deed (October 1894), she confessed to the police that she had shot the victim because he had taken "improper liberties" and had "insulted" (sexually assaulted) her. Ford, a mulatto seamstress, reportedly ate raw meat and often acted in a masculine role. She was fond of wearing men's clothes — as she had on the fatal day, of jumping on to fast-moving streetcars, and of carrying a revolver. The newspapers spread rumours of her unmaidenly past, but also stressed that as part-African one should look upon her as an outlandish child akin to a monkey. Ford clearly could not be defended by her clever counsel, E.F.B. "Blackie" Johnston, as a passive, chaste damsel defending her honour. Instead, he portrayed her as a poverty-stricken, defenceless woman, of African heritage and, therefore, childlike — who had clearly been taken advantage of in a long, duplicitous grilling by sophisticated, careerist detectives. The confession badgered from her was clearly useless and Ford's new story, that she didn't even know the victim, should be believed. The jury acquitted. This certainly approached nullification, since the trial judge had allowed the confession and expressed his belief in it during his charge to the jury. But it was also chivalrous: jurors, in a post-trial interview with the *Toronto World*, admitted their great reluctance to convict "a defenceless woman who was buffed and coddled by turns."

Carolyn Strange used the 1915 trial of a teenaged British maid, Carrie Davies, for murdering her employer, Charles Bert Massey, as a classic illustration of chivalry at work in the courtroom to preserve the feminine ideal. Davies confessed to the police and testified that one Friday night in February 1915 a drunken Bert Massey made lewd remarks. The following day he attempted to kiss her, insisted she accept a ring, and tried to wrestle Carrie on to a bed. That Sunday she visited her sister and brother-in-law, who advised she return and fulfil her duty to the prominent Massey Family. Fearing disgrace, she shot her master to death as he walked up to his house on Jarvis Steet, on Monday evening. This seems to have been an open and shut case of murder or manslaughter, but it was not to be.

Davies's counsel, Hartley Dewart, did not dispute the confession and Carrie testified to its substance. Instead, Dewart portrayed Carrie Davies as a young woman of unimpeachable character, defending her honour. Her father, a disabled veteran of the Boer War, had died in 1913; she had been sent to Canada to help support her three younger sisters and partly-blind mother. This she had done with remarkable sacrifice. She was lonely — awaiting faithfully the return of her boyfriend who had joined the Canadian Expeditionary Force to fight in Europe. Carrie Davies was a dutiful maiden, serving valiantly on the home front — torn between duty to the Massey household and losing her precious virginity to a cad. As Strange put it, Dewart did not so much deny guilt as make "a sentimental appeal for fatherly forgiveness."

The jury acquitted, ignoring the law and the strong case for manslaughter made by the prosecution. When the verdict was announced, the jurors cried as did trial judge William Mulock, who later remarked to the ecstatic assemblage that the decision "was not absolutely in conformity with strict rules, but they have rendered substantial justice."

As Ford had done, by praising "the boys of Toronto" for their loyalty to her, Davies recognized the male chivalry involved by thanking the judge and the "gentlemen" who made up the jury.

It is in the area of treason that this kind of "chivalric" injustice has most often prevailed. But, as no Canadian woman has faced trial charged with treason, we examine various murder trials to see if there were similar distortions of the law.

The case of Teenie Maloney, in 1916-7, a servant in her early thirties, of Austrian origin, who worked for the elderly Mary Ann Hamilton and her son William on their farm near Hamiota, Manitoba, (northwest of Brandon) provides an example of a similar miscarriage of justice.[2]

On the morning of March 21, 1916, William saw his mother alive and in good health about 9:00 a.m. before leaving for town to have a horse shod. Two hired hands ate breakfast with Teenie, leaving to do their chores just after 8:00 a.m. They returned at noon, followed shortly by William. Except for the accused and deceased, the house was apparently empty between William's leaving and the hands returning, during which time Mary Ann was killed with three blows from a blunt instrument and one from something sharp. The blows probably would not have killed a younger woman, but Mary Ann was almost 84. She was found by her son in the cellar, amidst bloodstains, with her clothes rumpled — suggesting a struggle. There were also bloodstains on the kitchen floor, partially washed away. Teenie had a cut or scratch on her nose — which had not been there at breakfast. She said it had been caused by a flying splinter when she was chopping wood for kindling.

For motives, the prosecution pointed to a history of constant bickering over minor domestic matters and the accused's belief that if Mary Ann died she might well be able to marry "Bill," an assumption strongly corroborated in a letter later written to Judge Galt by the lead counsel for the Crown.[3] The record also hints, somewhat ambiguously, that Teenie told a girl friend she intended to kill Mrs. Hamilton, whom she sometimes called "An old devil." Teenie's defence was to deny all knowledge of what had happened. She claimed to have been sent upstairs to quilt by Mary Ann who was to prepare the noon dinner. Teenie came downstairs about 11:30 a.m. There was no Mrs. Hamilton, no dinner being prepared, and so she set out to prepare it. She had heard absolutely nothing, which must have seemed far-fetched to the jurors. Teenie might well have escaped conviction for murder had her lawyers argued for manslaughter. In the circumstances, Judge Galt ruled out manslaughter as an option. The jury brought in a verdict of guilty, but with a strong recommendation for mercy.

Fortunately, Judge Galt was merciful and clearheaded. He expressed his thoughts forcefully in his report to the government. It seemed "almost incredible ... the prisoner could suddenly have changed from a competent and useful human being into a cruel and savage murderess ... [and then] revert once more, in the short space of an hour or less to her usual every day behaviour." The true facts had probably not been disclosed at trial, Galt believed, and he now thought it possible, or even likely, that Mrs. Hamilton, following a quarrel, "struck at the prisoner with either a pair of scissors or ... Other object ... and hurt her on the nose, whereupon the prisoner lost all control ... and determined to make away with the old lady once and for all." Galt concluded by hoping the jury's strong recommendation to mercy may save "this unfortunate woman, who had probably had little or no advantages of civilized training, from paying the extreme penalty."

The official report from the department to the Minister of Justice noted that the facts suggested retaliation and in any case there was no proof of intent to kill. Judge Galt had not allowed a manslaughter verdict as an option. This was a material error, a dubious proposition, and had the option been open, given the jurors' recommendation, "it is more than probable they would have found 'manslaughter.'" This report concluded that given the facts and the strong recommendation by the trial judge, clemency should be extended. Maloney's death sentence was accordingly commuted to fifteen years imprisonment. She was released early in 1924.[4]

It seems clear the law ended up being improperly applied in this case. At fault were the prisoner and her lawyers, but despite the report and in view of the plea, not the trial judge. A murder verdict could have led to the gallows, had the jury been hostile or Galt less merciful. In any event, Teenie Maloney had to live with the reputation of a convicted murderer for the rest of her life.

In his address to the jury, Julia Murdock's lawyer raised the question that should always be related to capital punishment — the possibility of executing an innocent person. Unfortunately, Sherwood's argument has not survived verbatim, but he contended that the only proof against Julia Murdock was circumstantial. He then went on, citing "several cases where prisoners accused of murder have been executed upon the strongest circumstantial evidence, who, as it was afterwards proved, were innocent of the crimes laid to their charge." Despite not knowing Sherwood's precedents, it is clear that the Crown in England, by 1837, had sent innocent people to the gallows.

It is important to understand that in the cases we are examining, we are trying to establish possible or probable moral innocence, not simply that, as in many cases, proof of guilt beyond a reasonable doubt was not given in court. To do this, we have used all available evidence.

Sir Fitzroy Kelly appeared as the principal witness on judicial error before the Royal Commission on capital punishment, appointed by Queen Victoria in 1864. A famous advocate, he was also a former attorney general and a former solicitor general. As paraphrased by the commission, Kelly testified that it could not be:

> reasonably doubted that in many instances innocent men have been capitally convicted, and in certain numbers of instances, few of course, but yet formidable numbers, have actually been executed ... Well remembered that there were, between the years 1802 and 1840, 22 cases of capital convictions, seven of which resulted in the execution of the convicts ... in the whole of the 22 cases the innocence of these persons was ... established satisfactorily to those who investigated the matter, and in most of the cases to the satisfaction of the advisers of the Crown.[5]

According to Kelly, the twenty-two cases were but the tip of the iceberg. Interesting English cases, of the "almost certain" variety, are described by Arthur Koestler and Judith Knelman. The first tells of a man condemned to death in 1835 but transported to Australia, where by chance he encountered the real murderer nearly forty years later. After two parliamentary debates, he received the Queen's pardon.[6] Knelman deals with the conviction and execution of a twenty-one year old servant Eliza Fleming in 1815 for the attempted murder by arsenic poisoning (a felony in England by statute law) of the whole family she worked for. It is clear she was sent to the gallows because of the prejudice against persons in her station. There was no adequate proof of motive. She had tasted the poisoned dumplings herself and important medical testimony was given that the blackened knives proved arsenic had been used, when in fact it proved the opposite. There was another suspect, the mentally unbalanced son, and as the years passed it came to be more and more accepted among those who took an interest in the matter than an innocent young woman had been hanged.[7]

Most of these examples predate major reforms in criminal procedure: the right to make full defence in felony cases by legal counsel (1836); the right of appeal (1848, 1907); and the right of the accused to testify (1872-1898). Until the 1836 change, trials for murder seldom lasted more than a day; for other capital offences, an hour or so usually did the job.

Modern scholarship, however, has added several possible, probable or near certain examples from the second half of the nineteenth century and the twentieth, prior to the abolition of capital punishment (except for treason) in 1965. The most notorious and absolutely convincing case was the sad fate of London resident Timothy John Evans in 1950. He had allegedly murdered his wife and baby, and was executed for the latter crime. His neighbour, Reginald Christie, appeared as an important Crown witness in the trial. After it was discovered that he had murdered six women, Christie confessed to killing Evans's wife and baby. Twelve years later the Home Secretary responsible for the Evans case admitted this gross miscarriage of justice to the House of Commons, which instigated a parliamentary inquiry. Consequently, Queen Elizabeth issued a posthumous pardon — the only one of its kind in British history.[8]

The largely unexplored area of pre-Confederation women who were factually innocent but found guilty includes two quite comprehensive vignettes from early Canadian history and two from the twentieth century.

Among those pre-Confederation women executed, Frank Anderson believes two were innocent: Catherine Snow who, as seen, pled her belly, but went to the gallows in St. John's in 1834, and Mary Aylward in Belleville in 1862.[9] Anderson was apparently unaware of the fate of Julia Murdock, for her trial was not mentioned in his *Dance with Death*. At a time when the Roman Catholic Church refused to allow the bodies of executed parishioners to be buried in parish cemeteries, both Snow and Aylward were given sanctified burial as non-murderers by local authorities of the Church.

In the Catherine Snow case, it is clear that two men fatally shot her husband, John, on his own fishing stage (or dock) at Port-de-Greve, Newfoundland on August 31, 1833.[10] One was her twenty-five year old cousin and lover, Tobias Mandeville, who regularly acted as the Snows' weekend bookkeeper; the other was the hired hand, Arthur Spring, who felt John was cheating on his wages. When arrested both men confessed, although each claimed the other had done the actual shooting. Both admitted dumping the weighted body in Conception Bay, west of St. John's — it would never be found. They also implicated Mrs. Snow in the plot. They were convicted without controversy, sentenced to hang and their bodies ordered to be hung in chains near the site of the murder. Execution took place three days after the trial, on January 13, 1834. According to the *Newfoundlander* of St. John's, both men "admitted the justice of the sentence which the laws of their country had awarded."[11]

Proof of Catherine's guilt was far more problematic. But it is clear that the confessions of the two men accused played a major role in the jury's thinking and these, therefore, require analysis. The *Newfoundlander* claimed that Spring's statement, when arrested, asserted that "his master had actually been murdered, at the instigation of his own wife!"[12] Neither Spring's nor Mandeville's admission implicated Catherine to quite that extent, but implicate her they certainly did.

Spring confessed that the three of them had planned the murder about a month before. Mandeville had initiated Spring into the plot, but at the critical moment Catherine gave him rum, told him to take the always-loaded gun and shoot her husband when he landed on the dock after picking up Mandeville. Spring had been induced to join in because Mandeville had promised full wages to him, without any of Snow's deductions. Mandeville admitted he'd had regular sex with Catherine since October 1831 — despite the difference in ages, she being in her early forties. From the beginning, the two had plotted to murder her husband and then marry. Catherine Snow had brought Spring into the scheme. At the trial, Mandeville retracted everything and "endeavoured, as much as lay in his power, to clear the character of the female prisoner."

Both Spring and Mrs. Snow made statements during their trial, but they were not recorded in the newspapers. Catherine's statement to the police, however, was presented to the jury. She denied any knowledge of the murder plan and further stated that on August 31 she saw Spring take the loaded gun, thinking he was going to shoot at dogs, which often went after the fish. She did not admit to any sexual liaison with her cousin.

The confessions were of course unsworn and not subject to cross examination. Each could therefore speak only against the confessor himself. Chief Justice Henry John Boulton correctly instructed the grand jury that "nothing said by either of the prisoners, Spring or Mandeville, upon their examinations, can be admitted to implicate her in the act." He went on to note that if other damning evidence existed, they could "indict her as accessory before the fact," which they did.[13] At trial, Attorney General James Simms acknowledged that the "confessions could not be admitted as evidence against her yet her own ... statements, and ... actions were to be accounted for on no other ground ... than that of her being a principal accomplice in the murder." True, he had no direct proof of guilt, but did have a persuasive "chain of circumstantial evidence to adduce against her."

Mrs. Snow's lawyer, George Everson, might have asked for a separate trial, simply because the confessions were lethal. Mandeville, whom Everson also represented, had changed his story by trial time. Who knows how Spring would have testified? He might have been induced by the prospect of a commutation to repeat his confession. Or he might have followed Mandeville's lead. In any case he could not testify to the adultery and Boulton would have been bound to warn the jurors about the reliability of an accomplice's testimony. A separate trial was certainly worth the chance.

A few suspicious bits of proof emerged. Catherine had exerted herself to get bail for Mandeville and Spring. She had initially discouraged the police search for her husband and had disappeared from home for some days after Spring's arrest. Perhaps the most damning legal proof against her was given by the Snows' servant, Kit White. She and the two eldest children, daughters in their mid-teens, had on the fatal evening been sent to a wake in the neighbourhood. The idea had clearly not been the servant's: "she did not ask to go to the wake but her mistress told her to go with the children ... [and she did] not know whether she wished to go to the wake ... [but] supposes she did when her mistress told her." The three had therefore been absent when the killing took place.

It seems clear that these circumstances, although suspiciously consistent with guilt, could be explained away. And that legal proof against her — beyond a reasonable doubt — was not made. But the confessions were available and adultery undoubtedly gave the jury a motive for the crime as well as stimulating disgusted hostility. The confessions also manifestly implicated Snow as a leading plotter, perhaps even the instigator. Overall, it is highly improbable she was not guilty.

After Catherine Snow had delivered her child, rumoured to have been fathered by Mandeville, and recuperated, the court on July 10, 1834, ordered her execution for June 21. Catherine Snow maintained her innocence to the grave.[14]

And, some suggest, even after it. Paul O'Neill records that on the "night of 15 February 1890 officials reported seeing a ghost on the premises [of the St. John's court house]. There were many who felt it was Catherine Snow ... Others wondered if the spirit which was troubling the officials did not originate from among other bottled spirits."[15]

"The Case of the Missing Hen" or "The Wandering Hen" could well metaphorically summarize the tragic events leading to the execution of Mary and Richard Aylward for murdering a neighbouring farmer, William Munro.

Frank Anderson expressed little doubt of Mary Aylward's innocence. But the trial reports and ancillary material in the two Belleville newspapers, the *Intelligencer*[16] and the *Hastings Chronicle*[17] make the question a difficult one. Anderson's opinion of probable innocence is best given in his own words. Continual disagreements between the Aylwards and the Munros had led to enmity which:

> climaxed on the afternoon of Monday, May 19, 1862,
> when William Munro and his son [Alexander] rode
> into the Aylward farmyard armed with pistols.
>
> Seeing their armed approach, Richard Aylward ran
> into his cabin and emerged with a rifle. His wife, who
> had been working in her garden, came to stand by him
> with a scythe ... it is clear that Aylward shot both

William and his son. In defence of her husband Mary attacked the older man with the scythe, inflicting severe wounds.

Munro later died from the wounds inflicted by Mary; Alexander recovered.

When tested by the trial reports, this account proves to be riddled with errors. The murder took place an acre and a half from the Aylward house and on May 16, not 19. Richard Aylward had a shotgun, not a rifle. William was not shot. The Munros were not on horseback, but on foot. Most important, they were initially unarmed — a fact confirmed not only by the younger Munro's testimony at the trial, but by Mary's post-conviction letter to her eldest daughter.

The precise roots of the disagreement between the families are unclear. From the trial record, they seem to have included vicious name-calling, unspecified threats by William Munro, the seeking of criminal warrants by Richard, and resentment that the neighbours' hens were eating the Aylwards' grain. In a letter to all three of her daughters, written two days before her execution, Mary wrote she had suspected Munro threw a dead dog into their well and recalled he later asked "how I liked the soup of it."[18] In another letter, addressed only to her eldest daughter, she claimed the deceased was in the habit of throwing stones at her, threatening to "do her," and calling her gross names, such as "d—d w-h—e." At least once he threatened to beat her up and there is the suggestion of religious and ethnic conflict: Catholic against Protestant and Irish against Scots. By mid-May they were not on speaking terms, according to the solicitor-general, and if we put any faith in the letters, matters had descended into a bitter feud. On May 16 the hen problem came to a boil, with fatal consequences.

According to Alexander, the main crown witness, he and his father were working their farm when they heard a shot. Returning home, Mrs. Munro told them one of the hens was missing. Off they went to the Aylwards' house. After an argument, in which Richard denied shooting the hen but admitted that he wished he had, the three men began walking to the wheat field in search of the missing bird. About an acre and a half along the way, Aylward turned the shotgun he was carrying on the senior Munro. A scuffle for possession broke out. The former then drew a pistol that Munro kicked out of his hand and

Alexander retrieved. As the son rose, Aylward shot him in the back of the left shoulder with twenty-six pieces of lead. He ran home, but not before spotting Mary: "She was 11 or 12 yards from me, about the same place where my father and Aylward had been scuffling; did not see Mrs. Aylward come up; did not see her till I was shot; couldn't say whether she had anything in her hand or not." A Dr. Yoemans testified that in examining the body of William Munro, who had lingered for twelve days, he had found two wounds, a fatal one on the head and another deep cut on the upper left arm, which could have been administered by a sharpened scythe.

There were no eyewitnesses to the scything and no professional forensic evidence linking Mary to the murder weapon. In fact no murder weapon was produced at all. The stories of other witnesses, however, appear damning — although they are not conclusive.

There were two other main thrusts to the prosecution. First, a close neighbour, Mrs. McCrea, swore that a week before the attack, the prisoners came to her place to sharpen the scythe, although there was then no hay to cut, a point emphasized by both Solicitor General Wilson and Chief Justice Draper. But as defence counsel, James O'Reilly, observed in his closing remarks, it was "usual, for farmers at this season of the year, when their spring work is done, to prepare for the coming harvest" or, we may add, a summer haying. In a letter to her children Mary Aylward claimed "the scythe was sharpened for cutting underbrush and not for any other purpose." Second, Mary angrily boasted about what she had done. William Johnston, another neighbour, testified that she had informed him of the older Munro's death and proceeded to explain: "she did not mean to strike him on the head, but on the neck, and cut his head off — and showed ... how she intended to do it." She had also said, "'Dick shot young Baldy [Alexander] ... May God almighty increase his pain.'" These kinds of statements were of course taken by the lead prosecutor and the chief justice as the confessions of a premeditating, bloodthirsty monster.

Why did Mary say these damning things, filled with hate and bragging about vengeance? There are, at least, three possibilities — beyond mere stupidity. She did not fear repercussions because she had acted in defence of her husband. When crown witness Margaret Glenn warned she would get into serious trouble, the prisoner responded that "it will not cause me any trouble." Or, she simply did not care because she was so angry. Or, she suffered from a temporary mental derangement deriving from the bloody deed.

These distinctions are necessary. O'Reilly did not offer a plea of insanity. This would have entailed offering proof to meet the very stiff test of the M'Naughten rules laid down by the judges of England in 1843.[19] These required acquittal and confinement in an asylum if the accused at the time of the offence suffered from a disease of the mind so that he or she could not understand the physical nature of the act or could not understand it was morally wrong. On the evidence given Mary was not labouring under the illusion of, say, slicing up a hedgehog, but knew she was hitting a neighbour's head with a scythe. She had, though, possibly convinced herself the actions were perfectly moral. Had it been possible to prove that this state of mind existed immediately prior to the act, an insanity defence would have been reasonable. But there was no evidence given of it. O'Reilly did not bother to examine any of the witnesses to Mary's confessions, at least five of whom knew her prior to the murder.

O'Reilly argued, rather, that the statements resulted from a deranged mind: "the utterance of these sentences ... is enough to make one's blood turn cold, and they are rendered doubly so by being uttered by the mouth of a woman. Is it not reasonable to suppose ... her mind was perfectly shattered, and she was rendered frantic at the thought of the deed she had committed ... Is it not ... the babbling of a maniac, or of an insane person?" At this distance, and given our lack of expertise, it is impossible to be sure, but the confessions do suggest an analogy to a form of paranoia where, as *Black's Law Dictionary* defines it, "the delusion is as to wrongs, injuries, or persecutions inflicted upon the patient and his consequently justifiable resentment or revenge."[20]

Be that as it may, it really doesn't matter. While exalting in her revenge and revealing the depths of hatred, none of Mary's confessions in fact ran contrary to her counsel's argument that in an emergency she had grabbed the first available weapon and rushed to the defence of her husband, who was about to be overcome by a very powerful man.

The most convenient way to start understanding is by thinking through her own words to her eldest daughter, remembering that by the law of the time and until 1893, neither prisoner was permitted to testify in court. This means that the only testimony to the fatal events given under oath in court came from a person, the son of the victim, with a serious grudge against the prisoners. Mary wrote:

he and his son walked away quite a piece up the road halloong to your Pa, the hens are in there now, if you want to drive them out. So your Pa took the gun and pistol and went out through the woodshed, and up to the wheat and Munro and his son crossed the fence into the wheat; they came close to him and they commenced kicking him and throwing him down. In his bosom he had the pistol. I heard Munro telling Alex to pick up the pistol and shoot him, and then your Pa hallooed for me. I heard Munro swearing by his Jesus that he would shoot him with his own gun in place of him shooting his hens. I was going to run away, and your Pa called and said don't, you see Alex is going to shoot me with my own pistol. I turned back and run up towards your Pa, when I saw Alex having the pistol cocked. I saw the old scythe lying on the ground a few rods ahead of me. I took it and ran up and hit Munro with one stroke. I did not know which one I had struck at the time. Your Pa sprang backwards and the next thing I heard was a shot, and your Pa turned around and asked me if I was shot. I said no, are you, and he said no. Alex and his father ran away. I will go and get my pistol from him, I said; no you will not go, for he might shoot you ... I looked after Alex and saw his back on fire, and I told your Pa that Alex's back was on fire, and to look at his gun. The charge was gone out of the gun. I did not mean to kill Munro, for it was in my own husband's defence that I struck the blow.

This concrete story could be a true version of events and there are certain factors possibly corroborating it. Alexander did not describe the scything or the threat to Richard, if any, as he himself was running away with the pistol. It was he alone, of course, who testified that Aylward had turned the gun on his father and that assertion did not appear in the *Intelligencer*'s report. Alexander also swore that his father was the more powerful of the two scuffling men and that the shotgun had been discharged at him before the scything. Most curious of all, William lingered for twelve days before dying of his abscessing head wound. A crown witness, Mrs. McCrea, who visited the dying Munro regularly, swore he never told her what had happened. The only defence witness, John Rouse, who knew Munro, visited on the fifth day and "advised him to have these folks arrested ... When I said the parties ought to have been arrested, he said he had no business interfering with them." Munro's reluctance — and that of his son — to go to the authorities do not jibe with the behaviour of men convinced they have been grievously wronged. The Alywards were not arrested until well after the death of William, having made no attempt to escape or to hide the weapons.

Nevertheless, the jury, which was out for two hours, returned a verdict of guilty with a strong recommendation for the Crown to show mercy to both. The verdict is understandable, given the one-sided testimony to the events and Draper's almost vitriolic attack on the defence and particularly Mary, portraying her as a cold-hearted monster, without any redeeming human qualities. Other factors may have involved religion. The jury's origins were almost certainly Anglo-Saxon with such names as Walsh, English, Clark, Brenton and Hawkins. The reasons for the recommendation are quite unclear: Mary's madness, her gender, extra-judicial knowledge of provocation, doubts that Alexander had told the whole story?

The recommendation, dismissed by Draper as having nothing to support it, was ignored by the government and, as were all petitions for clemency.[21] They were executed, on December 8, asking the crowd for their prayers, having never expressed contrition. Thus, Mary Aylward and her husband were quite possibly sent to the scaffold as innocent people. Certainly, they would have had a better chance to avoid execution if they had been legally permitted to testify on their own behalf and had done so.

There are over a dozen dubious executions of men and undoubtedly many more unsettling capital convictions in the post-confederation period. Certainly Abraham Steinberg, executed for murdering his business partner in 1931 appears to have been innocent.[22] Two cases involving women warrant investigation: Elizabeth Coward was condemned to death in British Columbia in 1915, but was not hanged, and Marguerite Pitre of Quebec, the last woman executed in Canada, in 1953.

Elizabeth Coward came to central British Columbia in June 1915 with James, her common-law husband, to take up a homestead five miles south of Fort St. James.[23] Her life to that point had not been an easy one. Married at thirteen, to a miner named Dell in the Utah-Colorado area, she became a single mother a year later after Dell had been reportedly killed in a mining accident. Within months she married again, this time to a man called Calabrise, by whom she had three children. The marriage was acrimonious and more than a decade later divorce proceedings began. Whether they were finalized is dubious.

Elizabeth was extremely naive about legalities — a matter the prosecution would raise time and time again during her trial. She believed the divorce was final because she had been shown a sheet of legal-looking paper. Later, she displayed a similar insouciance, maintaining she had married Coward although she had not appeared before any minister, priest, rabbi or justice of the peace.[24]

A city-dweller most of her life, Elizabeth had little preparation for pioneer life in northern B.C. To make matters worse, the Cowards were seriously underfunded; within a month after their arrival James was forced to work off an accumulated debt to the Hudson's Bay store. A vivacious woman, Elizabeth became increasingly lonely. She had little in common with her nearest neighbour, Lucetta McInnes, a mere 285 yards away, and by July her misery had reached such a point that James sent for one of the children she'd been forced to leave behind in San Francisco.[25]

Sixteen year old Rose arrived in Vanderhoof in mid-July and almost immediately little things went awry. Her trunk would not fit onto the wagon James had borrowed. He arranged for an acquaintance named Sullivan to deliver it. Sullivan, however, sub-contracted the job to two men from the Carrier nation, promising them a dollar on delivery. James refused to pay; his bargain was with Sullivan. Threats by the Carrier men led to counter-threats and a considerable amount of acrimony.[26]

The living conditions for Elizabeth, James and newly-arrived Rose may have made tempers short. While they built their own cabin, a generous neighbour had lent them his. It was about ten feet by fourteen, with two bunk beds built against the back wall. One person may have managed comfortably — two, tolerably. For three people, it was impossible. Recognizing this, James made himself a makeshift bed some distance from the cabin using an old sleigh and rigging a mosquito net and a tent over it. Maintaining marital relations thus became extraordinarily difficult.

Rose and her mother spent increasing amounts of time with Lucetta McInnes. "Indianphobic," Lucetta would happily provide tea and regale the two with stories about aboriginals, in much the same way that ghost stories are told over camp fires. And so the summer passed. There was no sign of acrimony in the relationship between Elizabeth and James; no one heard them arguing. To all intents and purposes they were a happy family. One neighbour in fact testified they "were very friendly ... living happily together."[27]

The only recorded incident contradicting this picture involved a puppy someone had given Rose. She loved it, James despised it. Matters reached a point where he threatened to shoot the small beast. Rose retaliated in kind. If he shot her puppy, she'd shoot him. A disgruntled James took the threat seriously enough to record it in his diary.

Florence Whitehouse arrived on September 3 to spend a couple of weeks with Lucetta. For the next few days the women visited back and forth. On Monday the sixth, James, Elizabeth, and Rose worked on their almost-completed cabin in the morning, then he walked into Fort St. James. The Coward women went across to Lucetta's, where they had a marvellous time scaring Florence out of her wits with their Indian stories. At one point in the afternoon, Elizabeth confided that she thought "something bad" was going to happen. Furthermore, whenever she felt like this, something bad did happen.

After the Coward women went home, they made their evening meal, left some food out for James, and began preparing for bed. James arrived back about eight o'clock, ate his supper, washed his dishes, set his place for breakfast, and then went outside to the sleigh bed. At nine-thirty, Elizabeth's premonition proved true as a gunshot shattered the quiet.

Shortly afterward they heard the gunshot, Elizabeth and Rose pulled wrappers over their night clothes and ran across to Lucetta, pleading with her and Florence to give them support while they checked on James. Florence refused, fearing an Indian lurking in the forest might grab her. Lucetta eventually acceded, and the three crept fearfully along the forested path back to the Coward cabin. There, Lucetta balked. She would not go near the sleigh bed for anything, but proposed a compromise. They should shoot their guns off while Elizabeth called to James. If James was injured he could shout to let them know. There was no answer to the gun shots and Elizabeth's calls went unheeded. Finally she announced, "He is dead, if he is there, so there is no use going up and looking at him and getting a fright, we might as well go home."

When they went back the following morning, Elizabeth walked out to the sleigh bed then screamed, "Oh he is dead." James had been shot, a bullet fired up his left nostril into the brain, killing him instantaneously.[28] Remarkably, there was little blood. None of the women wished to remain with the corpse, so they went back to the McInnes cabin where they decided Rose and Florence Whitehouse should go for help. Elizabeth seemed distraught, walking up and down, wringing her hands and muttering, "Oh if he had only listened to me ... he wouldn't sleep outside."

The nearest male neighbour, John Roberts, arrived within a half hour. After a superficial examination of the body, he went to get another neighbour, Freeman Stewart, who would stay with the women while he reported the death to the justice of the peace in Fort St. James. The police arrived the following day, September 8, in the person of Constable Rupert Raynor from Vanderhoof. After looking at the body and deciding it was a murder case, he called for reinforcements from his local headquarters in Fort George (now Prince George). In the meantime, the four women walked into the fort with their suitcases, while neighbour John Vachon hauled the body along in a wagon.

While awaiting help, the inexperienced Raynor conducted his own investigation, trying to find the bullet cartridge from a .32 revolver, searching the grounds and cabin.[29] His reinforcements arrived on Friday, September 10, more than three days after the murder — William Dunwoody, described as "Chief of the Provincial Police," and a Vanderhoof justice of the peace, D.H. Hoye. After Raynor handed Hoye a .32 revolver with four chambers loaded with .32 ammunition and a "shell which probably belonged to an automatic pistol" in the fifth, the hunt intensified for the missing cartridge. Teaming up with helpers from the vicinity, the men searched high and low, trashing the women's belongings and even tearing up the planks from the cabin's floor. Finally, Dunwoody appeared to have a brain wave.

Taking the fatal bullet, which had been extracted by Dr. Ross in the autopsy, from his pocket he appeared to examine it carefully and then announced the searchers should shift their hunt for a .38 revolver. Hoye went outside. Almost immediately he looked under an iron washtub lying on the ground and, like magic, found a slightly rusted .38 gun.

From the moment of Dunwoody's arrival, Elizabeth had become the prime suspect. Hoye's discovery seemed to solidify Dunwoody's suspicions. The problem was proof. He decided to allow Elizabeth and Rose to return to the cabin to collect clean clothes the following day.

When Elizabeth, Rose, and Mrs. Murray, wife of the local magistrate, arrived, Constable Raynor hid from them in the stable, but he had a clear view of the washtub. The women exclaimed bitterly at the state of their belongings and about the presence of packrats. While Rose fed the chickens, Elizabeth made a futile search for clean clothes. Finding none, they decided to go back to the fort and almost at the last minute, Elizabeth walked around to the side of the cabin and looked at the washtub on the ground. Raynor later testified she made "a sharp glance ... and kind of hesitated in her steps and then ... made a pause over this tub I should say [for] nearly a minute." That hesitation almost cost Elizabeth Coward her life.

When she tried to explain that she had only looked at the tub while wondering if it was possible to wash some clothes, Dunwoody would not listen. He knew what he knew and that was it. But there was no motive for the crime. Even the most vengeful witnesses, as Lucetta McInness and Florence Whitehouse became, could not point to any quarrel or change in the outward behaviour of the Coward family. On Monday, September 6, everything had seemed normal.

In his eagerness to gain a conviction, Dunwoody decided against the slow route of gathering forensic evidence. He made no effort to get fingerprints from the gun or to perform any ballistics tests.[30] Even the rudimentary step of connecting the fatal bullet to the rusted .38 was not done. Instead, he went on an expedition for background information, first to San Francisco, then to Watsonville, California, to Iowa, then to Manitoba, and, finally, to Clinton, back in B.C.[31] This odyssey took three weeks and became a vital part of the case against Elizabeth Coward.

The trial took place almost a month after the murder. Elizabeth and Rose, taken into custody on September 13 after their abortive search for clean clothes, had then been driven hundreds of miles to Kamloops, B.C., and then transported back to Clinton for the fall assizes of the B.C. Supreme Court — all in the space of three weeks. An inexperienced lawyer, William A. Scott, was assigned the case and did his best, eliciting several facts through cross-examination. The most damning was that Lucetta and Florence had talked over their evidence, smoothing out discrepancies so that their stories dove-tailed. Scott intimated, after Dr. Stone had admitted it was only his second murder case, that the body of James Coward might have been moved after death. When dealing with Raynor, Scott made him admit that, until Dunwoody suggested they look for the .38 revolver, he had "never noticed the tub" and "would not say it was or was not [there], but I never noticed it at the time."

The tub should have been in plain view as Raynor and the others walked back and forth from the sleigh-bed to the cabin. It should have been obvious, when they searched for the .32 casing. It seems extraordinary that not one man noticed it during those five days. But while Scott picked up the discrepancy, he was too inexperienced to make the jury consider it.

The crown's most surprising witness came from San Francisco. William Hart, "an operator for the Pinkerton National Detective Agency," tried to establish that in November 1914 Elizabeth had written an anonymous letter which resulted in James Coward being demoted from his position as a security guard at the San Francisco Panama Exposition. According to this theory, Elizabeth had hurt James once and would do so again.

Her carelessness regarding legal documentation of her relationships became a huge factor, as she was portrayed as a scarlet woman who might still be married to Dell or rather "Dellaquadra." The prosecution next placed doubt on the validity of the divorce from Calabrise. The Crown's stress on the "foreignness" of her last names cast subtle racial undertones that obviously resonated with the jury.

Rather than producing any scientific evidence, the prosecution concentrated its case on innuendo and character assassination. The jurors deliberated a mere twenty minutes before agreeing that Elizabeth Coward had murdered James. A single woman juror might have changed the verdict because, it must be asked, What pioneering woman would have placed her iron washtub on the ground when there was no running water? Before using it, Elizabeth would have had to take the tub to the stream, wash it and then carry both it and fresh water back to the cabin. Washtubs were invariably hung on nails either inside or outside cabins — never placed on the ground face down.[32]

After the death sentence was passed, radical Vancouver lawyer, J. Edward Bird,[33] took up Elizabeth's case, producing a six-page affidavit from Rose declaring that Coward had propositioned her. She claimed to have been too embarrassed to have brought it out at trial and years later, as a throw-away comment in her voluminous correspondence with the Minister of Justice she began, "Now we all know my mother was guilty. I think my Mother had her cause. Of course it may not seem that way to you." Elizabeth had been pregnant at the time, Rose wrote, and Coward had treated her so badly that her mother "was out of her mind." She explained why she had not talked about the family's so-called troubles: "I guess you think it was funny I did not tell of myself on the trial, well I was backward, it seemed awful to say anything like that in front of a lot of people." Thus she provided a motive for the crime and an admission that she thought her mother was guilty.[34]

The case against Elizabeth Coward, as pointed out in a Department of Justice memorandum of December 9, 1915, was "entirely circumstantial, and establishes no adequate motive for the crime." Consequently her death sentence was commuted to life imprisonment and Rose worked tirelessly to get her mother out of Kingston Penitentiary. In 1922, she wrote her last letter to the Minister of Justice extending her family's thanks that their mother had been restored to them.

Elizabeth maintained her innocence at all times — in her many letters to the Department of Justice and to all she met. She was "an awful liar," though, as the department acknowledged, and her sexual relationships were too immoral for the times. These factors may have persuaded a conservative jury to convict her but the case should have been thrown out of court before that point.

Marguerite Pitre, of course, actually did "Swing and Sway with J. Albert Guay."[35] At her trial, again in the Court of Appeal and in the Supreme Court of Canada, the principal question was whether the accused knew she had transported the fatal bomb to the baggage depot of Canadian Pacific Airlines. The appeal court upheld the verdict by a three to two margin, and the highest court, consisting of seven judges, unanimously agreed with the appellate majority.

Pitre denied all knowledge of the package's contents, claiming Guay had told her it contained a religious statue and was to be carefully handled. There was no direct proof made of her awareness and she professed her innocence to the grave. This stance, while worth considering as a possible factor, is far from conclusive. Both Catherine Snow and Florence Lassandro also maintained their innocence to the end.

The indirect or circumstantial evidence against Marguerite Pitre was very heavy indeed. She was intimately involved with Guay's life. Her brother, Généreux Ruest, worked for the jeweller as a watchmaker; she let J. Albert and Marie-Ange, Guay's mistress, use her place for trysts, in one case mediating a reconciliation. Furthermore, she owed Guay $600 in the form of two promissory notes. In the days before the airplane crash on September 9, 1949, she was seen talking to Guay and her brother behind closed doors. Early in August, she told Marie-Ange that Guay intended to poison his wife Rita; a fortnight later, using a false name, she bought ten pounds of dynamite, some caps and a wick; and in the same month she tried to enlist the paid services of a friend and neighbour, a taxi driver named Beaulieu, in a plot to blow up the taxi when Rita Guay would be a passenger. The driver declined and later testified that Pitre showed him a package that was to be placed in the "rear compartment" of the car. The prosecution also produced evidence that Guay, on September 8 or 9, promised to rip up the promissory notes if Marguerite took a parcel from the C.P.R. station to the Lorette airport, a ridiculously high payment for such a short trip. Pitre did not deny this; she simply did "not remember." The taxi dispatcher swore that she had told him three times to be very careful with the box. Her own husband testified that on the very day of the fatal crash, Pitre confided to him that Guay had told her the parcel inside the packaged box was dangerous. And there was proof that Rita Guay would be on the very plane for which that box was destined.

If Pitre did not know what she was carrying, she must have been extraordinarily naive. Her two hundred pages of testimony do not indicate this supposed naiveté. But, according to the Montreal *Herald* the "fantastic mass-murder of 23 innocent people might have passed as just another plane crash had not Mrs. Pitre attempted to take her own life." Surely, it could be argued, this attempt at suicide, after the destruction the parcel had caused, may show that she was not aware of its contents. She went to the gallows on January 9, 1953, "angry and defiant."[36] Her innocence is, at the very least, somewhat arguable.

The innocence of Julia Murdock is much more likely than that of Marguerite Pitre. While Henry Sherwood mounted a good defence of

Miss Murdock, it must be given a letter grade of B-, rather than an A. There was much in Dr. King's evidence that could have been exploited in a way to help his client. King proved that arsenic was everywhere — in the various foods, on various utensils, and, significantly, in the bottle of water that Henry had given his wife during the night. He had also testified that four to ten grains of arsenic would probably have been needed to kill Mrs. Henry, but that much less would have been fatal, if she had had an empty stomach. Evidence showed clearly that she had vomited continuously during the night, during the time she was being given the arsenic-laced water by her husband. There was absolutely no evidence that linked Julia Murdock to that bottle of water.

There was also no evidence of food in Mrs. Henry's stomach. King described everything else in gruesome detail. But, no food. Were the potato cakes and the floured fish important or were they red herrings? The prosecution did connect Julia with the gruel, but was that the substance that killed Mrs. Henry? To some extent, the matter was similar to a shooting squad. When the assembled squad fires at a condemned person, which bullet is the fatal one?

What became of the husband, James Henry, whose role in the murder was at least as questionable as that of Julia Murdock? After he had his trial successfully separated from Julia's, he found a sympathetic jury that acquitted him — although providence may have squared the equation, as he died a few days before Julia's execution.[37] Had he tired of his marriage to Harriet? Did he wish to strike out on his own? Would he benefit from her will? Unfortunately, there are no answers to these questions. After a thorough search in land and probate records, we were unable to find anything concerning the Henrys.

Julia Murdock was found guilty on two counts: that she had "jointly with Henry poisoned the deceased, and secondly, as having induced Henry to do it." As Sherwood pointed out in his address to the jury, there was never any proof of "criminal conversation" (sex) between his client and James Henry. Nor did the prosecution produce any evidence of any kind of relationship between the two. Therefore, conviction of the second count makes no sense at all, and if Julia was found guilty for having murdered her employer jointly with her employer's husband, James, why was the latter acquitted? Furthermore, if the latter was acquitted, surely a good defence counsel with a client whose life hung in the balance should not have ceased his efforts to save that life, even though political glory beckoned.

The ultimate answer as to why Julia Murdock was executed may lie in the simple fact of close associations among some of the main people connected to the trial. Her defence counsel and Dr. Charles Widmer, who testified for the prosecution, would join forces to regulate the medical profession.[38] The other doctor, John King, lived next to Murdock's lawyer's father, Judge Sherwood,[39] a colleague of the presiding judge. It would have been natural for these men to talk with each other. King, himself, admitted that he and Widmer were friends. And so, a conviction held by Dr. Widmer may have put the noose around Murdock's neck. The Toronto newspaper, *The Constitution*, had no hesitation in printing, "We were not in Court but learn that Dr. Widmer's testimony was not only positive as to her guilt in the case of Mrs. Henry, but that a strong suspicion lay on his mind that she had not done what was right towards Mrs. Roddy, whose sudden death was not easily accounted for."[40]

So, there it was. The suspicion that Murdock was a serial killer. An unproven suspicion — but, given the fact that Chief Justice Robinson did not even make mention of the jury's recommendation in his report, it may be the reason for the execution of a young woman with no resources to fight for her life.

Julia Murdock may have murdered Mrs. Harriet Henry, but like so many others in this chapter who may have been innocent, the charges against her were not proved beyond a reasonable doubt. Other considerations lean in her favour. She thus remains, at least, as a possibly-innocent victim of the hangman's noose.

Chapter Six
"Sham Chivalry": Canadian Women and the Criminal Jury in Capital Cases, 1867–1962

It seems ironic that, during the entire period in which Canadian women were subject to the death penalty, only two defendants (Christina Guay, tried in Sudbury, 1956, and Lina Thibodeau, an Acadian found guilty of fatally shooting her husband in 1955) had the chance of even one woman juror deciding their fates. Whether or not mixed juries would have altered the majority of decisions can never be known, but a jury with at least one woman on it might have been stalemated when deliberating the fate of battered-wife Elizabeth Workman. A woman on Elizabeth Coward's jury in Clinton, B.C. might have pointed out the unlikeliness of a washtub sitting face down on the ground, collecting rust, and thus cast doubts on the prosecution's case.

But all-male juries sometimes benefited individual female defendants through chivalric recommendations to mercy. This sham chivalry had not operated in a major way, apparently, in the pre-Confederation period (e.g., Julia Murdock and Mary Aylward), but it did, with one major exception, after 1867. This chapter deals with both the above issues — female jury service and mercy recommendations.

With the appearance of Carolyn Strange's stimulating collection of essays in 1996,[1] the number of studies in print on the royal prerogative of mercy in Canadian capital cases has reached double figures. All published in the 1990s, they take the form of essays, articles and in one case a dozen pages in a book; there is as yet no monographic study. Three works present single case studies of executive discretion related to female accused;[2] substantial portions of four others treat the same subject more broadly.[3] These include analyses of the gender-based differential favouring women in granting clemency, a closely related topic.[4]

One article only (by Strange, 1996) deals comprehensively with the question of executive leniency to females capitally convicted after Confederation and until 1962.[5] It establishes a huge discrepancy: twelve (eleven, in fact) of fifty-seven women went to the gallows, a rate of 21.3%, while 47.5% of 1,455 condemned males suffered a similar fate. Striking as it is, this difference is perhaps slightly understated.[6] In this article, Strange also qualifies John Beattie's thesis with regard to early modern England, in which he rejects the idea of chivalry in favour of arguments that women's crimes were usually perceived as not particularly threatening.[7] Strange warns that this generalization — while entirely accurate for that period, the eighteenth and early nineteenth centuries, when capital offences against property abounded — needs qualification. In post-Confederation Canada, capital convictions for murder dominated overwhelmingly and, in fact, all fifty-seven women were convicted for that crime.

This caveat has merit. In the second half of the eighteenth century and the first half of the next, women's capital crimes were, other than infanticide, predominantly petty property offences: stealing forty shillings or more from a dwelling house, shoplifting, and pickpocketing. Compared to men, women were very seldom convicted of the more serious offences of murder, horse and cattle theft, forgery, burglary, and robbery. And no woman was found by the courts to have been a traitor.[8] Executions for petty property crimes were rare, with those for the heinous ones more common — although the rate declined through the period. In London and Middlesex, in 1785, sixty-four persons, male and female, went to the gallows: fifty-five for major property offences; three for minor. In the same jurisdiction, from 1800 to 1804, forty of 222 convicted of serious property crimes were hanged, while only three of the 109 minor criminals found guilty met the same fate.[9]

Strange offers a persuasive argument to explain post-Confederation leniency to women: expectations of proper gender roles. In particular, the attitudes of male judges, lawyers, officials, jurors and politicians were based on feelings of chivalry — usually towards chaste and submissive women. But these heavily emphasized their inferiority: emotional excesses, the ease with which they could be manipulated by men, and so on. The most graphic expression to cover this attitude we have encountered comes from the British Commons' debate on the Sex Disqualification (Removal) Bill of 1919, where one member referred to a "sham chivalry" extended towards women in the criminal law.[10] While this was said to counter the notion of protecting females from hearing certain unpleasant trials as jurors, it fits as well as a commentary on both inequality in jury duty and jury or executive leniency. Strange notes that lawyers commonly defended female accomplices of male murderers as dupes of the latter. Sir Wilfrid Laurier expressed the view in the House of

Commons, in 1917, that there was "something revolting in the idea that a woman should be sentenced to death."[11] Strange also refers to the Joint Parliamentary Committee on Capital Punishment of 1956 as concluding that murders by women had been committed in circumstances warranting the exercise of mercy. Thus gender-based leniency was officially accepted, though not formally sanctioned.

Two topics — the surprising chronological evolution of gender equality in criminal jury duty and the incidence and impact of jury recommendations to mercy in favour of both men and women capitally-convicted of murder or high treason — support this thesis. Jury recommendations, somewhat surprisingly, have been given only passing mention in the studies of the royal prerogative cited above and in other works bearing on the history of capital punishment in Canada.

As the historian, A.J.P. Taylor aptly put it, World War I was, for the United Kingdom, "a decisive moment in women's emancipation," both socio-economically and a little later, legally.[12] During this period, women entered the public service and work force in droves. Over 100,000 joined the auxiliary armed services, while twice that number entered government departments. A quarter million worked the land and 500,000 replaced men in clerical jobs done for private firms. Fully 800,000 were recruited by engineering shops.[13] As Taylor observed: "Women became more independent and more enterprising," giving as an example the new custom whereby the female munitions worker "paid for her round of drinks at the public house." Many of the wartime positions proved temporary, but certainly not all. Female shorthand typists, for instance, permanently replaced male clerks, they of the quill pens.

Male gratitude and respect for women's roles during the First World War — both actively and as keepers of the home fires[14] — resulted in major statutory liberalizations of their legal status. The common law of course disenfranchised them politically and prevented women from holding any public office — except as queen or regent. In 1918, females over thirty were granted the vote and all adult women were made eligible to sit in the House of Commons.[15] Seven years later, the demeaning, sham chivalrous defence of spousal coercion was eliminated. It had, for several centuries, created a rebuttable presumption of innocence where a married woman committed a crime, other than treason or murder, in the presence of her husband.[16] More far-reaching was the Sex Disqualification (Removal) Act of 1919.[17]

This statute made existing permissive practices mandatory by law.[18] In some cases it created new rights and duties for women, such as those to become barristers and to sit on juries. The operative words read as follows:

> 1. A person shall not be disqualified by sex or marriage from the exercise of any public function, or from being appointed to or holding any civil or judicial office or post, or from entering or assuming or carrying on any civil profession or vocation, or for admission to any incorporated society ... and a person shall not be exempted by sex or marriage from the liability to serve as a juror.

The right and duty to act as a criminal juror was qualified. At the behest of either side or on his own initiative, the judge could decree that a jury would be composed of men only or women only. A woman summoned could apply to be exempted because of "the nature of the evidence to be given or of the issues to be tried." These provisions were principally designed to protect females from hearing or seeing the "disgusting" things that might arise in trials for incest, carnal knowledge, buggery, bestiality, murder, and rape, among others.[19] In the end, though, restricting references applying to judicial discretion ("the nature of the case and the evidence to be given") were deleted by amendment.[20] The woman's option was retained but exemption had to be granted by the judge.

With the exception of one province, Canada followed Britain's lead with glacial slowness. Prior to conferring eligibility on women to sit, most provinces excluded them through express disqualification of females or by requiring a juror to be "male." British Columbia and Nova Scotia used the indeterminate "person(s)" which in law was generally thought (until 1929) to exclude women. Change began, very hesitantly, in the 1920s.

Alberta, home of pioneering women's rights activists Nellie McClung and Emily Murphy, first emulated the British initiative in 1921. They did so only conditionally. A puritanical legislature required the exclusion of women on juries until Parliament eliminated the possibility of sequestering the jury overnight. Alberta repealed this provision only in 1966.[21]

As befits a province that had been in the forefront when granting rights and protections to women, British Columbia led the way to women serving on juries. In 1873, for example, females had received the right to vote on a municipal level. Along with the prairie provinces and Ontario, B.C. was among the first to grant equality between genders in provincial voting, and eligibility for jury service soon followed.

The jury duty bill of 1922 was introduced by former Attorney General, Liberal John Wallace de Beque Farris, and was supported by Liberal Minister Without Portfolio, Mrs. Mary Ellen Smith, the first woman member of a cabinet in the British Empire. This initiative came naturally to Farris, who despite being a member of one of British Columbia's most socially and politically prominent families, was something of a radical when female rights or protections were in question. As attorney general, he had initiated several reforms — many intended to improve life for women: for example, minimum wages and the Testator's Family Maintenance Act. He also appointed suffragist Helen Gregory Macgill, from whom he drew many of his reforming ideas, to be the first female judge in the province.[22] Macgill's biography does not, however, mention women on juries, so presumably she was not overly concerned with the issue.[23]

The jury duty bill was passed by a margin of 28 votes for and only 14 against, with almost solid support from government members. The terse report of the debate reveals little in the way of attitudes for and against the proposed law.[24] Farris indicated his general aim to move significantly towards equality, while Mrs. Smith thought the measure was not an interesting innovation: "women served on juries in Scandinavia, in many of the states of the United States, in England and in Alberta." There were more objections, unspecified, she could make, but she "thought wise restrictions [also unspecified] could overcome these." Hardly a ringing endorsement. A Member of the Legislative Assembly, N.A. Wallinger, noted that the women of Cranbrook had studied the issue and were in favour of Farris's proposal.

The only concrete opposition reported was the forward-looking one made by H.F. Kergin. Referring to the opting-out clause (referred to below), he said, "This is not a case of equal rights for women. It is a case of giving them superior rights." One member declared "that the negative arguments reminded him of the class of arguments used against woman's suffrage," which can be briefly summarized below.

Women, it was often alleged before 1923, were too irrational and indecisive to enjoy the vote. Such a right would knock women off their just place on a pedestal and "emotionalize balloting."[25] But, equally common were contentions that women did not want the vote. This was manifestly disproved by 1916 at the latest in the five provinces west of Quebec. Other objections were that it was against nature, the Bible, or both, and that women's household duties were sacrosanct. The many themes here included marital discord, even breakup, and neglect of children. In 1914 Sir Rodmond Roblin, the Premier of Manitoba, asserted that politicized females would "throw children into the arms of servant girls." Almost two decades earlier, a Nova Scotia legislator used divorce statistics from the United States to forecast on ominous future should women vote.

Some arguments were even more absurd. In the British Columbia Assembly of 1913, a member attacked a bill by trying to prove that the most atrocious parts of the French Revolution were due to women and not Robespierre, St. Just, and others who made massive use of the guillotine. In the 1918 federal debate, one M.P. from Quebec thought female political emancipation meant a lower birth rate and much greater "promiscuity between the sexes." The prize for sham chivalry was taken, however, by another M.P. from Quebec, Guillaume Amyot, who asserted that women were "the point of connection between earth and heaven. They assume something of the angel. Let us leave them their moral purity, their bashfulness, their sweetness ... it ill becomes the community to change her sex and to degrade her by the exercise of the franchise."

The 1922 B.C. jury act is remarkable, not only for its early date but for the pioneering reach of its provisions. In the United Kingdom, under its 1919 statute, a woman could ask the judge to decide upon an exemption for her because of the unseemly nature of the case. A similar proposal was made in British Columbia. Farris agreed that he personally "should hate to see a woman on a murder case," but she could opt out, and in any case "practically every woman's organization in Vancouver had gone on record" in support of his bill. Former Premier and Opposition Leader, William J. Bowser, obviously influenced by the Alberta Act of the previous year, confessed he had difficulty with the notion of mixed juries spending three or four days together on a long murder trial. Yet no

"Alberta amendment" was made, and Bowser nevertheless voted for the bill.[26] Another aspect of the bill provided that a woman could opt out of jury duty within fifteen days after receiving a registered letter from the sheriff informing her that she was on the annual jury list. This kind of procedure surely made more women compellable than in other provinces that later allowed opting out at the point of an actual summons, as mentioned below.

Despite its radical nature and given the times, neither the bill nor the act caused much stir. Neither the minutes of the University Women's Club of Vancouver nor those of the Vancouver Council of Women, 1919-23, contain any record of discussion of female jurors.[27] The *Daily Colonist* of Victoria devoted about half a column to the debate while the *Vancouver Daily Province* called the session "uneventful."[28] The *Vancouver Sun* was lukewarm in its assessment of the act: "There can be no possible harm in empanneling [sic] women on juries and there might be a great deal of good." After this opening, the editor devoted most of the column to denouncing juries for taking the law into their own hands, citing a recent Alberta murder case that had, despite allegedly flawless proof of guilt, ended in an acquittal. He concluded by arguing that Criminal Code changes be made to allow judges to examine all prospective jurors to ensure they would abide by the laws.[29] The *Canadian Annual Review of Public Affairs* for 1922 did not even mention the act in its 1046 pages of text.[30] It would be a generation before other provinces began catching up with their pioneering Pacific counterpart.

The only other province to qualify women before 1950 was Nova Scotia; this was achieved by a peculiar, passive and entirely theoretical route. From the beginning, the provincial legislation made "persons" eligible for jury duty, without defining the term.[31] When the Privy Council reversed the Supreme Court's unanimous ruling in the famous *Persons* case of 1929, holding that females were persons,[32] women in Nova Scotia, at least propertied ones, became legally eligible for jury duty. But in practice, women were apparently not called as jurors in that province until sometime in or after 1951. A bill of that year — expressly to exclude women from jury panels — met with such protest from women that it was withdrawn.[33]

For more than half a century after the British breakthrough in 1919, Canada's Federal Parliament remained silent on the subject of the exlusion of women from criminal juries — entirely with respect to legislation and largely so in debate. Under several numbers, what became section 921 of the Criminal Code in 1906 had existed since 1869 and continued to exist, with numerical changes but without substantive amendment, until 1972. From the beginning, section 921 had transferred power over jurors' qualifications to the provinces, despite Parliament probably enjoying dominant jurisdiction.[34]

Part of the reason for this long hiatus lies in the breakup of suffragist organizations once the right to vote had been achieved. The Manitoba Suffrage League, the first to achieve success in Canada, disbanded in 1917.[35] The same happened in Newfoundland in 1925, and undoubtedly elsewhere.[36] The Quebec League of Women's Rights in the 1930s, of which the late Senator Thérèse Casgrain had been president, included female eligibility for juries as one of its objectives. This aim was quietly stillborn in a province where married women could not sue or enter into contracts without consent of their husbands, where a man could obtain a marital separation by proving his wife's adultery but a woman had to prove, until 1955, that her husband had brought his mistress into the family home and where, until 1940, no woman could vote provincially.[37] M.P. T.L. Church of Broadview, Ontario, recalled bringing the matter before Parliament some twenty years before 1948 and being attacked in the Toronto *Globe* on the grounds that "women were too temperamental."[38]

In the 1948 session, Church introduced a bill requiring one third of the jurors to be women when a female accused was tried. Church denied women were more temperamental than men. In this, he was supported by Jean-François Pouliot, M.P. for Tomiscouta, who argued that as a rule women were better read than men. Pouliot agreed to support the bill if women with small children were exempted from serving. Two members, one from Alberta the other from New Brunswick, claimed there was no female demand for any such reform, with the member from Alberta insisting that since women were such "delicate people" they should never be forced to serve on juries. The Minister of Justice, J.L. Ilsley gave Church's initiative the *coup de grace* by noting the bill's rigidity and the practice since Confederation of leaving these matters to the provinces. This latter, disingenuous ground probably indicated the cabinet did not think political points could be scored. The early post-war years, after all, had seen the highest peacetime degree of centralization in Canadian history since the 1870s.[39]

Things, though, were bound to change, sooner rather than later. After women had proved themselves capable of "men's work" in two world wars, in the professions, in business, in politics, and in voting, as well as jury duty in various places in the world, the C.C.F. government of Saskatchewan under Tommy Douglas followed British Columbia's lead in 1950.[40,41] Ontario, never one to lag too far behind Canadian legislative opinion, was next. The debate in 1951 was essentially passionless, the main opposition being an expressed dislike of the option given women, and not men, to avoid jury service. The government's case was entirely practical. Women had proved themselves in the ways mentioned in the preceding paragraph; there was no insuperable problem regarding separate overnight accommodation; women on the jury rolls would take the burden off men and indeed the court system. The option of exemption was given because most were homemakers.[42] Unlike British Columbia in 1922, the act followed the imperial model by allowing judges to exempt compellable women if the subject matter of the trial was "unseemly."[43]

Manitoba and New Brunswick soon followed Ontario's lead.[44] Alberta and Prince Edward Island caught them up in the 1960s, as did the two territories.[45] In the Northwest Territories, many male defence lawyers worried that women fact-finders would prove ultra tough in rape cases. This did not occur, as territorial judge W.G. Morrow soon pointed out in print. He noted also that women, he had heard, held their own with men on questions of evidence and asked many intelligent, technical questions from the jury box. They also helped spread the burden of jury duty in a sparsely populated land.[46]

Thus by 1970 only Quebec and Newfoundland had not permitted eligibility. Neither jurisdiction was renowned for supporting women's rights, being the last two provinces to grant them the vote. Indeed, Quebec provides an excellent example of sham chivalry. The first female graduate from the law school at McGill, Annie Langstaff, was refused entry to the Bar in 1915. The Superior Court judge held that to admit a woman as a lawyer

> would be nothing short of a ... manifest violation of ...
> public decency. Let us for a moment picture ... a
> woman appearing as defending or prosecuting counsel
> in a case of rape and putting to the complainant the

questions which must of all necessity be asked ... No woman possessing the least sense of decency could possibly do so without throwing a blur upon her own dignity and bringing into utter contempt the honor and respect due to her sex.[47]

Women were not admitted to the Quebec Bar until 1941.

Prior to 1970, no jurisdiction qualifying women as jurors — except Nova Scotia in strict law (since 1929), British Columbia (1964) and the territories — made jury service compulsory.[48] Two provinces, Alberta and New Brunswick, had opting in clauses, the latter's reading that "no female inhabitant shall be qualified and liable to serve ... unless ... she files with the sheriff of the county where she resides, a request ... to have her name listed on the jury list." The remaining statutes allowed opting out. Saskatchewan's was reasonably typical: "a woman who ... does not desire to serve as a juror shall within three days after ... [receiving a] summons notify the sheriff in writing ... that she claims exemption from service as a juror for a period of one year ..."

It cannot be shown how often women exercised their options, but considering the well-known reluctance of men to do their jury duty and the American experience, the rate must have been high. In 1971, Senator Elsie Inman, supporting a bill to eliminate such options, remarked that in Prince Edward Island "it is considered by the judges and officers of the courts unsatisfactory for women to be allowed to decline to serve on juries." An Island judge had told her that "in one case 200 names were 'in the hat', so to speak, many of them belonging to women, but few of the women would serve, and it was difficult to empanel a full jury."[49]

The Royal Commission on the Status of Women in Canada, which reported in 1970, summed up the situation:

In Quebec and Newfoundland, women are not eligible for jury duty. In some provinces, if they do not wish to serve, they are excused solely on the ground that they are women. In others, they are not required to appear unless they give notice of their

willingness to serve. In only two provinces, Nova
Scotia and British Columbia, do they serve under the
same conditions as men. In the Yukon and Northwest
Territories men and women are equally eligible. We
see no reason why women should not in all cases
carry the same responsibility to perform this
important duty as men.[50]

If twenty years before women could be stereotyped as housewives, it
was no longer so.

The *Report* brought fast action. Alberta and Ontario eliminated the
exemption option in 1971 and 1972 respectively.[51] In Quebec, after a
decade of the Quiet Revolution, male lawyers began to complain of the
injustice of prohibiting female jurors.[52] The result was a 1971 statute that
simultaneously created eligibility and compulsion.[53] Newfoundland, the
same year, finally agreed to eligibility but, amazingly, enacted an opting
out clause in the teeth of the *Report*.[54]

Equally important were developments at the federal level. These
began early in February 1971 with Thérèse Casgrain initiating a
Senate debate to complain that women were not called for jury duty
in Quebec and Newfoundland. She made the elementary case about
eligibility existing in the United Kingdom, France, and most of the
United States.[55] Senator Muriel Fergusson, though, greatly increased
the pressure on the federal government. If John Farris might be
called the "Father of Eligibility" in this field, Fergusson would
certainly be the "Mother of Equality." She had long taken an active
interest in the issue, even as a member of the delegation that in 1954
induced the New Brunswick government to enact legislation putting
women on jury lists.[56] In 1963, a lawyer from Justice and adviser to
the Council of the Northwest Territories, R.B. Olsen, successfully
convinced that Council to reject women jurors. He was quoted in the
Ottawa Journal as saying that in rape, murder, and like trials "women
tend to have an emotional and not [the] ... intellectual approach
needed in such cases." Fergusson fulminated, asking if disciplinary
action would be taken. No, answered the government's Senate Leader
before agonizing about difficulties such as providing separate living
facilities and the need for matrons.[57] Less than two years later,
Fergusson won her contest with Olsen.

Citing the Royal Commission, she argued in 1971 on the principle that exclusion denied gender equality, as guaranteed by the United Nations Convention on the Political Rights of Women, ratified by Canada in 1957 and by the Canadian Bill of Rights in 1960. It also denied representativeness to juries trying the most serious crimes. She cited and quoted several statements asserting that women had performed with as much if not greater competence than male jurors and with no less ability to control emotion and to assess intelligently complex facts. Equally important, she anticipated the government trying to hide behind provincial rights, as it had in 1948, by making a very persuasive case that Parliament, under section 91 (27) of the B.N.A. Act of 1867, had jurisdiction to deal with the composition of juries in criminal trials. Government Leader Paul Martin Sr. promised to consult the law officers on the point.

When the debate resumed, Martin informed the Senate that the law officers agreed with Fergusson and thanked her for clarifying the matter.[58] On May 13, 1971, Fergusson moved second reading of a bill amending the criminal code to make women everywhere in Canada absolutely equal to men in rights and duties relating to criminal jury duty. One "dinosaur" ridiculed women jurors as overly sentimental and none too smart — he was Senator Lionel Choquette, a practising lawyer for thirty-nine years. He told this story about an Ottawa automobile negligence case, at which he had acted for the plaintiff:

> five of the 12 jurors were women. These women were very sympathetic towards my client, who was the father of a large family and who had met with a terrible accident ... those five women ... used to go home at night and tell their husbands what a poor man the plaintiff was, and how disabled he would be for the rest of his days.

When the case ended, one of the jurors, with great enthusiasm, "told her husband they had been very generous to this poor, unfortunate man and awarded him $11,000." The husband was less than overwhelmed, replying "that is not what the afternoon paper says. It says that the case was dismissed ... [because] you found no negligence on the part of the defendant." Choquette went on to explain:

> These women said ... the reason they did not find any
> negligence on the part of the defendant was that they
> knew that if he did not carry insurance at least the
> Government of Ontario would pay from the Unsatisfied
> Judgment Fund ... two or three thought if they said that
> ... the defendant was negligent, the police would put
> him in jail.

Although comical, this anecdote proves nothing about the abilities of female jurors. An inexperienced all-male jury, especially if not properly instructed by the judge, might well have made a similar error. Indeed, this jury's unfortunate verdict was agreed to by a male majority. In fact, Choquette was saying that all jurors were irrational — the women a bit more so — and juries should be abolished. In ending his speech, Choquette reiterated, for almost the last time in Parliament, that "women should stay away from them [juries], because their duties as housewives should be given priority." But the time had passed when such sentiments would find much agreement. By now there was general approval for Fergusson's initiative. This included Martin, who hoped the two opposing Senators would reconcile their differences over tea that day. The bill passed easily.[59] In the Commons it was read a first time and, significantly, ordered to be printed.[60]

On April 27, 1972, the Minister of Justice, Otto Lang, moved second reading of an omnibus bill to reform the criminal law, consisting of seventy-five amendments to the Criminal Code, including the substance of Fergusson's bill. Lang justified the latter only on the basis of the Royal Commission's Report, although he later commended the New Brunswick senator for all the leadership she had shown. Only three other members — Grace McInnes (Vancouver-Kingsway), Warren Allmand (Notre Dame de Grace) and David McDonald (Egmont, P.E.I.) spoke on the issue. The first two praised Fergusson for her efforts and the last emphasized how archaic the existing system was. Seventeen other members, all men, spoke in the debate, on topics such as capital punishment, hijacking aircraft and the abolition of whipping. None mentioned women and juries. So, even at the end, gender equality in jury service had not become a political issue of importance.[61]

The bill received royal assent on June 15, 1972, thereby amending the Criminal Code to read that "no person may be disqualified, exempted or excused from serving as a grand or petit juror in criminal proceedings on the grounds of his or her sex."[62] Thus, all provincial statutory provisions to the contrary were voided in criminal law. Manitoba, New Brunswick, and Saskatchewan, following the spirit of the act, hastened to provide equality for civil juries.[63] Incredibly, Prince Edward Island and Newfoundland did not do this until 1980 and 1981, respectively.[64]

The arguments for and against including women on all juries were much the same, in Canada and the United States.[65] American advocates of equality, though, put more stress on the importance of including women's distinctive experience and point of view in several types of cases, such as those involving religion, child abuse, female embarrassment and violence arising from the eternal "love" triangle. Some arguments against were met head-on by women. A Detroit judge, driven by chivalry, had excluded women from rape cases or others involving "revolting or gruesome details" in the 1920s, until women on the panels showed themselves "very indignant" over the discrimination. To the common objection that it was improper to sequester both genders, Eleanor Roosevelt publicly retorted in 1937 that "it never occurs to us to be disturbed if we are all locked up all night in an airplane." Some thirteen years earlier, a pamphleteer pointed out that the country had in fact "survived the test of men and women travelling together in sleeping cars, in the care of a male porter."

One of the most distinctive features of the American experience was the use of constitutional argument in and out of court. The relevant provisions were the fifth and fourteenth amendments that no one should be deprived of life, liberty or property except by "due process of law," with the fourteenth amendment adding that the states could not "deny to any person within its jurisdiction the equal protection of the laws." The sixth amendment calling for a criminal trial to be held before "an impartial jury" was to prove even more important.

The existence of these fundamental laws, which could not be amended by Congress or a state legislature acting alone and had considerable popular appeal led to three differences from the Canadian evolution: the existence of a national movement for women on juries, earlier successes, and the use of the courts to advance the cause.

Certainly there was a national movement from after World War I, and perhaps before, that resulted in the issuing of pamphlets, the making of speeches, the writing of letters to editors and going to court, for example. From the 1920s to the 1950s, two organizations, the League of Women Voters and the National Woman's Party, were prominent activists. The American Civil Liberties Union became committed by the early 1960s and became the principal player in the lawsuits thereafter. By the late 1960s, the National Association for the Advancement of Colored People, worried about the difficulty of getting blacks registered for panels, lent its public support to the women's jury movement.

This and the aftermaths of the suffrage movements led to rapid early success in the area of eligibility. By the end of World War I, five states including California, had joined pioneering Utah (1898) to put women on the rolls. By 1923, when only British Columbia had made women unconditionally eligible in Canada, eighteen of the forty-eight states and the Alaska Territory had followed suit. Only three states held out to 1961. None of these reforms was instituted by the courts, but by legislatures responding to normal political pressure.

In the early days, the courts did not offer much help. In *Strauder v. West Virginia* (1879) the Supreme Court held that the only categories excluded from discrimination under the fourteenth amendment were racial. A Massachusetts decision in 1921, confirmed in 1934, prevented eligibility in that state for a quarter of a century. As late as 1961, the Supreme Court in *Hoyt* upheld state opting in or out provisions. There were, however, victories. In 1946 Justice William Douglas in *Ballard* spoke for a majority on the Supreme Court to the effect that the sixth amendment's requirement of "an impartial jury" meant representativeness and hence the Federal Courts could not exclude women. Within a few years those courts, logically, had made female jury service an obligation. In *White v. Crook* (1965-6), the U.S. Court of Appeals, fifth circuit, held that under the fourteenth amendment Alabama, or any other state, could not deny women the right to appear on jury lists. Finally in *Taylor*, 1975, the Supreme Court voided state opting in or out provisions on the basis of the sixth amendment. Equality in this crucial area had been achieved.

Except in part, with regard to the options, Canada lagged behind its southern neighbour. The Americans fought for juror equality; Canadians did not. Americans lived under the equalizing notion of citizenship. Many well understood the power of appeal, as well as the legal implications of fundamental laws guaranteed in their constitution.

Canadians were British subjects until 1947 and governed by no relevant fundamental laws.

How does this chronological analysis relate to women and capital crimes? The absence of women on criminal trial juries no doubt occasionally worked to the prejudice of the female accused. Such likely occurred in the case of Jennie Hawkes,[66] convicted in Alberta, in 1915, of fatally shooting her husband's mistress, Rosella Stoley. Washington Hawkes had invited the woman, together with her husband and children, to live with them towards the end of 1914. Women on the jury, thoroughly shocked by this behaviour, would likely have opted for a verdict of manslaughter, which usually carried a short jail sentence. As it was, the jury recommended mercy and the federal authorities commuted the death sentence to ten years in prison. Jennie Hawkes, of course, carried the stigma of a convicted murderer for the rest of her life.

If male dominated juries occasionally prejudiced female defendants, they benefited them more often — particularly in regard to the incidence and impact of jury recommendations to mercy in capital cases from 1867 to 1962, the last year the sentence of death was carried out. Examples drawn from secondary and primary sources suggest, although not precisely, that recommendations had some importance.[67] But not in all cases. Private intervenors for mercy, including lawyers, sometimes ignored recommendations.[68] The printed form of the order-in-council commuting the death sentence had no section to indicate that a recommendation to mercy had been made.[69] More important, judges, and the statistics suggest responsible officials and politicians as well, did not automatically presume in favour of clemency simply because there was a jury plea.

In the case in 1942 of Edward Roy Kolesar, for instance, Judge C. Plaxton mentioned the recommendation, a mandatory procedure, but was "unable to find in the evidence anything in extenuation."[70] Concluding the trial of Olivier Gallien for murdering his lover's husband in 1874,[71] Mr. Justice Weldon told the accused that while he had to forward the jury's recommendation, "No mitigating circumstance has appeared in the Evidence to call for or give you any claim to the merciful prerogative vested in the Crown."[72] A precise assessment of the impact of jury recommendations would require months of work in the National

Archives' Capital Case Files and other primary sources. The jury's plea, though, almost certainly brought about a commutation of the death sentence for Jennie Hawkes.

The Inventory to the Capital Case Files provides some statistical precision by summarizing the 1,533 capital convictions from Confederation to the abolition of capital punishment in 1976. There are 1,058 relevant murder cases and two treason convictions up to 1962, the last year of execution.[73]

In the first place, jury recommendations were frequent, accompanying almost one third of the relevant convictions (31.32%). Secondly, the statistics show that recommendations definitely had importance, but much less than anticipated. Those not recommended were executed in over two thirds of the cases (67.31%). With a jury plea, slightly more than a fifth went to the gallows (21.99%). In the twenty-one proceedings where the inventory records that the jury asked for mercy and the judge disagreed, the jury prevailed in twelve.[74]

These results are surprising.[75] Most people assume, rather naively in retrospect, that rejecting a jury recommendation was a very rare event, dependent on obvious and strong political motives. But the statistic of more than one in five suggests an authoritarian administration of capital punishment, 1867-1962.

The statistics show a remarkable gender disparity — remarkable not for its existence but for its size. Men received recommendations in thirty per cent (29.89%) of the trials. The women's rate was about double — almost six out of ten (58.49%). Even more striking is the fact that of the thirty-one women recommended, only Elizabeth Workman went to the gallows.[76] Of the 301 men receiving jury intercessions, seventy-two were executed — approximately one in four (23.92%).

Outstanding examples of this double standard are the cases of Angèle Poulin and her lover Olivier Gallien, both convicted of murdering Angèle's husband in New Brunswick, in 1874. The jury in Gallien's trial recommended clemency on the grounds he had confessed and expressed remorse. Poulin's jury wanted to recommend, but was dissuaded from doing so when Judge J.W. Weldon established that the jurors had no specific grounds. At the trial, Judge Weldon referred to Poulin as having acted out of "lusts and passions" and having "grossly violated ... [her] marriage vow." In his report to the Secretary of State, Weldon asserted she was the more guilty. Despite this assertion, Poulin's sentence was reduced to life imprisonment, while Gallien was executed.[77]

This obvious differential corroborates Carolyn Strange's argument of "chivalrous" leniency, when the executive commuted death sentences imposed on women. Evidence in literary sources supports this interpretation. "A Male Reader," complaining in the *Calgary Herald* about male indifference to the fate of the recently convicted Jennie Hawkes asked, "Where is chivalry?" Had it all gone to the war front?[78] Angelina Napolitano, convicted in 1911 of murdering her physically abusive husband who had tried to force her into prostitution, elicited much active sympathy throughout North America and Europe. One intercessor, Toronto lawyer James Fullerton cited "her womanhood" as a reason for clemency. A.C. Boyce, M.P. for the Sault, the site of the murder and trial, wrote the Minister of Justice to announce that "Ones [sic] mind naturally revolts against the idea of the death sentence upon a woman."[79]

The same motif played a part in Elizabeth Coward's commutation. Her post-trial lawyer, J.E. Bird of Vancouver, compared her to British nurse Edith Cavell, executed by the Germans in Belgium, in October 1915, for underground activities. Both women, he wrote, had been convicted by legally constituted authorities for offences meriting the death penalty. Cavell's sentence had been widely reviled. As had Coward's in B.C.: "The sentiment of the community evidences that women shall not be treated in this manner, notwithstanding laws to the contrary."[80] Even more interesting is the report of Trial Judge Denis Murphy to the Secretary of State, which includes this telling passage: "beyond calling your attention to the fact the accused is a woman I have no recommendation to make."[81] A memorandum prepared by a Justice official for the minister echoed the report and Bird's letter in citing as the sole reasons for clemency the accused's gender and the sentiment of the community.[82] Coward's sentence was commuted to life imprisonment. Given the stress of the memorandum, trial judge's report as well as the Bird letter and the fact that the jury had not recommended mercy, it seems certain the commutation was gender based.

Chapter Seven
Elizabeth Workman —
Sinner or Saint?

Raucous music blared; beer flowed; couples danced with abandon. Everyone, it seemed, was having a great time. Maybe the music was too loud, but it was summer and this was a great party. During the night and into the early hours of August 31, 1986, the brooding host, Kevin Rust, watched his common-law wife as she circulated. Sometimes Angelique, known as Lyn Lavallee, laughed. Sometimes she got a little closer to a couple of men than Kevin would have liked.

Those who knew him well recognized the signals. Lyn had received medical treatment for various cuts, fractures and bruises several times over the three or four years she had lived with Kevin and each time he had been the abuser. As the party wound down, according to Lyn's own testimony:

> I ran in the house after Kevin pushed me. I was scared, I was really scared ... I went upstairs and hid in my closet from Kevin. I was so scared ... Next thing I know he was coming up the stairs for me ... OK then he turned and he saw me in the closet. He wanted me to come out but I didn't want to come out because I was scared. I was so scared. He grabbed me by the arm right there [she pointed to the inside of her right forearm], there's a bruise on my face also where he slapped me.

At this point in her statement, she indicated the visible facial bruising before continuing with a crucial admission, "All I thought about was all the other times he used to beat me, I was scared and I was shaking as usual."

But this time would not be usual. After Kevin had shouted that she was his woman and had to do what he wanted, he gave her a gun. From that point Lyn remembered:

he started going like this with his finger and said something like 'You're my old lady and you do as you're told' or something like that. He said 'wait till everybody leaves, you'll get it then' and he said something, to the effect of 'either you kill me or I'll get you' ... He kind of smiled ....[1]

To Kevin's short-lived surprise, Lyn took the first option. She pulled the trigger.

Lyn Lavallee was subsequently charged with second-degree murder. At the well publicized trial in Alberta, her lawyer offered the defence of "battered-woman syndrome." The judge and jury accepted it and the Supreme Court of Canada upheld the verdict.[2] *R v. Lavallee* thus became a precedent for women charged with killing abusive partners.

More than one hundred years earlier, Elizabeth Workman was hanged for the murder of her husband, James. Societal norms and tolerances were different. Most importantly, there was no *Lavallee* precedent and she had no money to hire a competent lawyer. Elizabeth lived constantly with verbal abuse and periodically with physical violence. Unlike Lyn Lavallee, no pointed gun catapulted her into killing her husband and when she faced trial, her defence depended on a young, inexperienced lawyer, appointed by the court only hours before the trial, who was unprepared to fight for her life.[3] Furthermore, this trial occurred in a period when male attitudes to battered women were ambivalent and at times insensitive, particularly amongst the elite.

British examples of these then-prevailing attitudes can readily be found. In 1856 Dorset, Martha Brown killed her carter husband after years of being beaten with a whalebone whip. A local vicar wrote *The Times* to assure its readers that the death penalty was quite appropriate, while the *County Express* of Dorset lamented the passing of "poor Anthony Brown" and, after the execution, predicted its readership "would take comfort in the condemnation of a husband murderer, however abused." Judith Knelman concluded that "Martha Brown was a scapegoat, an abused wife who had to be punished as an example to others in the same positions."[4] Edward Cox's influential guide to sentencing in England (1877) portrayed working class wives who got beaten as almost always deserving of it; this was, after all, appropriate punishment for swearing, drinking, neglecting their husbands, and so on. Only those rare ones who were morally pure and utterly submissive deserved protection.[5]

In late nineteenth century North America, New York City social workers readily believed battered women were often to blame for being slothful, drunken, or adulterous.[6] Their counterparts in Boston meted out more praise to abused wives who stayed with their abusers rather than move out — where that was possible.[7] In the Montreal of the 1870s, magistrates punished the illegal sale of liquor and abusive language by women more severely than wife battering.[8] Other Canadian examples include Judge Britton and Justice Minister Aylesworth in the Napolitano case. In Alberta, during its first fifteen years as a province, enforcement was a farce. Even for recidivist husbands, the norm was token fines and occasional short prison terms, often of only one month.[9]

But there were many offsetting examples and these indicate the growing strength of an emerging concept of the husband as a protector, not the "manly" aggressive owner of his wife. In the United Kingdom, explicit wife-beating legislation was enacted in 1853, enabling magistrates in aggravated cases to order imprisonment, with hard labour, for up to six months.[10] Female victims of serious spousal assault could obtain a separation with maintenance under the Matrimonial Causes Act of 1878.[11] Thus the state had spoken its values; the preamble to the 1853 Act, for instance, asserting "the present Law has been found insufficient for the Protection of Women and Children from violent Assaults." In addition, a Society for the Protection of Women was active in the field of prevention, for example, having representatives observe some trials as early as the 1860s. Throughout the latter half of the nineteenth century *The Times* campaigned against wife-battering, described in an 1853 editorial as the work of "brutes," "ruffians," and "tyrants" — such "monsters outrage every law of civilized man, and violate every instinct of human nature." As the century wore on, more and more London magistrates adhered to this viewpoint as Cox's harsh attitude gradually became archaic.[12]

By 1900, wife-beating was illegal either by enactment of the legislatures or judicial decisions of the state courts in most of the United States. Other illustrations can be given of changing attitudes among the elite in late Victorian times. The Boston chief of police, for example, testified in many aggravated battery cases and the American Bar Association "chivalrously" resolved in 1886 that "the interests of society would be promoted by the general use of the whipping post as a mode of punishment for wife-beating and other assaults on the weak and defenceless."[13] Linda Gordon effectively summarizes: "Contrary to some common misperceptions, wife-beating was not generally accepted as a head-of-household right at the time [c. 1870], but was considered a disreputable, seamy practice."[14]

It must be emphasized that, while wives were protected by law, enforcement was generally very poor and not only where magistrates or prosecutors considered battering a venial sin. While Philadelphia in the 1880s (but not a decade later) was a model, other areas in the state were not. Baltimore, 1883-5, had 313 arrests — but only two convictions.[15] The same lack of enforcement characterized London (U.K.), Montreal, Halifax, and several American cities. The reasons often lay in the reluctance of even desperate wives to carry matters to trial — arrest being enough — due to internalized guilt, affection, fear of retaliation, the danger of losing the breadwinner, or some combination. In Montreal, necessary disbursements acted as a brake. It cost a wife a dollar (a sum equal to a labourer's daily wage) for an arrest warrant and, if she did not appear at trial or refused to testify, court costs of four dollars or so were added to the bill.[16] Cost was also a deterrent in Halifax in the later nineteenth century.[17]

The few secondary sources relating to turn of the century Canada do contain examples of positive sympathy for battered women on the part of elites, but they are less clear-cut than those revealed in the scholarship on England or the United States. In Halifax, there was a Society for the Prevention of Cruelty to Children which, by 1880, logically concerned itself with brutalized women as well. The main effort was a caution to the husband implying a possible threat of criminal charges.[18] In 1909, the Canadian Parliament enacted a law expressly making wife-beaters who caused actual bodily harm liable to two years in jail and a whipping.[19] This added to a generic provision in the Code of 1892 (and antecedent law) punishing aggravated assaults with up to three years in prison.[20] The 1909 Act was progress in a symbolic sense, but came a full fifty-six years after explicit legislation in England. In Alberta, the whipping sanction seems to have been still-born during the early years at least.[21]

In Canada, situations involving murder did galvanize public attention and by doing so revealed that in general, as expected, the Canadian elite was adopting the emergent attitudes of Britain and the United States. On October 25, 1873, the day after Nova Scotia logger Peter Mailman was convicted of murdering his wife, whom he had repeatedly beaten with gross brutality, the *Halifax Evening Reporter* was moved to outrage: "If any one ought to be able to live securely by another it should be the wife by the husband ... this the closest relationship which exists in public life should be most amply protected by the law. On this ground and this ground alone we believe that the guilty man should be left to his fate."[22] Mailman was indeed hanged at the end of the year.

In 1882, Clara Elliot was convicted of manslaughter at Sweetsburg, Quebec, for having assisted her brutal husband in beating their seven year-old servant boy to death. She was sentenced to ten years. Five years later, her trial lawyer interceded with the justice minister for a full pardon on the grounds that at the time of the killing she had been a "mere girl ... [who] lived in brutal fear and dread of her husband, who often treated her with great harshness and brutality." This appeal was seconded in a petition from the "citizens of Sweetsburg" who stressed her "constant fear" and the fact "she was often severely beaten" by her spouse. The government responded with a free pardon.[23] There was a massive, world-wide outpouring of sympathy for Angelina Napolitano — although more of the sympathy was stimulated by the attempts at forced prostitution than the murderous assaults. As in the United Kingdom and the United States, elite attitudes percolated down the social scale.[24] But as late as January 1999 wife battering remained a problem for Canadian society. In a 1999 *Globe and Mail* article Bill Catucci, president and CEO of AT&T Canada, asked why it is still largely hidden. He cited current statistics showing that only 26% of women report their battering to the police and, even worse, an estimated 22% of battered women never tell anyone about it.[25]

James and Elizabeth Workman lived with his eight year-old son, Hugh, in Mooretown — a small rural neighbourhood a few miles east of Sarnia. Their lives were marked by "unquiet desperation." Elizabeth was the local washerwoman and housecleaner. James, a butcher and occasional labourer, rarely found work — although he was "a good sized strong and active man." When he did, he seemed unable to keep it, which, at age 55, must have been galling. His closest neighbour, David Patterson, described him as "hard-working and industrious" but with the caveat that he "drank a great deal." To support his habit, James forced Elizabeth to hand her earnings over to him. Whether or not his family had groceries seemed immaterial as long as he had his liquor.

Their family situation was no secret in the neighbourhood. The Workmans quarrelled loudly and frequently. Many times, the quarrelling and fighting would begin about ten at night and last up to six hours. Obviously, the Pattersons were kept awake — a situation that should have demanded redress of some sort. Apparently, Sarah Patterson once worked up the courage to confront James about his drinking: "Workman and I had not been very good friends for some time before his death because I had checked him for drinking and he would abuse his last friend when he was in that state." Other than that one instance, nobody seemed to have intervened in what was obviously a worsening situation.

Maybe people were afraid of James. A violent man, he would lash out as readily with his fists as he would with his tongue. Maybe the dictum of a man's house being his castle held true and this situation might have continued indefinitely, but fate intervened in the persons of a couple of itinerant black barbers who set up business in Mooretown. Using many towels in their work, they thus became Elizabeth's customers. Eventually a friendship formed between the barbers and the Workmans, with the barbers visiting the Workman house outside of business hours. Sarah once heard one of them, Samuel Butler, "Sing a song with Mr. Workman" and her husband saw "him going to the Workman's house at different times." According to young Hugh, "The barbers were in the habit of coming in ... the evenings and would sometimes stay until a late hour or until after I went asleep. Sometimes they quarrelled with my father." Butler brought "Whiskey at night more than once."

Elizabeth apparently found a special rapport with Sam Butler. Maybe she felt a bond through their both being outcasts — she, as a victim of domestic tyranny; he, through the colour of his skin. There could be little doubt that Butler was aware of Elizabeth's disintegrating family life. James was drinking almost non-stop and his violence, verbally at least, had become constant. Unlike others in Mooretown, Butler was prepared to do something about it — as shown by an incident shortly before Workman's death.

According to several residents, on Thursday, October 24, 1872, James Workman showed up at Butler's shop. He had come for his wife who was, presumably, scrubbing and cleaning the establishment. Workman demanded that Elizabeth leave Butler's shop and return home, which she wasn't ready to do. So James stood, his hands against the door jamb, arguing loudly until Butler "stepped up and shoved Workman against the wall and told him if he did not leave her alone" he would kick him. According to a witness, Peter Mayhew, Workman mumbled something, then Butler did indeed leave him alone. A cowed Elizabeth "went for her shawl & she and her husband went away together."

Shopkeeper Samuel Judson's story was much more dramatic and may well refer to a totally different incident. In Judson's version, after Workman put his hands on the door, Butler pushed him. As James "came out he fell on the sidewalk on his head and shoulders. He fell by a somersault over some timber then got up, swearing at Butler, who told him he had better go home and mind his own business." Elizabeth stayed put, "scrubbing and cleaning," because Judson testified that "she did not then go home." Hugh Workman remembered that quarrel taking place on the Thursday night when "Butler shoved my Father out of the shop and he fell." His mother then had gone home with them.

However difficult it may be to reconcile these accounts of the "row," there can be no doubt that it happened and would have fatal repercussions for James Workman. Within less than forty-eight hours he would be dead.

David and Sarah Patterson lived above the Workmans on the second floor of the shared house, separated by only a wooden ceiling. Not only did they overhear the frequent violent arguments of their downstairs neighbours, they also had no compunction about opening their doors to see what was going on. In fact, from their own testimony at Elizabeth's subsequent trial, they seemed almost totally preoccupied by their neighbours' comings and goings to the point that one must wonder if they did anything else. But their accounts provide a fairly detailed picture of the events leading up to James Workman's death.

Elizabeth had not appreciated being brought home from Butler's shop. Indeed, that very public row may have been the immediate provocation for her to change from victim to attacker. James's son, Hugh, testified that he didn't think Elizabeth slept in their communal bed that Thursday night. Sarah Patterson remembered that she'd heard "Workman scolding during the night;" Hugh had said "Father" several times but she did not hear "the Wife's voice."

David Patterson's unsubstantiated evidence about events early the following morning proved damning for Elizabeth, particularly for the suggestion of infidelity it firmly planted in the judge's mind. Patterson identified Butler and testified he'd seen him at the Workmans's house several times. Then he told his version of events early Friday morning:

> about 4 o'clock [a.m.] I heard some one pulling his boots on in the room below. I thought the sound was too heavy for a boy's foot and that Workman must be getting up to go to do some butchering. I went to [the] head of [the] stairs of our landing outside of the house. I saw a man going up the embankment ... I took that man to be the prisoner Butler. He was 3 or 4 feet from the stairs when I first saw him & I was at the head of the stairs. I was 12 to 16 feet from him [and] it was dark. I could see the man had on a gray coat. I did not see his face. I thought it was Butler from his size & footsteps. When he got to the road he went up to the village. That is where he lived.

If this indeed had been Butler, he would have been extraordinarily busy that Friday morning for Patterson recalled that about 6:45 a.m. he again saw him leaving the Workman's house with a "bowl in his hand filled as I thought with pickles." When Butler went off in the same direction as the previous visitor, it confirmed Patterson's belief that it was the same person. Hugh Workman, though, supplied a perfectly logical reason for the barber's visit that morning, recalling him coming between seven and eight o'clock with a load of laundry.

Later, while Elizabeth was hanging out that washing, Sarah Patterson heard "her husband talking loud to her from his bed."[26] Then, at two o'clock she overheard Elizabeth ask James "if he had got enough. He made answer & called her some abusive name." Titillated by the exchange, and like her husband had earlier in the day, Mrs. Patterson went out onto the landing so that she could look down into the Workman's part of the house. Then, after seeing Elizabeth walk out of the bedroom, Sarah

> went back to my place & I heard again blows downstairs & words. I went again to my landing and saw her come from the bedroom. I went back to my place again. The blows commenced again. I went the third time to the

landing but the door below was shut ... [Then she heard] a heavy blow ... and Workman scream out that he was killed. Before that it was only groans ... this time it was a scream.

From her part of the house she heard one more blow, then ominous silence.

The entire incident, she thought, lasted about two hours. That evening, Elizabeth brought her up a plate of pickles and raised the subject herself by asking if Sarah had heard anything that afternoon. After receiving an affirmative reply, Elizabeth said "she had given him what he would not forget for a while."

"Yes. Mrs. Workman, if you have not given him too much it will be all right," Sarah answered. What was "too much" would never be defined. Nor would the Pattersons' lack of concern regarding James's possible injuries, particularly when later that night, David heard James complaining of being beaten but "he did not speak violently." This seemed to go on intermittently between ten and midnight and after that the Pattersons heard no noise at all from the Workmans until Sarah summoned them to her house, Saturday afternoon. By then James Workman was dead.

Hugh, of course, had the closest view of the situation as he slept in the same bed as his father. He hadn't seen his father out of that bed since the Thursday. On Saturday morning, when James asked for some water, about ten, he could not lift himself up to drink it. Hugh thought he was ill and Elizabeth told him she thought his father "was going to die." Then he "saw her strike ... father on Saturday with the mophandle. She hit him with the handle of it on the shoulder" after Hugh had given him the drink. Although she had mentioned an earlier beating, this was the only time he saw his stepmother hit Workman.

From that point, events escalated quickly. At two o'clock, Elizabeth called out to David Patterson, who was in the back yard cutting wood, asking him to "come here and see what is the matter with Father." After seeing the body, Patterson immediately sent Hugh for his wife. As he described in court, he came:

in & put my arm under his head and put my hand to his heart. It was not beating & he was cold and had been dead some time. I felt as I put my hand to his heart that his shirts, such as they were, were wet ... I thought he had been washed. The right shoulder was black and brown as if he had got a hard beating. The shoulder was swelled awfully. He had two cuts on the right side of the temple and one on the left temple — all three cuts about the same size. I did not examine him further.

Patterson noticed that the "areas back of his hands and fingers were badly beaten" and later that evening, after the doctor had left, he examined the legs, finding that "his shins were beaten & his toes were awfully used up."

When told that James was dead, Elizabeth "got herself across his body & said 'Father Father won't you speak to me.'" After Patterson ordered her to "come off that the man is dead," Elizabeth "came off as if she were crying but I [David] saw no tears." True to his previous pattern of non-interference he "did not ask how it happened nor did she tell" him. But he recollected her words of the previous evening when she had told his wife that "she had given him what he would remember for a while." The doctor's examination bore out Patterson's testimony, noting there were twenty to thirty blows on the body and legs.

The puzzle for the prosecution would be threefold: exactly when had Workman died; which of the many injuries had been fatal; and how had such a slight woman as Elizabeth managed to inflict such massive damage on her larger and stronger husband.

Dr. Edward Oliver attempted to answer this last question:

> I should think the legs must have been bound by a cord
> ... and that the abrasions were perhaps caused by his
> struggling against ... [it]. I think the blow on the temple
> was the last given. He might have been killed instantly
> by the two injuries on the nose & temple — or he might
> have lived 12 to 24 hours ... [but] after getting those he
> would not be able to speak ... [and would] lie in a
> comatose state.

Dr. Oliver noted a small amount of liquid in the stomach and a considerable amount of what he termed "dissipation." But, as poison was not suspected, his examination of the stomach was cursory.

Elizabeth and Sam Butler were subsequently arrested and stood trial in Sarnia, May 1873. The presiding judge was Adam Wilson, Mary Aylward's prosecutor. After resigning from the position of Upper Canada's solicitor general in 1863, Wilson received an appointment to the judiciary.[27] To defend Elizabeth, the court chose a very young and inexperienced lawyer, John A. McKenzie, then gave him only a few hours to prepare his case.

McKenzie actually did a reasonable job with cross-examination, drawing out some mitigating circumstances. But he also adduced damning testimony that would paint Elizabeth in Judge Wilson's eyes as an unfaithful woman. For example, he had tried to establish Workman as an abusive individual from David Patterson's cross-examination, a man who had become so abusive that the Pattersons did not socialize with their closest neighbour. This he did. But he also allowed Patterson to put the following words into the record: "Workman had a bad tongue at times. Many persons were in the habit of visiting their house. A man ... [named] Stewart stayed there 6 or 8 days when Workman was at Point Edward." And then Patterson continued with his characterization of "Workman [as] a hard-working industrious man" who "drank a great deal."

Maybe Stewart was related to or a friend of Elizabeth. But Judge Wilson put his own emphasis on this testimony, concluding that Stewart was Elizabeth Workman's lover. This, together with placing her and Butler in frequent contact, confirmed his conclusion that she had "impeached" her "conjugal fidelity."

Even though evidence about the row the Thursday before Workman's death was contradictory, McKenzie should have been able to tie some of Workman's wounds to that incident. Judson, in particular, had testified that Workman hit the sidewalk on his head and shoulders. Given Dr. Edwards' vagueness about the time the fatal wounds were inflicted, surely McKenzie could have at least suggested that this incident might have resulted in a fatal wound. This might well have been clutching at straws, but it might also have raised the thought in at least one juror's mind that the initial cause of death was accidental.

As mentioned earlier, Hugh testified that he slept with his father. Judge Wilson, in his letter to the Minister of Justice dated May 8, 1873, acknowledged that he:

was perplexed for a time, how she a small slight woman, could have gone, time and time again to her husband in bed, who was a good sized strong and active man for his age, and inflict upon him such serious injury without his rising from bed or protecting himself in any way — but if his legs were tied [as according to Dr. Edward's suppositions] that may partly remove the difficulty — and so also would the fact if one of the very severe blows given at the beginning ... remove the desire and also the ability to rise.

If Judge Wilson was so perplexed by this, why didn't he ask Hugh? Given the close sleeping quarters, Workman might have told Hugh that Butler and/or Elizabeth only inflicted the severe beating because his legs had been tied.

According to Sarah Patterson's testimony, Elizabeth beat up Workman on Thursday afternoon. If Judson's account is correct, he would have had head and shoulder injuries by this time. This time frame would explain why he offered little or no resistance. If, however, the evidence of Mayhew and Hugh is accurate, the quarrel happened Thursday night. Thus, the fatal wound might have occurred after the "row." There were enough discrepancies for an experienced lawyer to have planted the seed of "reasonable doubt" in a jury's mind. In any case, although it found Elizabeth guilty, the jury added a recommendation to mercy.

The final problem with McKenzie's defence is that he did not bring even one witness to any physical abuse endured by Elizabeth Workman. Instead of an early "battered-woman-syndrome," McKenzie left the jury with the picture of a bound man being beaten to death by his unfaithful wife. Although Sarah Patterson testified that James "would illuse" his wife, the precise nature of that "illuse" was never specified. Furthermore, Hugh declared on cross examination that his father did not beat Elizabeth: "He was cross to me and my mother when he had been drinking. I don't remember of his beating my mother. He has called her names. My Father was not very kind to my Mother. They used to abuse each other." Again, "not very kind" and "abuse" remained undefined. In his charge to the jury, Judge Wilson declared that Butler must be acquitted as the prosecution had produced no evidence against him. How convenient, as a co-accused Butler had been unable to testify. Wilson also claimed about Elizabeth that "she was not kind to her husband." He had thus taken Hugh's words and reversed them.

In his M.A. thesis, "The Female Killer and the Public Mind," Edward Stoddart paints a fascinating picture of Victorian attitudes towards female killers.[28] They were either saints or sinners and he used Elizabeth's trial and its aftermath to demonstrate this. As we have seen, the trial record hints at adultery. Judge Wilson didn't have one iota of doubt as to Elizabeth's infidelity. Furthermore, as there was "no special quarrel" between James and Elizabeth, he believed the motive for the murder must have been lust and he completely disregarded evidence that put Butler's relationship with her on a business and platonic footing. According to Judge Wilson, once Workman was out of the way, Elizabeth would consummate her relationship with Butler. But then, by his own admission, Wilson believed she had already done so.

Other, less biased observers at the trial interpreted the evidence very differently. In their eyes, Elizabeth became more of a saint — a woman who had reached a breaking point only after enduring years of abuse. As it led the campaign to save Elizabeth's life, the *Sarnia Observer*, on April 18, 1873, stated that "the deceased James Workman had for a long period of years been a most intemperate and tyrannical husband and father; that his wife had frequently to take refuge in the dwellings of her neighbours from his violence; ... that she was a quiet, industrious, hard working woman."

The *Observer*, however, had had months to write this dispassionately. And, unlike defence counsel McKenzie, who had only a few hours to prepare for trial, the *Observer* had time to do its homework by interviewing people who had known the Workmans and not testified at the trial. The reporter tracked down people in the nearby town of St. Mary's, where the Workmans had lived before moving to Mooretown; from these interviews, a different picture emerged: "it appears he [James] carried on the same system there; often coming home in a state of toxication, and dragging his wife out of bed, and forcing her to give him the pittance she had earned by working during the day, so he might spend it on liquor."

Petitions, from a broad cross-section of the Sarnia and Lambton County communities to the Minister of Justice requesting clemency, support this viewpoint. The petition from St. Mary's described Elizabeth as a "sober, industrious woman" married to a man who stole and then spent her earnings in "drunkenness and debauching." The citizens of Lambton county described a woman caught up in what a hundred years later would be called the battered-woman syndrome. Elizabeth had "quietly submitted" to her husband's demands for years until "her patience being exhausted she gave him blows that were fatal."

So why did Elizabeth Workman's life end on the gallows? After all, there were "extenuating circumstances" as the Lambton County Council resolved. Moreover, she was the only woman hanged, out of thirty-one, whom post-Confederation juries recommended to the Crown's mercy.

Until the *Lavallee* decision, repeated abuse by the husband, including serious assaults, was no defence if the wife intentionally killed him. If the abuse was sufficiently severe, it could, however, amount to provocation and reduce a potential verdict of murder to one of manslaughter, which of course was not capital and seldom carried a prison sentence longer than ten years. But the response to provocation had to be "sudden."

The 1911 case convicting Sault Ste. Marie battered wife, Angelino Napolitano, of murder demonstrated this thinking. The accused had obliterated husband Pietro's life and almost his body as well by smashing him several times with an axe while he slept.[29] Napolitano's lawyer desperately tried to prove abuse and provocation, citing a battering in November 1910, when Pietro had viciously stabbed her with a pocket-knife in the shoulder, arms, chest and face. Judge F.M. Britton remarked when ruling the evidence inadmissible that "if anybody injured six months ago could give that as justification or excuse for slaying a person, it would be anarchy complete."[30] Although clearly insensitive to battered wives,[31] Britton was legally accurate on this point. At the time, months or weeks of delay disqualified a plea of provocation. However, this did not mean that the reaction had to be immediate. If the delay was a mere few hours or days, the defence could be considered valid.[32]

Another exculpatory plea was self-defence: essentially using sufficient force, up to homicide, to repel another's violence to the accused. During the proceedings against Catherine Sabourine in

Ottawa, in 1880, the defendant's two teenaged daughters and the deceased's brother proved that the husband recurrently beat Catherine. On the fatal night, after another assault and having threatened to kill her, he made a rush at her. She responded with an axe-stroke to the head and he died three days later. The jury acquitted.[33] As defined then, actions in self-defence had to occur during a confrontation or when one was imminent. This does not fit the facts in Workman's case.

Therefore provocation or self-defence do not need analysis, but the evidence on battering and on adultery certainly does.[34]

In his charge to the jury, Judge Wilson accurately summarized the evidence when he stated that the two spouses "quarrelled — he did not beat her — but he was abusive in his language to her when he had been drinking." There was abundant proof of James Workman's tendency when drunk to curse his wife, but none at all clearly pointing to battery. Sarah Patterson did testify, on cross-examination by Mackenzie, that when James drank "He would illuse his own child or wife ... She has come to my place on 4 or 5 occasions to be away from her husband ... and to get away from his abusive tongue[.] he drank pretty heavy for a week or two before his death." She did not define "illuse," while her husband said nothing about wife abuse and Hugh claimed he didn't "remember ... his beating my Mother ... [although he] was not very kind to her."

Allegations of spousal brutality, more serious than foul-mouthing his mate, come from the many intercessions, mainly telegrams, a letter and petitions, to save Elizabeth from the gallows. A petition to the governor general from 118 people of Mooretown and the surrounding area, including many of the elite (and witness Judson),[35] portrayed the convict as "a sober industrious woman of good character who worked hard to support her husband and child though often deprived by her husband of her hard earnings as soon as obtained." On the point of wife-battering, the petition was vague but suggestive. James was "very dissipated and *cruel* and frequently ill treated her compelling her to take refuge" with neighbours. She submitted for several years but "at last ... her patience being exhausted she gave him blows that were fatal." She had indeed been "so sorely tempted" that the exercise of royal mercy was called for.

The accusation of wage stealing was supported in a petition signed by 464 residents of Elizabeth's former town, St. Mary's; several of these people, the document asserted, knew the family. Elizabeth was sober, industrious, and the main breadwinner. As for James, he "was a drunken dissipated man who often forcibly took the earnings of his wife and spent it in drunkenness and debauchery."[36] After the trial, the Grand Jury of Lambton County resolved that now the facts had become better known, it was clear Elizabeth had "been more sorely tempted than human beings usually are."

But what of explicit allegations of battery? The Capital Case file includes a letter, dated May 28, 1873, seeking clemency from Alexander Mackenzie to the Prime Minister and Minister of Justice, Sir John A. Macdonald. Mackenzie was then M.P. for Lambton County, leader of the opposition in Ottawa, and soon to replace Macdonald as Prime Minister. He was also a longtime resident of Sarnia. He portrayed the couple as drunken and coarse in language, adding that "blows were common." If this last were true it would certainly mean that Elizabeth got the worst of it, she being a frail, petite woman — while James was "a good sized strong and active man for his age."[37] The St. Mary's petition, moreover, expressly alleged that Mr. Workman "often beat and threatened the life of his said wife."

Justice Wilson's charge cited as suspicious the fight at barber's shop on the Thursday, when Butler threatened Mr. Workman with violence if he did not leave his wife alone, noting that Elizabeth Workman had been there the whole day and that James had come to take her home. Wilson also asserted that Butler on the Friday morning at 4 a.m. "was *seen* leaving" the Workman house; he concluded that "the evidence points to some kind of improper intimacy between the Woman and Butler." In his report to Ottawa, enclosing the charge and his notes on the trial, the judge elaborated: "The evidence suggested criminal or improper conduct between the woman and Samuel Butler the coloured man who was tried with her — I mean conduct impeaching her conjugal fidelity and that may have been the motive for her violence — as it may also explain the purpose which she wished to accomplish."

The "evidence" simply does not support these damning statements. The fact that Elizabeth had been at Butler's barber shop all day Thursday, cleaning, signifies nothing more than business. Mrs. Workman did Butler's wash and the latter sometimes drank with the couple at their home. No one testified that Butler and Elizabeth had gone into a private room for sufficient time to have intercourse.

As for the so-called identification of Butler leaving the Workmans' at

4:00 a.m., in itself far from conclusive,[38] this came solely from David Patterson, who saw a man in a grey coat leaving the house from a distance of about fifteen feet. He took this man to be Butler. But how trustworthy was this identification? Judge Wilson assumed it was, but Patterson concluded his testimony on point, by admitting "it was dark ... I did not see his face. I thought it was Butler from his size & footstep." And later: "many persons [men] were in the habit of visiting their house."

It is clear that far from proving adultery beyond a reasonable doubt the Crown did not prove it at all; and Wilson's conclusion — that such proof had been made, perhaps grounded in local gossip — moved Elizabeth Workman closer to the gallows.[39]

There are two possible explanations for Mrs. Workman's execution. The legal and political establishments in Canada thought husband-murder such a particularly atrocious crime that wives needed continuing deterrence by the sight of executions. Or, possibly, Elizabeth Workan's fate is found in the late nineteenth-early twentieth century insensitivity to the plight of battered women.

In her book, *Twisting in the Wind*, Judith Knelman claims that wife killers were treated far more leniently in England during the nineteenth century than husband killers. Her evidence, drawn from the 1840s to the 1870s, is anecdotal but not unpersuasive for that period. A striking quotation by John Stuart Mill and Harriet Taylor, which appeared in the *Morning Chronicle* of March 29, 1850 sums up Knelman's thesis, if with exaggeration: "is it because juries are composed of husbands in a low rank in life, that men who kill their wives almost invariably escape [the gallows] — wives who kill their husbands, never." This alleged differential contrasts strikingly with the execution rates for all capital crimes: 27.2% for convicted women (1843-82). The general rate was much higher for men. In some years it reached 67% and higher from the mid 1850s to 1899.[40]

Canadian statistics give no support for transferring Knelman's concept across the ocean.[41] They indicate that, unlike England, husband killing, for reasons yet unknown, was treated less harshly than wife killing by Canadian authorities in the nineteenth and twentieth centuries.[42] These same statistics, though, indicate that dispatching her spouse to eternity was considered the worst kind of murder committed by females; a generation or two earlier it had been legally deemed a form of treason. No wonder, as the law and its administration was largely the preserve of men, exclusively so before the twentieth century. Perhaps because husband murder was deemed such a dastardly act, the nature of the offence affected Ottawa's judgment on mercy when Elizabeth Workman's worthiness to live was decided.

If wife battering was not generally condoned by Canada's elites in the late nineteenth and early twentieth centuries, as explained earlier in this chapter, the post-trial evidence should have worked in Elizabeth Workman's favour. Why didn't it?

The explanation of Workman's execution seems quite simple. Like so many poor and capitally-charged at the time, Elizabeth was not properly represented by counsel.[43] Today, under the Charter, she would have to be told by the arresting police of her right to counsel and of legal services available free to the poor. It is not clear, though, whether provinces are required to supply legal aid at all, much less at a high standard, or, failing that, that the court is required to supply a lawyer free of charge.[44] Elizabeth Workman's lawyer was appointed by the court — a very old tradition in Canada — only a few hours before trial.[45] Had he had the time to prepare effectively, Mackenzie would surely have done two things: produced one or more witnesses to Workman's actual battery of his wife and argued there was no evidence of adultery. The first might have prevented Judge Wilson from reporting that he had "nothing to say of the case favourable for the prisoner" (May 8, 1873). The ministry of justice would certainly have weighed more sympathetically proof of wife-beating, sworn to on oath and subject to cross-examination, than assertions contained in post-trial pleas for mercy. Suspicion of adultery was then often fatal to female accused.[46] It is even possible Mackenzie could have mounted a persuasive defence of provocation, reducing the verdict to non-capital manslaughter.

Today, a woman in a situation like Elizabeth Workman's could not be executed. Indeed, she might well be discharged following acquittal. In the precedent-setting unanimous decision, rendered in May 1990, *R.v. Lavallee*, the Supreme Court of Canada liberally expanded the meaning of self-defence available to repeatedly battered wives, legal or common law, who kill their spouses.[47]

Under Canadian law, then and now, a persuasive self-defence counter to homicide must establish three elements of reasonableness: relating to the degree of force used to repel, the apprehension of death or grievous bodily harm from an assailant, and the perception there is no workable alternative to avoiding harm. The courts were traditionally guided by the masculine norm of a barroom brawl — a fight of unarmed equals. These criteria of course would not protect a battered wife, who like Workman and Lavallee, killed their defenceless mates with weapons. Justification was found by making an exception to the norm.

Trial evidence was offered that Lavallee's experience fell under the rubric "battered woman syndrome" deriving primarily from the work of American psychologists, particularly the pioneering studies of Dr. Lenore Walker, often and favourably cited in the Supreme Court's decision.[48] Walker depicted the battering relationship as accompanying three-part cycles: growing tension accompanied by minor assaults; an uncontrolled bout of beating; and loving contrition. A battered woman was defined as one who had suffered through at least two of these cycles with the same man. Such considerable experience was supposed to give the woman "heightened sensitivity" to an impending and possibly lethal attack by her partner, a perception reasonable to her if not obvious to an outsider.

A second concept, which Walker borrowed from psychologist Charles Seligman's electro-shock experiments on dogs, is "learned helplessness." Just as the dogs selected for shock eventually gave up hope of escape, even when made easy, battered women lose any motivation to act prudently and become paralysed by fear. The only way out often seems to be homicide. Dr. Fred Shane, the expert witness for the defence in the Lavallee case, gave as his opinion that the defendant "had been terrorized by Rust to the point of feeling trapped, vulnerable, worthless and unable to escape... 'I think she felt ... in the final tragic moment that her life was on the line, that ... unless she reacted in a violent way that she would die.'"[49] The Supreme Court accepted both "heightened sensitivity" and "learned helplessness" as relevant. It further held that given these factors and the differences in strength, shooting Rust while he was helpless was lawful.

Acceptance of the battered woman syndrome allows intolerably battered wives to justify preemptive strikes as reasonable in certain circumstances and begins to undermine the common male stereotype that failure to leave the relationship indicated female masochism. This decision certainly helped right the balance in law. But scholars and legal commentators are beginning to criticize the "syndrome" based both on its lack of legal logic and feminist fears that a new patriarchal stereotype might replace the old.

Like a bride going to her husband, Elizabeth Workman climbed the steps to the gallows on June 19, 1873 grasping a bouquet of white flowers. She had killed only in self-defence, she informed the small group of police and reporters and the official witnesses, to those who had helped her since the death of her husband, she was "remarkably grateful."[50]

A graceful ending to a distasteful episode in Canadian history.

Chapter Eight
Annie Robinson —
"More to be Pitied Than Censured"?

As parishioners in the Methodist church in Warren, Ontario sang the farewell hymn, "Abide With Me," few noticed if Annie Robinson sang along and fewer cared before the dreadful days of 1909.

Annie was the wife of James Robinson and, to outsiders, the Robinsons seemed happy and contented. If the opinion of the local justice of the peace, Ernest Wright, can be accepted, the people of Warren thought James "honest" and "virtuous."[1] Wright could have added hard-working. After all, in just seven or eight years, Robinson had taken a tract of bushland seven miles from the village and systematically hacked a farm from it. But Wright should have wondered why the family kept so determinedly to itself, because, in contrast to their parents, the ten children rarely went to church or into Warren. None visited or played with neighbouring children.[2] If questioned, they answered that their father had ordered them to stay at home to do their chores.

There was, of course, another explanation.

When James Robinson first met Annie, she had lived in Westmeath, in the county of Renfrew, Ontario. Her father, a "middling poor" farmer, was very kind to his family as befitted a stalwart of the local Presbyterian church. His pastor, Rev. C.A. Ferguson, later described him as "one of the most honorable and most strictly upright" men he had "ever known" and the family was "respected for miles around." Strictness certainly applied — for Annie had been brought up in a home "where ... rigid discipline prevailed."

As she watched two of her brothers become ministers, Annie must have wondered when and if her time would come to leave home. James Robinson's courtship doubtlessly seemed an answer to her prayers. She was twenty-four, an age by which most of her peers had long since begun their families. Although she later described her marriage to James as a "love match," there was undoubtedly an element of desperation about it. To outsiders, her marriage seemed happy. Her family had no hint of trouble and certainly the children came fast and furiously, with the three eldest being born in the first four years.

During this time, James maintained his industrious façade — working hard and keeping himself relatively sober. But after three children and four years of marriage he changed, beginning to drink hard; everything deteriorated. Although he rarely abused his family physically, he ruled them with an iron fist. Annie, used to her father's rigid philosophy of "spare the rod and spoil the child," accepted this as a matter of course. She would also acquiesce to James's decision to move to marginal farming land in what was then called the "new Ontario" — an area about fifty kilometres east of Sudbury. There they built a small farmhouse with only one bedroom.[3] She was now seven hundred kilometres from her parents, family and friends and Annie must have reasoned — a new place, a new start.

The Robinsons had been married more than fourteen years, by this time, and had had eight children. The marriage bonds were beginning to show signs of strain and there were hints that James had been unfaithful and not kept to his marital vows. Summoning her courage, Annie had once asked him about his unfaithfulness, but cowered when he answered that if she "ever said anything about it again that he would make it worse" for her — that he would indeed give her "reason" to complain.

Complaining did not seem to be in Annie's nature. She worked hard, as a house wife, in the fields, and, with increasing difficulty, in the marriage bed where she could not seem to satisfy her husband sexually, although she never refused him "if she was well." The move to "new Ontario" changed little. James soon began to drink excessively and Annie, finding her courage again, confronted him with it — but in a "kind" way. As she later explained, she "considered kindness ... the best way with him, for if I would scold him it would make him worse." Maybe she should have asked herself if things could have been worse.

Unknown to Annie, James Robinson had become a sexual predator. His prey weren't random persons or acquaintances. He kept his deviance in the family, systemically molesting his daughters, "tampering" first with Jessie, the oldest, when she was five, and then, with his other daughters after they reached the age of nine, "making ... efforts to have carnal intercourse using his fingers till connection [penetration was] effected."[4]

The terrified girls did not tell their mother immediately, so effective were their father's threats. But at some point Annie became aware of the situation because Jessie testified at her mother's trial that "she and her mother talked it over at odd times." Annie seemed "broken-hearted" when she found out but did not confront her husband. James continued, seemingly insatiable, having intercourse, or in Jessie's words "something to do with her," inside the house, the fields — in fact, "all over."

As the girls grew older they found resistance futile. Jessie, Ellen, and Maggie "occupied one room with 2 beds and the father came to the room, chose one of the 3 and the other two remained listeners."[5] James didn't often beat his girls, "just ... when we wouldn't do it for him," and many times enforced his will with just a glare. They talked about leaving the farm, but according to Ellen, "He said, if I threatened to go off ... for a living, he would shoot me before I could get off the place." Ellen tried to stop the abuse by saying that she would tell someone but, again, her will was broken when James kicked her into submission. She, like the others, quit school when aged twelve and was confined to the farm.

Only when James left the farm was there a modicum of happiness. Generally, life was dreary. Annie fretted most of the time and "nearly always cried when she started to talk" to the girls. The prosecutor at the trial aptly summed up the atmosphere when he asked Ellen, "Were there plenty of tears in that home." She answered simply, "Yes."

In 1905-6 the inevitable happened.[6] Both Jessie and Ellen, then aged approximately fifteen and fourteen, became pregnant. Jessie's child died, but Ellen's was added to the Robinson brood. Annie could no longer shut her eyes to the problem.

Annie would later testify that she had only become certain of the situation one evening when, while nursing her baby, she had seen "him and Ellen go into the bush together, and they were only a minute or two, or a few minutes, and they come back again ... something, I can't tell what, aroused the suspicion that there was something wrong and I asked Ellen ... and she wouldn't answer." And so her suspicions grew. She searched her mind but couldn't find any reason for her husband to molest his daughters and she was too afraid to ask him directly. She'd make her mind up to question him "time and time again," only to lose her courage at the last minute. Isolated, and with no friends, Annie couldn't tell anyone, as she "was afraid he would find out before anything could be done." Neither could she write her mother, because "that was the first disgrace brought on the family." So Annie endured her own cowardice, "borne down by sorrow and shame ... as though there was a smothering feeling" around her heart. The girls and their mother had to wonder if this was all the future would bring. The small farm was already supporting twelve people. Within months there would be fourteen and, with Maggie getting older, would there be seventeen in three years?

After the first pregnancies, the girls tried hard to escape. Once, Jessie had "started on the road" when "her father seen what was going on and went ahead of them and turned her back." Annie couldn't run away from that "lonely place" either. There "was too many of them, so many of them for me to take, and I couldn't go and leave any of them behind." The eldest son Johnny also tried ineffectively to help, promising to find enough money to send Jessie, at least, to her grandparents.

1907 proved to be a momentous year. James Robinson had become sufficiently prosperous to hire a few men to help clear his land and those men could not help noticing that both Jessie and Ellen were pregnant. This created much gossip and endless speculation among the workers and the people of Warren.

Jessie's child was born on March 17, 1908, with Annie in attendance. Soon after the birth, Jessie began crying "and lamenting ... 'Oh, if I had not been made to do this, this would not have happened.'" According to Annie, she repeated this "two or three times, or maybe more" before "she said, 'Oh mother, if this could be only kept hid.'"

Annie accepted the baby initially, planning to bring it up with her own children as she was doing with Ellen's son, who had been born in 1906. She tried to soothe the new baby's cries, dandling it on her lap and giving it some liquid with a spoon. As the time for the midday meal arrived, she handed the baby over to Ellen and fed her family. But during this time, Jessie's pleas must have reverberated in her mind. As Judge Magee said in his charge to the jury: "This daughter Jessie was the one for whom she had the most affection ... One can well conceive the feelings that at that moment actuated her, that she was ready to do anything to save the reputation of her daughter Jessie; ready to do anything to prevent a further addition to the family of an illegitimate child, the continuance at least of an illegitimate child in the family." Annie herself said she felt the "shame — of it being her child, and her own father, its father, which just driv [sic] me that I didn't realize — what I was doing at the time." Driven by this shame, her sense of guilt and compassion for Jessie, at some time in the afternoon Annie Robinson took the infant, placed it between two mattresses and smothered it. Almost immediately she had second thoughts, feeling "the awfulness of what I had done." If she could have revived the child, she would have.

James Robinson, working outside, found out later. He did not berate his wife or seem to grieve. Instead he began making the baby's coffin; ominously, it was large enough for the bodies of two babies. He must have seen Annie's act as a godsend; once again, he was escaping the consequences of his actions. So, when Ellen went into labour six days later, he was present at the birth and made no bones about what he wanted done. "Go on ahead and do the same as ... with the other one," he ordered. Annie replied, "no Jimmie, I can't." But, as usual, James's will prevailed. Ellen heard her second son cry, but never saw him. Nor did she ask what had become of him.

With the burial of the two babies, James probably thought life would go on as normal. But the reclusive family had become of interest to the people of Warren and, once there was no evidence of the new babies, gossip began. Those who had worked at the farm the previous year insisted that both Ellen and Jessie had been pregnant. The local physician, Dr. Dixon, had been told by the girls and Annie that two men who had worked in the camps the previous years were the fathers. Yet, there was no sign of their offspring. What had happened?

As the rumours about the babies' whereabouts and their parentage swirled, becoming more colourful and improbable, James Robinson went into Warren. When confronted, he laughed, inviting anyone interested to go out to the farm and see for themselves. That offer deflated the gossip for a while. The talk, however, persisted. On Sunday, August 8, 1909, Ernest Albert Wright, Justice of the Peace, Crown Lands Agent, and clerk of the Division Court, saw Robinson in Warren. He had to visit the farm, he told James, to "satisfy himself about some rumours." Fine, James replied, seemingly unconcerned.

It may have been fine but Robinson was clearly uneasy about the proposed visit. The next morning, Wright and Dr. Dixon set out. Wright would later testify that his sole intention was to arrest James Robinson for concealing the births or deaths of the babies. But once they reached the farm, Robinson was nowhere to be found and, after searching the woods for the rest of the day, the men returned to Warren. They rounded up a couple of constables; over drinks at the hotel, they discussed the situation, deciding to return to the farm about midnight. Not wanting to tip their hand and spook Robinson, they left their rigs about a mile or so away and walked in. The constables entered the house while Wright waited outside to catch James if he should try to run. Fifteen minutes later, when it became clear that Robinson wasn't going to "make a bolt for it," Wright walked through an unlocked door with a "none of your nonsense expression."

Wright thought that this would "stimulate the women" — but it nearly killed Annie, who collapsed with fright.[7] She had a history of heart trouble and, as she lay gasping, the men dragged her outside and sat her in a chair. She promptly vomited. Wright, seeing "she was choking ... took her by the shoulder or by the arm." Obviously this did nothing to help, because "her face became quite dark and her eyes looked very dangerous ... bulging out of her head." Rather than offering platitudes of reassurance, Wright "started to strike her between the shoulders with my open hand in order that she might breathe — she wasn't breathing; she was gasping and I struck her several times pretty sharp and finding that it wasn't doing her much good ... I closed my fist and struck her hard and continued until she did breathe." Altogether he hit her about forty times. Annie didn't complain. When she revived she thanked him for saving her life. Then they got down to business.

"We must know the truth, Mrs. Robinson," Wright began. "We want to know the truth ... we believe that there have been two more babies born."

"I will tell you the truth. I will show you," she replied.

Wright stopped her by saying he wanted to see the bodies and then he would hear the story. So the party wended its way outside, with Annie looking like she might faint again at any moment. Finally, they reached the spot at the back of the barn where James had buried his children/grandchildren, including Jessie's first born, their graves marked by a stump with a crooked root. The men began digging, retrieving two well-made boxes. The top box had some rotting woollen clothing. The second contained the babies.

Once back at the house, Annie began the story and Wright and the other men must have wished at some point they had never come to the Robinson's farm. She was known as a truthful woman and they had no doubt she told the truth now. And, once started, she kept talking. Part of it would be her confession, then she would drift off "on to something regarding Jimmie Robinson and ... her family connections." Soon, Wright realized he should be making a record and, after asking John to get him a writing pad, he began paraphrasing her words: "she told me and then I would say 'Now is that what you mean,' and I would break it down into a shorter sentence ... and in each case she would say 'Yes, that is exactly it.'" She had borne her troubles too long and couldn't wait to unburden herself of them.

It must have been an extraordinarily emotional scene. Threatening, as well. Men had stormed into her house at midnight; Wright had thumped her excessively. Now he and the other men crowded around her as she spoke with at least Wright "taking some drink off and on."[8] Cautions about the possible legal ramifications of her words (or, the paraphrased ones) were never brought to her attention.

When she finished and signed Wright's documents, Annie felt a tremendous sense of relief. It was about 3:30 a.m. Almost immediately, she reverted to the role of good farm wife — making breakfast for everyone. When breakfast was over, she calmly climbed into one of the rigs for the ride to Warren. Once there, the men initially held her in the hotel before transferring her to Wright's own house because they "didn't feel like putting her in the lock-up." Later, she attended an inquest where Dr. Dixon decided that Jessie's first baby had died of natural causes and that the two babies born in 1908 had been killed. At 5:10 p.m. Wright and Constable Chapman finally put her on the western train, bound for Sudbury. She would be charged with two separate counts of murder.

It seems certain that many wished Ernest Wright had not investigated the matter so thoroughly. By the time Annie came to trial, Jessie had given birth again[9] and Ellen was within days of delivering her third child. As the details of the incest came to light, public reaction ran the gamut from titillation to outrage to horror. The first trial, for the murder of Jessie's child, began on September 21, 1909, with the public galleries packed.

The case was easily proved. Annie never denied the facts. Her confession was accepted, although Wright had been either too intoxicated or flummoxed to warn her that it might be used against her. The motive for the crime was obvious to all: Annie, in an impossible situation, had reached an unbearable point. If she could not stop the incest, she would eliminate its consequences. The key question for her defence would be her state of mind.

Annie testified that the child's screams had haunted her and that still "today, I can hear that cry." She had attempted to soothe the infant "on account of Jessie's trouble, her sorrow, and then there was other little children in the house" and she wished to keep them ignorant of the birth. Ernest Wright admitted on cross-examination that Annie had said, "I know I did wrong, I should not have done it, but I did not know at the time that I was doing wrong." The precise meaning of that statement — and Annie's capacity for understanding it — would be argued between Mr. Justice Magee and defence counsel Mulligan.

In his address to the jury, Justice Magee began by reminding the jury that Annie was charged with homicide — "the taking of human life by an illegal act." He summarized Annie's motives for the crime, then asked "what was the reason for her silence? Was it not, as she says herself, the very shame and disgrace of it to her family, rather than any fear of her husband?" If Annie's motive was to avoid disgrace, that would be "evidence of intelligence on her part." The law excused people who suffered from a "disease of the mind" or "natural imbecility" and could not therefore appreciate what they had done. But Annie had known that she had done wrong when she testified: "I knew that only One [her God] had a right to take that life, but I was just in such a state of sorrow for Jessie and the shame of it being her child and her father its father, it just drove me until I did not realise what I was doing." Magee accepted that Annie's act may have been driven by impulse; but, he told the jury, "if we were to allow impulses to relieve people from the consequences of their acts, I am afraid we would have a state of society that you and I would not care to live in."

Mr. Justice Magee had an inkling that the jurors found the case repugnant and would have trouble condemning Annie. As a result, he attempted to prepare the jurymen thoroughly: "You are not called upon to pronounce the death sentence upon this woman. It is not part of your duty, nor of mine, to punish her for anything she has done. Your duty is to try the issue whether she is responsible for the death of that child." The jurors could not evade their duties; they should not "give way to sympathy," nor lose their common sense to it. The "rule of law, that rule as I may say of common sense, of right, of justice, does not enable jurors to escape from their duties." As "reasonable men," applying their knowledge "of human affairs to the evidence ... heard, unless you can say that you are not convinced that this prisoner is guilty, then you have no right to relieve yourselves from the consequences of bringing in a verdict of guilty." Magee acknowledged that he, himself, had "some feeling of compassion for this poor woman," but that she could not put the burden of evading responsibility of her actions "upon you or upon me." Only rarely did a criminal regret committing a crime, Magee advised, "but the fact of regret, the fact of remorse, the fact of all this unhappiness caused by someone else in that family, cannot relieve us from dealing fairly and properly with the evidence, according to our judgment."

Magee made his position clear: "the law does not recognize merely an impulse of the moment to which persons give way, and which impulse they may think is irresistible ... The question is ... Was she at the time of sound mind, or ... suffering under disease of the mind so as to be incapable of appreciating the nature and quality of the act, and of knowing that it was wrong? That is the whole question."

With this in mind, the jury retired and shortly returned with its verdict: "That Annie Robinson is not guilty of murder, on the ground that she was not responsible for her action at the time the deed was committed." Magee, aghast, chided them: "I do not think you are warranted in bringing in such a verdict." Annie had admitted that she knew what she had done was wrong, he reminded them, and then instructed them to reconsider. Mulligan objected and Magee asserted, "I decline to receive the verdict of the jury."

So much for common sense and the jury's sense of understanding their responsibility. By now, it was obvious to all that the jurymen's compassion drove their common sense. They did not want to convict Annie Robinson and thus have the mandatory death sentence passed on her. By now, though, it was supper time and Magee adjourned the court until 8.00 p.m. Twenty minutes later the jury returned to the courtroom.

Magee asked if they had "reconsidered the matter ... and come to any different conclusion."

"No," the foreman replied.

The judge was chagrined. Determined to wring a guilty verdict from this most recalcitrant jury, he would permit no jury nullification of law in his court. He now told them that their thinking was entirely wrong, that they were "finding upon a different principle" than what he had outlined in his charge to them. They believed obviously that "she was not responsible for her action at the time the deed was committed." Now he asked them: "are you prepared to bring in [a] ... finding ... that her mind was diseased to such an extent that she was incapable of appreciating the nature and quality of the act, and of knowing that the act was wrong?" He then sent the jury off for a third time, withholding their dinner until they reached their decision.

The deliberations lasted another two hours. At 10.35 p.m. the weary, hungry jury returned with a different verdict: "We ... find the prisoner Annie Robinson guilty, and as we unanimously agree and believe that the prisoner committed the deed while laboring under a heavy mental strain, we therefore recommend her to the mercy of the Court." Mulligan immediately asked for leave to appeal. He was outraged that the judge had refused the first two verdicts and forced a third one. Mr. Justice Magee amended the jury's verdict so that Annie was properly recommended "to the mercy of the Executive." He thanked the jurymen, saying that he regretted they had "been deprived of [their] evening meal until this late hour."

Had someone on the jury known enough law to convince his fellow jurors to render a simple verdict of Not Guilty, the first time, Annie Robinson would have been discharged. Magee had to accept a general verdict and could not question the jurors on their findings. But when they added words implying temporary insanity they introduced a concept outside the Canadian Criminal Code. The second verdict was the same. In both cases, the judge was correct in asking them to reconsider and hence the final verdict was correct in law as well. Magee, however, clearly feared that the jury wished to nullify his instructions on the law and not convict Annie.

Even with the desired decision, Mr. Justice Magee was not finished with Annie Robinson. Although Mulligan protested his intention to appeal, Magee decided that in the interests of expediency and expense, the second trial — for the murder of Ellen's baby — should commence the following day as "the witnesses are all here, the tale has been told; it would be a pity, it seems to me, as might possibly happen, to have to in six months' time at another Assizes, tell all this tale again... Besides that, the witnesses might separate, some might die."

Mulligan asked if Annie might get a fairer trial if the date was postponed because "a new jury empanelled in this court, who have heard the evidence in the preceding case, would be more likely to be convinced of the guilt of the prisoner at the outset of the trial, rather than being filled, as the mind should be, with a conviction of her innocence." But argument was useless, as Magee reminded everyone again, for Annie had confessed to the crime.

So began the trial the following day, with Ellen in hospital anticipating the birth of her third child. The second jury had learned from the first, finding Annie guilty, although it too recommended her to the "full mercy of the Court." Again, Magee amended this to the mercy of the privy council. Then the time for sentencing came. Annie, "a woman of 45, a broken and dis-spirited human being" offered no pleas or excuses. Magee, acknowledging that he wished "this task had fallen upon some other shoulders" told her that she had been found guilty of almost the "highest offence known to the law" of which he was "only the mouthpiece." He then went on: "The dread sentence of the law is that you must lose your life and die ... and I can hold out no hope ... that the sentence which the law decrees will not be carried out." During Annie's remaining days on earth, he announced, she should "look to [her] Creator for that mercy which is shown to all who are ready to ask for it. There alone can [she] find comfort, and ... in [her] last days obtain the consolation of that ... can be obtained from that Divine source." The execution date was fixed for November 24, 1909, two months away.

The verdict angered many, many people, leading to an outpouring of emotion that was unknown in Ontario to that point. There was virtual unanimity that Annie Robinson should not pay with her life. As Judge Magee feared, compassion triumphed over common sense and strict law. There was a deluge of letters from Methodist and Presbyterian ministers, led by Annie's brother Rev. Peter Mathieson of Kinross. Newspapers printed petition sheets by the thousand. Mrs. Elizabeth Wilson of Toronto made the ultimate offer: "Will you allow *her* to go to her home at once, and allow me to take her place in the Sudbury jail and to bear any punishment it is decided she ought to have. Mrs. R. should be with the daughter who is *enceinte*." She declared herself "absolutely sane (passed all the *tests*)," and advised the Minister of Justice that she was not looking for notoriety and was a sister-in-law of the late Chief Justice Sir William Wilson.[10]

As petition after petition deluged the ministry, a Mr. G. Evans notified the clerks that a memorandum "from state" advised that it was no longer necessary to answer each and every one. Annie's plight had captured thousands of hearts. Signers of these petitions included publishers, travelling salesmen, barristers, undertakers, doctors, teachers, tailors, cheesemakers, and housewives. The petition from the town of Warren, with close to a hundred signatures, was headed by the remorseful Ernest Wright — who also verified those who signed with a cross. Women's organizations, such as the Women's Christian Temperance Union and the National Council of Women, took up the cause strongly. Advocates for clemency from the latter included Lady Tilly from New Brunswick, Mrs. Sanford from Hamilton, and Mrs. Adam Shortt, wife of the well-known economist and archivist.

Some, however, agreed with the verdict — "Sigma" wrote in the *Ottawa Citizen*, on November 1, 1909, that the offence of killing infants seemed to be "all too common." James Robinson had been acquitted of murder and, in Annie's case, "twelve men" did "their utmost to acquit her and find her guilty only under compulsion of the judge ... Immediately on her conviction the country goes into hysterics. Press and people unite in demanding her pardon. A special clerk has to be appointed to receive and file the petitions for clemency ... She is spoken of as a martyr ... Does this not mean that child murder ... has become common among us, even among our 'best families,' that the putting to death of an infant is no longer looked on as murder? Are we not abandoning our Christian standards of morality and reverting to those of paganism?"

In her article, "The Lottery of Death," Carolyn Strange wrote about the capriciousness of the judicial process when it came to putting the sentence of death into effect. To prove her case, she used examples from 1867 to 1976. The period after Confederation, though, merely continued what had gone before in colonial times — as shown by the following four cases, nearly a decade apart in the 1830s and 1840s: Grace McManus, Grace Smith, Julia Murdock and Grace Marks. Each of the convicted was young, in her teens or early twenties, and the crimes involved the employers of these young women. All were sentenced to death. And, yet, all suffered different fates.

Grace McManus worked as a servant for Richard and Sarah McGinnis, "two old and infirm Persons" in Montreal.[11] According to the Montreal Chief Justice and Judges' report of June 21, 1831, her crime was "one of great turpitude ... having robbed [with fellow servant Catherine McNaughton] a respectable family in which she was engaged as a Servant of a large Sum of money in specie and bills" in the summer of 1830. The total theft was staggering, given the times: £560 in banknotes; 144 pieces of silver valued at £36 and French half crowns, equivalent to £19.10.0. This was the kind of crime — stealing to high value from a dwelling house, involving insubordination by the lower classes — that the authorities usually singled out as exemplary. This meant the punishment should be so terrible that others, tempted to commit a similar wrongdoing, would be deterred. The mandatory death sentence was given and an execution date set for September 10, 1830.

McManus, however, was extremely fortunate in her employers. Not only wealthy, they were also compassionate. They petitioned for a reprieve, writing that if they had known "that the Punishment of the crime committed by Catherine McNaughton and Grace McManus would have been death, no earthly consideration would have made us ... [appear] as the Prosecutors at their Trial ... we would rather have sacrificed all than to have placed the lives of our fellow creatures in Jeopardy ... if either of these two unfortunate women are executed we shall neither of us ever enjoy a happy moment and two respectable families to whom these wretched creatures are connected will be plunged into misery and Disgrace."[12]

Once the death sentences had been rescinded, McManus began a campaign to free herself and McNaughton from jail. In a petition to Lady Aylmer, dated December 13, 1830, she acknowledged her crime and claimed to have found Christ. If pardoned, "like the prodigal son we will Return to our parents and live and honist [sic] and Sober Life ... through faith in our Lord Jesus Christ." Covering her bets, McManus implored Lady Aylmer to "consider our weak frames as females." Neither she nor McNaughton had ever been "Subject to the like [i.e.

prison] before.' Her plea fell on deaf ears. Undeterred, she tried again. In her second petition she reiterated that she had always been of good character until the theft and asked Lord Aylmer "to liberate her out of this miserable Place of confinement having no friends to bring her any thing for what cloaths i [sic] had when i was apprehended I have wore them out and i have not one stick to ware if i had the look to get out of this place." Neither had she "friends that would fee a lawer."

On June 21, 1831, less than a year after Grace McManus had been sentenced to death, Chief Justice Reid and Judges Pyke, Uniacke and Rolland cautioned that, while granting an unconditional pardon was inadvisable, they "would respectfully recommend ... a pardon on condition of their departure ... from this province." Three days later "the said Grace McManus" received her pardon provided that she would "forthwith depart and transport herself by way of the River and Gulph of the River Saint Lawrence and out of Our Said Province of Lower Canada, to some place or Country other than and not comprehended in Our Province of Upper Canada and also other than not comprehended within the State of Vermont, one of the United States of America."

For Grace McManus, a death penalty meant confinement in prison for less than a year and banishment from the Canadas and Vermont.[13]

When Grace Smith, a black sixteen year-old, pled guilty to arson (then still a capital crime) October 16, 1839, it was suspected that she was responsible for other fires.[14] She was the daughter of a "very correct well conducted woman who [had] taken great pains in bringing up her children to honesty, industry and correctness of principle." Apprenticed at fourteen to a dressmaker, Mrs. Morris, Gracie soon became dominated by her employer — "unfortunately" becoming "too compliant with the directions of her actual guardian." Although she confessed to the crime of arson, with an "inimitable tone of sincerity," some wondered where she had gained "such inventive genius" as shown in the total destruction of her employer's workshop. Once she received the death sentence, various people besides her family intervened.

One was Dr. Lucius Bennet, a justice of the peace, who claimed to have made an extensive inquiry before "presuming" to write his petition. Various "Ladies of Toronto" vigorously championed Gracie's cause: Lady Campbell, Mrs. T.G. Ridout, Mrs. W. Baldwin, Mrs. J.S. Baldwin; there can be no doubt that their petition, dated November 11, 1839, was taken seriously. They pointed out that Grace's character up to the incident had been "unexceptionable" and felt that His Excellency, the Lieutenant Governor, should extend mercy "which may be the means of saving a despairing creature from an awful doom — and preserve a sorely afflicted family from the lowest depths of misery and woe."

Grace's sentence was commuted to life imprisonment in the newly built Kingston Penitentiary. She entered the prison in early 1840 but, as in the case of Grace McManus, life imprisonment meant something else. She received her pardon on July 25, 1840, and was released after serving only a few months.

Grace Marks, whose story Margaret Atwood made famous worldwide through her novel, *Alias Grace*, should have been so fortunate.[15] Suffice it to say that Grace Marks was implicated in one of the most sensational Canadian murders in the nineteenth century, that of Thomas Kinnear and his mistress, Nancy Montgomery, on July 23, 1843. She and James McDermott worked for Kinnear and, after the murders, they ran to the United States. Captured, they stood trial for Kinnear's murder on November 11, 1843. Both were condemned to death. McDermott was duly hanged on the nineteenth. Grace's lawyer, Kenneth MacKenzie, managed to raise doubts about Grace's actual complicity and the resulting petitions stressed her youthfulness, mental incapacity and "feminine frailty." Her sentence was commuted to imprisonment in Kingston Penitentiary and, like that for Grace Smith, the stated term was "life."

Grace was not a model prisoner, being disciplined twice in 1847. Nor was she well, as shown by the following extract from the Hospital Patient Diary for the same year:

> [Grace had] a healthy appearance, florid complexion and sanguine temperament but was often observed to be labouring under the influence of gloomy remorse and was frequently brought before the surgeon for occasional indigestion, accompanied generally by headache and mental despair. At other times and during the intervals of these indispositions she appeared [with] a healthy appearance with the high and fine complexion natural

to her. About the beginning of last Jan. she suddenly begun to exhibit evident signs of Insanity which have since become more manifest. From being quiet and well behaved and industrious she all at once [became] noisy and excitable. For several days displaying the highest state of Exulting viz singing laughing and rapid talking, which would be followed by a shorter period of gloom and despair. She has ... illusions, imagining she sees strange figures invading her. She slaps [her] body and wanders about her room for most part of the night in search of the subjects of her false visions. Her ... appetite [is] generally bad and sometimes for days together nearly suspended. Complains often of pain.

In April 1852 the warden lamented that Grace Marks was destroying "the order which must be maintained in this institution, therefore it is important that [she] ... be sent to the Lunatic Asylum with the least possible delay." Three weeks later, the relieved warden wrote to the Minister of Justice, A.-N. Morin that Grace Marks had been "safely handed over to the Superintendent of the [Provincial] Asylum." She was returned to the prison in three months. Unlike Grace Smith and Grace McManus, Grace Marks's sentence of life imprisonment was almost carried out. She was pardoned only in 1872, spending a little less than thirty years in the Kingston Penitentiary, her term only alleviated by time spent in the Provincial Asylum. Maybe, considering this, Julia Murdock's suffering was less.

Julia Murdock, after being convicted of murdering her employer, was hanged on the gallows in December 1837. Obviously Mrs. Henry's death did not excite as much notoriety as the Kinnear-Montgomery murders — but, then, Upper Canada was in a state of rebellion at the time. What sets Julia Murdock apart from the three Graces — McManus, Smith, and Marks — is that no one petitioned for her life. It cannot be argued that Toronto was in such an uproar that petitions went by the board for there are literally hundreds from the time in the National Archives of Canada. Most came from citizens affirming their loyalty. But the Upper Canadian Sundries collection contains one set of petitions for the commutation of a death sentence passed on a William Brass in October 1837, almost the very time of Murdock's sentence.[16] There is no record of the executive council or the governor even considering a reprieve for Murdock. She alone, of the female murderers of the nineteenth century, seems to have had no one to plead for her life.[17]

The Queen of Hearts in *Alice's Adventures in Wonderland* might be the best person to define a sentence of death. "It would mean," she might say, "exactly what I intend it to mean." For there seems to be no rhyme or reason to commutations.

Certainly, as with Annie Robinson, if the cause were taken up by the rich and powerful, a reprieve would likely result. But not necessarily. Alexander Mackenzie begged Sir John A. Macdonald to spare Elizabeth Workman "for my sake." She was nevertheless executed. Division among appellate judges meant little in the Marguerite Pitre case. Louis Riel's execution was more a statement of Macdonald's political will than justice, despite the thousands of petitions and the doubts about his mental capacity. The lottery of death reflected provincial standards as well. Part of the huge outcry after the sentencing of Elizabeth Coward was that she would be the first woman to hang in British Columbia.[18]

A host of factors were taken into consideration when the cabinet considered Annie Robinson's fate. A letter from "A.P." of the Department of Justice, November 4, 1909 to his minister, Sir A.B. Aylesworth, outlined the dilemma. Agreeing that Judge Magee's "merciful recommendation" should be adopted, A.P. added the case called "for substantial punishment in order that the gravity of the crime may be marked." He held himself back from commenting though:

> on the communications and petitions which have overflowed the department. The poor guilty woman (deserving indeed of pity in the highest degree) is spoken of not merely as a martyr, but — as you, Sir, yourself have heard — as a heroine. In pity for the sad conditions of the poor creature's existence, the value of human life is entirely lost sight of; indeed, the taking of these two innocent lives is justified, as you have heard it justified, and that too by women. Fortunately the whole matter is not to be decided upon the more or less hysterical outcries of the press, or the more or less

competent judgment of those superficially acquainted with the real facts, but on the sober common sense of the Privy Council of Canada.

Common sense did prevail and Annie Robinson's sentence was commuted on November 10, 1909, to ten years imprisonment in the Kingston Penitentiary. Aylesworth, for one, was determined that Annie spend time in jail. Replying to Elizabeth Shortt in December 1909, he hinted at his opinion of the "more or less hysterical outcries of the press" and the "more or less competent judgment of those superficially acquainted with the real facts." Furthermore, he could not "think the killing of these two helpless babies was any less a crime because it was Mrs. Robinson who did it than it would have been if her son had killed them, and I can scarcely think if it had been the son who did it, people would be urging that <u>he</u> should go unpunished."[19]

But the issue and pleas for Annie Robinson's release would not die down. As early as November 2, 1910, "A.P." had announced he would not be against releasing her if it weren't for "the question of publicity. It would not be desirable that she be released *sans trompette*."[20] In January 1911, the department of justice told Mrs. William Craig of Kingston, who had written on behalf of her local Women's Christian Temperance Union, that the case had been considered "several times" but that insufficient time had elapsed to balance the need for punishment and the public's sense that Annie should not be in prison. Her four brothers, "very respectable people," guaranteed to "provide for her for the remainder of her life" and would willingly have posted bonds if that would effect their sister's release.

Finally the government gave up. On February 23, 1911, Aylesworth concurred with his department's recommendation for her discharge and Governor General Earl Grey approved it two days later — February 25, 1911. Although Annie had been in custody since September 23, 1909, her time in Kingston was, like Grace Smith's, extremely short. In Annie's case, the death penalty had meant less than two years in jail.

At his own trial for murder, rape, and incest, at the end of October 1909, James denied being present at the birth of the second baby and ordering Annie to kill it. If he had said to "go ahead and do the same as with the other one," he explained, he had meant that Annie should rear Ellen's second son along with her first born, George. Annie was not allowed to testify on the grounds that communications between husband and wife were privileged. James received the benefit of the doubt legally, being acquitted of the murder charged. He was, however, sentenced to fourteen years for incest with Jessie, another fourteen for Ellen, and twenty-eight years in prison to run concurrently with the others for the rape of young Maggie. And although he might have escaped the death penalty in court, the prison system had a way of balancing certain things. James did not survive two years in Kingston Penitentiary.

Chapter Nine
Jennie Hawkes — A Woman Wronged

Like many people in the Westaskiwin district of Alberta, near Edmonton, Washington Hawkes had immigrated from the United States. Alberta offered both land and an opportunity to start over. More than most of the newcomers, Hawkes needed that chance — for his reputation was sordid at best. As Mrs J.C. Ellis of Indiana would later state, his Oliver County (North Dakota) record was "not good, [his] affairs legion."[1]

That he dominated his wife of thirty-three years by force was an open secret. According to their adopted daughter, Mamie Rosser, "she seemed to think whatever he said or done [sic] was law [and] if she would ask him to leave these bad women alone, he would threaten her with a weapon."[2] Mrs Margaret Baye of Heusler, North Dakota, knew the scene well: "Mr. Hawks [sic] was cruel to her [Jennie]. When she objected to his relations with other women ... [he] beat her until she was covered with bruises having her eyes blacked and swollen ... At one time I saw her with scratches on her face and I have known him to kick her out. She had to seek shelter with neighbours." After several similar assaults, Jennie had been "in bed for days, caused by his, Mr. Hawks' [sic] abuse."[3]

With his aging wife terrorized into thinking his word was law, Hawkes felt absolutely no compunction about bringing mistresses into the family home. In Oliver County, his lover would not only visit the Hawkes' house, but eat and stay there. In fact, Mamie recalled that a special bed had been set aside for the woman and that "mamma had to sleep alone."

No female seemed safe if Washington Hawkes fancied her. Certainly neither youth nor pregnancy were barriers to his attentions. Once, he hired a motherless thirteen year old whose father couldn't support her. During her period of employment, "this poor girl had to put up with everything." Another time, Jennie had taken a pregnant teenager into the house to help her keep her plight a secret from her family. She had no defences against the predatory Hawkes. As Mamie later testified, "He forced the girl to sleep with him. He knew she would do anything to keep her people from finding out what shape she was in."

Even the presence of his mother, Mrs. Martha Long, could not deter Hawkes. On one occasion, she investigated noises coming from the teenager's bedroom. To her consternation, she found her son engaging in sexual intercourse. She might have expected contrition, even embarrassment. But rather than being abashed, Washington merely cursed his mother for her interference, telling her to get out of the room and mind her own business.

A Wetaskiwin neighbour, Mrs. Gibson, whose husband had personally witnessed Hawkes' behaviour in North Dakota, deposed that Jennie "although objecting to such work, tolerated it." That seeming toleration, though, had come with a high price. Again, according to Mamie, "Mamma and I always had to put up with such conduct. I have seen her get many a black eye when she objected to such carryings on in the house, knocked down and drug across the floor by the hair until ... [he was left] standing with ... [only] hair in his hand." This corroborated evidence from Mrs. Ellis; in Indiana, she had seen Hawkes knock Jennie "down and drag her out of the door by her hair in the rain and shut the door on her."

On the journey north to Alberta, Jennie must have wished for that proverbial new start. Both she and Washington were well into their fifties; at some time soon his sexual drive had to slow down. At the very least, she must have hoped he would be discreet while they struggled to establish themselves.

Unfortunately, this hope was not realised. Alberta provided the new start all right, but virtually no change in behaviour patterns. Jennie Hawkes quickly reestablished her reputation for being a good and kind neighbour and Washington continued to gratify his sexual urges whenever and wherever he chose. The only difference was that in 1914 he began, at last, to think seriously about his future.

On his farm, twenty miles from Wetaskiwin, he quickly established at least one cash crop — potatoes. More importantly, given his proclivities, he began working as an itinerant grain grinder and sawyer, taking his tools and machinery to various farms in the area and frequently staying overnight. During one stint in 1913, while working five and a half miles away from his home, Washington Hawkes met the Stoley family who had also recently immigrated from the United States. After some discussion, Henry Stoley agreed to buy twelve bushels of potatoes from Hawkes; a couple of weeks later, when he went to pick them up, he took his wife Rosella along with him. At first, the families interacted socially, playing cards and partying together.

Washington and Jennie's daughter, Mamie, had married William Rosser. Together, with William's brother David, and the Stoleys, they formed a group. By December 1914, it seemed natural they should have their Christmas party together. It was quite predictable that Washington should be seen fondling Rosella in a corner at this event. But such behaviour, while titillating, had never been enough for Washington Hawkes

By January 1915, the Hawkes-Stoley relationship had proceeded to a point where Hawkes proposed a questionable financial deal. He sold Stoley a quarter-section (160 acres) of his farm for $10 an acre on a pay-later deal.[4] Stoley gave a cheque in the amount of $200, post-dated to June 26, 1915, as a partial payment; he also bought a team of mules for $225, again without a down payment. Hawkes was so generous he even volunteered to share his home with the Stoleys. This in itself was not unusual. The Rossers, followed by a handyman, had lived in the back portion of the house. And, in fact, at some point before the Stoleys moved in, Washington had thought about putting a door or window between the two parts. He didn't finish the job, but left a large hole in the partition.

The offer was too good to turn down; Henry obligingly moved his wife and three young children into the back half of the Hawkes' house February 1, 1915. Later, Henry would testify that Jennie had moved most of her belongings out of that part of the house and had dinner waiting for them when they arrived.

The reason for this largesse on the part of Washington Hawkes must have been Stoley's wife. Aged 28, almost half Jennie's age, Rosella stood 5'10" and weighed 160-odd pounds. There was absolutely no doubt that she had caught Washington's roving eye. More than that, she somehow gave him the feeling of eternal youth. When Henry Stoley conveniently left on a trip, March 2, 1915, Washington's plans became definite.

Washington felt his wife was old, downtrodden and dumpy. Years of living with him, catering to his every need had left their mark. There was no challenge, only a sense of dreary obligation. He knew Jennie would never divorce him, although he had given her multiple grounds over the years. Worse, he could never divorce her.

On the other hand, Rosella invigorated him. Yet, how could he manage to live with her? They were both married. His bargains with

Henry, however, had shown the man was willing to turn a blind eye to Hawkes's advances towards his wife. Furthermore, Stoley had conveniently taken himself off on a trip. But what could be done about Jennie? While Washington had enforced his will most of his life, he knew that Alberta's morés would not countenance any manifest desertion of her. He was between the proverbial rock and a hard place. Without actually murdering Jennie, or paying for someone else to do it, there was only one way to free himself. He would have her committed to an insane asylum. Without caring that Jennie would hear, he outlined this idea to his new, exciting, and compliant mistress. And then, he implemented his plans to both enjoy Rosella's bed and to drive his wife to lunacy.

A situation witnessed by William Rosser could have been part of this deliberate strategy. On March 2, 1915 he came across the Hawkes arguing outside their house. With a piece of wood, about three and a half feet long in his hand, Hawkes stated, "Now, look here, I am going to sleep with that woman to-night, Mrs. Stoley, and I want you to go and put mother [Mrs. Long] to bed and keep out of my way." Then with menace in his voice as well as in his hand, he warned that if she didn't obey, Jennie would "never see daylight again." As usual, Jennie complied. This time, however, she added a surprising qualification: "I will for the present."

The present proved to be short-lived and was indubitably ended by the sight of Washington and Rosella having sex. As Jennie testified:

> one morning Mr. Stoley got up and went to the barn to do the chores and Mr. Hawkes got up and he goes right through this hole which is in the hall ... into Mrs. Stoley's part ... I heard her come out of the bedroom a little after he went in and then she started around the stove and I ... heard her say, 'Don't Mr. Hawkes, you hurt', as if he was hurting her and she was laughing, laughing awful and I could hear them both laughing and I slipped out of my bed and went around and looking in quick at this window hole and there he was with Mrs. Stoley, there was a kind of, oh, it is a space, I should judge may be so wide ... between the stove and where it goes into the pantry and there he had Mrs. Stoley up on this end, God

forgive me but I have to say it, it is the truth, there he had Mrs. Stoley up on there and her clothes up having intercourse with her.

Today, we understand people's so-called "flash-points" differ from person to person; 1915 was no different. In retrospect, it seems, Washington had crossed the mythical line Jennie had drawn in the sand. She would no longer willingly accept his infidelity, particularly in her own home. In likely the most courageous act of her marriage, and without doubt motivated by desperation, Jennie shortly afterwards moved into her daughter's house.

For a woman of her age, who had given her best years to a failing marriage, it was an unthinkable situation. During the next few days she fumed about Washington's ingratitude, his plans to have her committed, and his infatuation with Rosella Stoley. Ominously, she became obsessed with the woman who had callously stolen her husband, her house, and her belongings.

The climax to Jennie's story began relatively innocently. Once her mother had moved into the Rosser house and it looked like she would stay there, Mamie decided she should remove a couple of cherished items from Washington's house. To her surprise and chagrin, Rosella Stoley refused to let her take anything. Furious and defeated, Mamie stormed home and told her mother. Jennie, of course, was outraged. Rosella was not content with Jennie's husband and home, she had had the temerity to deny Mamie, Washington's daughter, her very own possessions. Determined to right the balance, Jennie took a revolver from William Rosser's trunk and, with the excuse that she wanted to get some geese and blankets, she began a slow, mile-long walk back to her old home about one o'clock that day, March 13, 1915.

As things worked out, Washington Hawkes was away and Henry Stoley soon went over to David Rosser's, about ninety yards or so away. Almost like an automaton, Jennie entered the Hawkes' part of the house. After exchanging platitudes, she complained to her mother-in-law, Mrs. Long, about Rosella's behaviour. Rosella must have seen Jennie coming down the path, as it soon became obvious that she was listening through the wall. As Jennie began complaining that neither she nor Mamie had been able to take their belongings, Rosella, through the hole in the partition, ordered Mrs. Long, "to tell her [i.e. Jennie] that Mr. Hawkes had told us not to let anything out of the place until he came back." Furthermore, she now claimed Jennie's possessions as her own. That taunt lit the fuse.

Jennie exploded. Taking William Rosser's revolver out, she fired a couple of shots blindly through the partition. One ricocheted through the kitchen, making a horrendous noise as it clattered against a frying pan. Then, rigidly pointing the gun in her outstretched right hand, she began walking round the house to the Stoley entrance. Two of the Stoley children were playing outside and Jennie warned them to, "Look out you little devils or I will shoot you." Terrified, the children scurried away.

The sound carried through the crisp air. Ninety yards away, Stoley looked up, saw the gun, his children in peril and began a frantic race home. Rosella, petrified, began retreating into her bedroom as Jennie walked calmly through the door, with the gun now pointing towards the ceiling. The eldest Stoley child, Elsie, aged eleven, cowered in the kitchen until Jennie threatened that if she didn't "get out of the house ... I will kill you." Elsie did not hesitate. She ran then stood, fearfully, in the doorway while Jennie walked through the kitchen to the bedroom and fired three shots into Rosella.

By this time, Stoley had almost reached the house. As Jennie retreated into the kitchen, he caught up with her. There he wrestled her to the ground, then took the revolver away. He would later testify that, "she had the gun in her hand like ... she was fooling with it or trying to load it again or some thing" and that she protested that his "wife was trying to take her husband away from her."

Then, he hurried into the bedroom. Rosella lay on the floor, doubled up in pain. After a quick survey, Stoley found a wound in her wrist and an infinitely more serious one on the right temple. Knowing that he alone could do nothing to save her life, he rushed outside urging the children to run for help. The Rossers were the closest neighbours, but they had no phone. So, Elsie began a mile-long dash, half-carrying, half-dragging her toddler sister and younger brother, to the Conroy farm.

The Conroys had difficulty reacting to Elsie's message. After the children had rushed into their house, "asking them to go quickly, that their mother had been shot," the Conroys never thought about using the telephone for help. Instead, they rode over to the Hawkes house. Thus began a series of blunders leading to Rosella's death the following afternoon.

At the post-mortem, the doctors found Rosella had died from pressure on the brain. The elusive bullet lay between bone and brain, "practically free in the cavity of the brain." It had penetrated from the outer angle of the eye downward until reaching:

> the bone of the ear ... and by that time it had gone outside, between the skin and the outside of the skull, there it had hit the bone and been deflected and taken an upward course and in back ... right up through the brain and leaving an opening which you could easily put your finger through, the whole brain cavity was filled with blood clots and that had caused the pressure.

Otherwise, Rosella had been in perfect health.[5]

For the legal authorities, the case seemed open and shut. There could be absolutely no doubt who had killed Rosella Stoley. Jennie Hawkes was arrested late Saturday night, March 13, and taken to the jail in Macleod. The trial was set for the following October.

Jennie was luckier than most people in her situation at the time. Mamie, her daughter, was intelligent, resourceful, and she enjoyed her husband's support. Emptying their bank account, she hired the lawyers W.J. Loggie and R.W. Manley to fight for her mother's life. Right away, however, the sinister forcefulness of Washington Hawkes and the international events of 1915 almost combined to thwart them.

John Davidson was the handyman who had lived in the back portion of the Hawkes house before the Stoleys. He had eaten with the Hawkes, seen their home life, and knew very well Washington's attitude towards women in general and to Jennie, specifically. He would have been a strong defence witness. Loggie and Manley knew that. So did Washington Hawkes. Once he realised the defence was talking with Davidson, Hawkes intervened. If Davidson knew what was good for him, he'd disappear. That Davidson took the threat seriously was obvious by his actions. After some reflection, he enlisted in the 51st Regiment, volunteering to go to Europe.

With Davidson safely in the army and training for the war in Europe, Washington Hawkes must have relaxed. Loggie and Manley did not. They applied successfully to Mr. Justice Hyndman for an order to take Davidson's evidence *de bene esse*. As Davidson could not attend the trial, his testimony would thus be available "for what it was worth."[6] In the presence of the Attorney General and crown counsel, who had the right to cross-examination, Davidson gave his evidence under oath, in much the same way as he might have done at the trial. Loggie questioned him about Hawkes' behaviour and conversations he had had with him without any objection from the crown. From this, Loggie's defence strategy became obvious.

He would argue that Jennie had been provoked by her husband for many years, certainly since she had come to Alberta. By his actions, Washington Hawkes had shown repeatedly his disrespect for his wife and their marriage vows. While his brutal behaviour may have cowed his wife into seemingly tacit acceptance, it had also provoked her into taking a stand. And so, driven by her husband's callous behaviour, Jennie had reached a state of temporary insanity — a state that began when she had moved into the Rossers' house, and which had lasted for three weeks after Rosella Stoley's death. Loggie later put this argument before the trial judge, Mr. Justice Ives:

> I contend through a systematic course of conduct by the accused's husband not only in connection with the deceased woman [i.e. Rosella] but in connection with other women for years back that he drove this accused into such a state of mind that she was practically not responsible for what she did when this matter occurred ... by a long system of years of continual infedility [sic], not only that but if my instructions are correct, worse than that, that this woman had to live with for many years ... with this man who was continually abusing other women even in her own presence, right before her and threatening her and talking to her about them and [even] threatening her on various occasions if she didn't allow him to have his own way ... and it ended with the deceased....

This long period of provocation, Loggie contended, "brought this woman to the state in which she was in on the 13th of March, that she didn't have a knowledge of what her conduct was; temporary insanity if that is the legal phrase for it." Therefore, Jennie Hawkes could not be held "liable for murder."

Rosella Stoley's death and the circumstances surrounding it had scandalized the Wetaskiwin area for months. The trial, when it began on October 5, 1915, attracted attention throughout Alberta. William Carlos Ives, the so-called "cowboy judge"[7] presided; W.H Odell led the prosecution.

In an unusual step, Loggie immediately asked that the courtroom be cleared of spectators and then brought in one of his witnesses, a sergeant-major of the 51st Regiment, who testified that Davidson was in England, or perhaps even France. That done, the spectators were allowed back in.

The prosecution began by calling on Henry Stoley. He testified as to the events of March 13. On cross-examination, Loggie elicited Stoley's dealings with Hawkes, particularly his buy-now, pay-later transactions. Mrs. Long, the next witness, couldn't remember when Washington had married Jennie or even when Jennie had moved to the Rossers. She claimed she had never seen any trouble between her son and his wife. Nor had Washington eaten with Rosella in the Stoley part of the house while Jennie ate in the front. Elsie Stoley, aged eleven, then testified about the events on March 13. Other than that, she couldn't remember if Washington Hawkes had eaten in their part of the house or not, but when he came "he didn't go in[to] any other rooms at all."

The problems with Loggie's defence strategy began to surface once he began his cross-examination of the next crown witness, Fred Conroy. Prosecutor W.H. Odell objected strenuously and successfully when Loggie tried to introduce conversations Conroy might have had with Washington Hawkes. Loggie, after obtaining a few details of Conroy's business dealings with Hawkes, next tried to get his conversations with Washington about Davidson into the record. This time Mr. Justice Ives ordered the jury from the courtroom so that he could listen to the argument.

Loggie detailed his strategy, "that through a systematic course of conduct or misconduct whatever ... the accused's husband had driven her to desperation and through a system of things he did from time to time ... his conduct was such as any wife could not possibly stand and maintain her mental equilibrium." Ives asked if he was suggesting a defence of insanity. Loggie answered that what he hoped to prove was that at the time of the shooting "the prisoner was so worked up by a long system of conduct on that day and for previous days that at that time she was not responsible for what she was doing." If that was Loggie's thinking, Ives responded, "That might be a defence going perhaps to a reduction of the charge or enabling the jury to find a verdict of manslaughter if she had shot her husband."

Those last few words, which would be repeated several times as the trial progressed, summarized the problem with the defence strategy. Jennie had not shot Washington Hawkes; she had shot Rosella Stoley. Judge Ives seemed not to think of the latter as a cause of provocation as the law understood it.

To some extent, this same exchange would be repeated at other times. Loggie would attempt to bring in Washington Hawkes' opinion and treatment of Jennie, saying such evidence was crucial as being "one of the links in the chain" of his defence, and Judge Ives would disallow that line of questioning because it was "no defence for shooting a stranger" — Rosella.

The prosecution concluded its case with evidence from Sergeant Michel of the Royal North West Mounted Police and Doctors Robertson and Dixon. Loggie's main witnesses were Mamie and her mother. Jennie certainly did not help her case, giving long rambling answers when questioned. She claimed to have no recollection of events from the time she stayed at Mamie's until coming to her senses in the Macleod jail where she thought she was being held as a kind of witness.

In his charge to the jury, Judge Ives explained the definitions of culpable homicide according to the criminal code; he told the jurymen that the "great ... distinction between murder and manslaughter is, Gentlemen of the Jury, that the offender ... intends to kill the person killed." Culpable homicide, he went on, could "be reduced to manslaughter by certain things" provided by the law. The first "thing" was a sudden provocation that would cause someone to kill another "in the heat of passion," such as an outburst of controllable temper. The second was a "wrongful act or insult ... sufficient to deprive an ordinary person of the power of self-control," providing, of course, that the person acted upon it before "his passion [could] ... cool." Whether these wrongful acts or insults amounted to sudden provocation, Ives continued, were matters of fact which had to be proved.

So the basic question for the jury was whether or not Loggie had proved his case. As he had stated many times during the trial, Ives now repeated that "Washington Hawkes is not on trial." Even if Hawkes were as contemptible as the evidence showed, and if that evidence were given "all of that weight, all the provocation which we as reasonable men can understand that that conduct would be to that woman," the bottom line was that Jennie should have acted at the time of the provocation — not ten days later. The period in which Jennie claimed to have acted as an automaton was not proved. During her evidence, Jennie had clearly remembered many of the events of March 13, particularly her exchange of words with Rosella Stoley and what she had said to Mrs. Long. Although she claimed to have fainted, Justice Ives pointed out that she couldn't go from her side of the house to the Stoley side "while in a faint."

The law did however acknowledge "a sudden mental oblivion." If Jennie was in that state, she "was not in a condition to realize what she was doing, to know whether she was doing right or doing wrong. She was in the eye of the law insane at the time she committed the crime." In Jennie's case, "if she was unconscious then she was not in a state of mind to know what she was doing and is therefore not answerable to the law for what she did do. It is entirely a matter for you, Gentlemen of the Jury, to say whether you believe that story or whether you do not."

The gentlemen of the jury, after some consideration, decided they did not believe that story. They brought in a verdict of guilty, with a recommendation for mercy. Having no other option, Ives solemnly donned the black cap before sentencing Jennie to death.

The sentence astonished the jury. Most of the men were American in origin and they had clearly not realized the death sentence was mandatory. Judging from Justice Ives's reaction, many must have wished they'd opted for a manslaughter verdict. It also shocked the people of Alberta. Some thought, and many prayed, that it would be reversed when Loggie appealed the case before the Supreme Court of Alberta. But such was not to be. In a split decision, the lower court's verdict was upheld.

Mr. Justice Beck dissented. He thought Jennie's story of losing her memory and only regaining it after a couple of weeks in custody was "not an unheard of happening." Medical authorities called it "hysterical or epileptic amnesia." Women, he went on, were "especially apt to be hysterical" as their emotions were "especially apt to be aroused," that is to say they were mostly less rational than men.

If Albertan women had been fully eligible for jury duty in 1915, their presence might well have helped Jennie Hawkes, particularly given the attitudes of male jurors. Many women would have likely empathized with Jennie's plight. Washington Hawkes' abusive domination would have struck a responsive chord, making them think that constant exposure to such behaviour was sufficient provocation to justify manslaughter, if not outright acquittal, whatever the law said.

Doubtless influenced by the stereotype, defence counsel Loggie threw all his energies behind a defence of insanity, which failed at the trial level and on appeal.[8] A better chance to avoid a murder conviction would have been to argue provocation sufficient to enable the jury to find manslaughter. Judge Ives did raise the question briefly in his charge, denying its relevance by noting that the accused "had not seen Mrs. Stoley for ten days and there is no evidence of provocation during that time." But, surely, Hawkes's bringing his mistress into the common domicile amounted to a constant provocation of Jennie on behalf of both lovers and it must have lasted through the ten days from Mrs. Hawkes moving out to the killing. There was, moreover, the final straw of provocation on March 13, when the victim refused to allow Mamie and later Jennie herself to remove some belongings.

It is true that some hours had elapsed between Jennie first learning of Rosella Stoley's refusal and the fatal shooting. Canada's Criminal Code of 1892 summarized the common law — which remains essentially the same today — by requiring the deadly act to be done "in the heat of passion caused by sudden provocation" and again "before there had been time for his passion to cool."[9] This was a question of fact for the jury, but it must be stressed that an immediate response was not required. The sixteenth edition (1952) of Kenny's Outlines of Criminal Law reads that "it may be plain" an accused "did remain beside himself for a relatively long time."[10] The seventeenth century jurist, Sir Mathew Hale instanced the case of two quarrelling men leaving to fetch weapons and returning to fight it out.[11] The noted common law specialist, Sir Edward Hyde East, who published in 1803, cited a partially true instance where B, forcefully dispossessed of his home by a mob led by A, returned three days later with his own gang. Had he shot one of A's men to death, East thought that "so recent and grievous a provocation would have reduced the offence to manslaughter at least."[12] Common sense, moreover, tells us that a continual history of provocation, makes the "last straw" much less easy to banish from the mind and a relatively modern case has held just that.[13] Manslaughter might well have resulted in a shorter term of imprisonment and would have removed the life-long stigma of having been a murderer.

The thought of Jennie Hawkes going to the gallows outraged the people of Alberta and western Canada. Annie Cheeseman of Rosetown, Saskatchewan, wrote a letter to the Minister of Justice that summed up the attitudes of many: "I am sure Your Lordship *can not* possibly believe that sentence just ... I myself would certainly have done the same thing as that poor lonely wife on the homestead had that fell to my lot, but thank God I have a good husband."[14] Organized petitions flooded Ottawa, appealing for mercy on the following grounds:

> That we are informed and believe that the Jury added a recommendation to mercy in bringing in the said Verdict. That the said Mrs. Hawkes is an elderly woman and as far as we know has been of good character previous to the said offence. That we verify because that her domestic life previous to the said offence has been, to say the least, very unsatisfactory and that many causes in her belief led to the fatal occurrence. That we believe under the circumstances of this case it would be most unfortunate for the said offence and we would humbly ask you to order the sentence commuted.

Literally thousands signed such petitions. Articles appealing to the emotions of their readers appeared in Alberta newspapers, refering to Jennie "lying in the shadow of the gallows at the Macleod jail." The *Morning Albertan* reported that letters on the subject choked its mail boxes and that "The whole country is justly aroused." It had circulated 18,000 copies of a petition in its Saturday edition and immediately four to five hundred people applied for more. The churches also took up Jennie's cause with "Extended reference" being "made from the majority of pulpits and in many cases the opinion was freely expressed by the clergymen, that there should be legislation giving women easier remedy in such instances of extreme provocation." Furthermore, it was precisely "that lack of an easier and cheaper remedy than is provided by the present law ... [that]

ultimately impelled the woman to take the law into her own hands and kill" Rosella Stoley.

An article in the *Calgary Herald* demanded "Equal Justice." Another, detailing the facts of Jennie's case, condemned the jury for its "too slavish adherence to the letter of the law ... without giving Mrs. Hawkes the benefit of the justification which the aggravating situation entitled her to." Jennie had "fired a shot in the defence of decency." She was a "pioneer of a new settlement ... yet because she defended her rights and the rights of all married women we allow her to pay the penalty of the blackest crime." The writer of the article then pointed out that a double standard was being enforced. In a "case over in British Columbia just recently ... a man had defended the decency of his home" and was acquitted. Thus Jennie's conviction was "a sad commentary upon the unevenness of justice in this country" and it illustrated "the fact that women must be on the alert to prevent its miscarriage." In cases such as the B.C. one, "the men were set free by 'the Unwritten Law.' Why doesn't that law apply to Mrs. Hawkes as well?"[15]

The case to which this article referred was a murder in Fernie in September 1915. Sam Watson, of the 54th regiment, had killed his wife's lover, Hugh McGill. At the October assizes, the spectators applauded when the jury acquitted Watson; the defence for its brilliance, the Crown for its fairness. The final words on the case came from Chief Justice Hunter: "Under the circumstances ... I don't think anyone regrets that the jury has been able to absolve ... [the defendant] from all blame and I can only say my hope is that you recover from the shadow cast over your life. I will further say, I think the fate of this unfortunate man ... ought to be a salutary warning to any man who in future sets out with the purpose of destroying another man's home."[16]

No wonder Albertans saw the law offering a double standard.

The Hawkes case is one where there can be no serious doubt that the jury's recommendation helped obtain a commutation, as shown by the conclusion to Trial Judge Ives's report to the Secretary of State:

> I would urge upon the department the most serious consideration of the jury's recommendation for clemency. This community is largely peopled by

American immigration and the juries are apt to be influenced by their knowledge and experience of the administration of the law in the community from whence their members came. In the present case the 'unwritten law' was strongly put forward and I think future trials at Wetaskiwin would result in an added impartiality and sense of duty on the part of juries if the present recommendation should be given effect to. In fact ... if the jury ... had realized that only one sentence was permitted upon a verdict of guilty or that their recommendation ... would be without effect, they would have returned a different verdict.[17]

Jennie Hawkes, like Elizabeth Coward in the same period, did not fare well in Kingston Penitentiary. Her health deteriorated to the point where the prison doctor became convinced that further confinement would "likely prove fatal." And, also like Elizabeth Coward, she was blessed with a daughter who fought hard for her release; in July 1920, the Chief of the Remission Branch had "the honour to advise that the prisoner be given a Ticket-of-Leave."[18]

One final note. Moralists would have loved to have seen the adage, "Cheaters never prosper" proved. Washington Hawkes had done everything in his power to get Jennie convicted from threatening potential defence witnesses to actively helping the Crown. But, shortly after the trial he "lost his life by being caught in the belting of a sawing machine."[19]

Chapter Ten
Annie Rubletz and Mary Paulette —
"The Far Side of Despair"

Do the majority of people "lead lives of quiet desperation," as Henry David Thorreau averred?[1] Certainly desperation provoked many women in this book to extreme action. Annie Rubletz, in 1940, and Mary Paulette, a little more than a decade later, faced the gallows after conviction for killing their newly born children. Although coming from different backgrounds, their motives were the same — desperation.

Annie Rubletz lived with her Ukrainian parents on a farm outside Hyas, Saskatchewan (about 250 kilometres northeast of Regina) until May 1940. Then, aged seventeen, she was sent to live with her sister, Kate Tetlock.[2] Kate's motives in taking her sister into her home may have been altruistic; the childhood home of the sisters was not safe for them. After being molested by one of her brothers, Annie had given birth in 1939. An elder sister, Helen, had had a child when she was fourteen.

Annie's own family had probably far more pragmatic motives: Annie, pregnant again, was expected to give birth toward the end of June or early July. The father, this time, was none other than Leslie Tetlock, Kate's husband. During the fall, while Annie helped with the harvesting, Leslie had had intercourse with her several times. As Annie later recalled, "After I became in the family way ... I told him ... and Leslie Tetlock got me some pills, little black pills — I don't know where he got these pills ... Leslie Tetlock, when he gave me these pills, told me that they were for to get rid of the child. I took some of these pills but they did not do any good." Accepting this result, Leslie owned up to paternity and, before he went to jail for receiving stolen grain in March 1940, he asked Kate to make sure Annie went to a hospital in Norquay "when she got sick."

Kate valued the help of her sister, Annie. She ran a household with thirteen children — eight were her own and five were from Leslie's previous marriage. Kate was herself also pregnant with a ninth child. A capacious woman, she accepted her sister into the household and, as

Annie's delivery date neared, the two sisters went into Norquay to see about getting a doctor. The doctor was out of town that day, but after some questioning they found a nursing home. When she came back to her home, Kate sold some pigs and a cow for almost $60 to pay the costs for Annie's impending delivery.

Annie, though, had an enemy in the Tetlock household. Norma Tetlock, also seventeen, a daughter from Leslie's first marriage, despised her. Annie's command of the English language could best be described as "fair." Norma viewed her as more of a servant than a step-aunt, maybe resenting the "attention" her father paid her. In any case, as events would show, Norma was unwilling to help the interloper in her house. More than that, she displayed real malice towards the somewhat slow-witted Annie.

On June 7, Kate left her house for a short stay at the Rubletz farm, in order to finalize details arising from her mother's death a few weeks earlier. About noon the following day, Annie went into premature labour. She called for Norma, asking her to get their neighbours to take her to Kate or the hospital in Norquay. Norma later testified that she thought Annie had "appendix trouble." Nevertheless, she treated the request casually, sending a younger sister over to the Danyluks, the closest neighbour, with a note. Then she started off for town to register for an amateur talent contest. On the way, she met Sarah who told her that the Danyluks could only drive Annie later that night. Norma did not turn round to tell Annie the news, nor did she try to get other help; she and Sarah continued into town. In town, she met Helen Skwarchuk, Annie's sister. After telling her that Annie was sick and needed Kate, Norma seemingly washed her hands of the whole affair. She met a friend, David Heska, and allowed him to drive her home. Heska stayed half an hour, during which time Norma did not bother to check on Annie. Only after Heska had left did Norma call up the stairs. Annie answered that she'd had a "haemorrhage." Still unconcerned, Norma prepared supper and, eventually, went to bed.

Helen Skwarchuck's behaviour seems equally callous. She later testified that she had called at the Tetlocks and found Annie making bread. Annie apparently asked for help and, at the very least, begged Helen to fetch Kate. Although she later delivered the message, Helen claimed she had never told her brothers or Kate that Annie had wanted to get to Norquay and that she had refused to take her. Once Kate heard she was needed, she set off immediately on horseback in the pouring rain. She arrived late that night. By then, it was too late.

As the contractions intensified and her baby's birth became imminent, Annie Rubletz must have felt quite desperate that Saturday afternoon, June 8, 1940. It was obvious to her that no one wanted to help and that Kate could not know she was needed. Annie must have wondered about the future. Her mother had recently died. She had been molested by at least one brother and by her brother-in-law. Her first baby had been adopted. What would become of this second child? Would it have any chance of leading a life other than that of depressing poverty and ignorance? As for herself, it seemed obvious that if she stayed in the Tetlock household, Leslie would probably attempt to have sexual intercourse with her again and the pattern would be repeated. She must have realized that Norma hated her and that she had influenced the younger children from Tetlock's first marriage. Would they possibly accept Annie's child? Could the household finances stretch far enough to provide for this new baby? Kate's ninth child was expected in August and, together with Annie's, this would mean fifteen children in all.

With no aid, solace, or future, Annie Rubletz smothered her child.

When Kate arrived shortly after midnight, Annie was in physical distress — in Kate's words, she had "ruptured." The dead baby, "kind of bluish" and with a bruise or "dinge" on its forehead, lay beside her. Kate bandaged Annie up, then talked about what they should do with the body. Annie said "to dress the baby up, put it in a box and bury it." So, the next morning, Kate put a diaper and a good dress on the body, wrapped it in a baby's blanket and "put it in a box" with layers of wool underneath. Annie had made a cross from wax candles and Kate, as a good "Greek Catholic," put this in the baby's right hand "just like we always do." Then she buried the child and the afterbirth near two small spruce trees, the only trees on the farm.

Norma Tetlock wondered what had happened. She and a brother unsuccessfully searched the farm for the gravesite. Eventually, in August 1940, she decided to write an "anonymous" letter to the police:

> to inform you about Annie Rubletz and her baby she
> had and no-body knows where it disappeared. She is

down to Leslie Tetlock's three miles South of Hyas. As the small kids know about this they said that the baby was sick and her mother took it out and carried it in the bush where there is a lot of spruce. So go up and find out more about it.

When the R.C.M.P. investigated, Kate, once again, would be unable to help her sister. The police arrived on August 10, acting on "confidential information;" Kate was in hospital preparing to deliver her own child. Left alone to cope with the questioning, Annie admitted to having a child in 1939 but denied giving birth in June. Leslie Tetlock was home however, having served his sentence and, wanting no more trouble with the police, took Detective Sergeant N. Bretherton, Corporal Gilliland, and Constable Fitzgerald to the grave. Tetlock dug up the small box and the officers returned to the house, collected Annie, and brought her to the site to identify the body.

While Gilliland then went off for a coroner, Bretherton interviewed Annie, with Fitzgerald taking down her statement. He made no threats or offered no inducements to her for this but he did warn her. Annie identified the corpse as her baby and then gave an expurgated version of the events leading up to the baby's death. She was arrested, charged with concealing the birth of a child, and escorted to prison in Yorkton. Not satisfied with Annie's version of events, though, the police continued investigating.

Statements from Norma Tetlock and Helen Skwarchuk confirmed the belief of the police that there was more to the story than Annie had admitted. When they interviewed her again, in the prison, on August 27, they read Norma's and Helen's statements to her, then followed with the one she had made on the tenth. Somewhat to their surprise — and supposedly after Sergeant Bretherton had warned her not to say anything — Annie blurted out, "Lots in that statement is not true. When the baby was born I put my hand over its mouth and it choked." According to testimony at the subsequent trial, the police warned Annie that she did not have to say anything, that anything she said would be written down and might be used against her in court. To ensure the legality of any statement, Bretherton asked the attending matron if Annie had understood the warning and the words "threat" and "promise."

This second statement of August 27 was damning and would be directly responsible for Annie's conviction for murder. While she had admitted in the first statement that the baby had been born alive, she was now describing her child's birth and death:

> I was standing up when the baby was born, beside the bed. The baby came from me and fell on the floor, hitting its head on the bedpost. I then picked the baby up. The baby was alive, and I laid my hand over her face to choke it, because I did not have anybody to look after it. I laid my hand on its face, over the mouth, for about five minutes. When I took my hand off the baby's face it did not breathe any more. Previous to doing this, I cut the belly-button with a knife. After the baby was dead I wrapped it up in a blanket and put it on the bed. There was only a year old baby in the house, my sister, Katie's child ... I did not tell Katie about having put my hand over the baby's mouth and choking it ... The reason that I killed my baby was because there was nobody to look after it ...

Only after signing her name to this statement did Annie receive any legal assistance; Bretherton arranged for a lawyer named McGregor to represent her.

With this written confession, Annie's trial in September appeared an open and shut case. The main prosecution witnesses were Katie, Leslie, Norma, and Helen Swkarchuk. Although Helen had an interpreter, she tried to use her halting English as a guard against difficult questions; for example, she denied knowing that Annie was pregnant and that she had refused to help take her to Norquay. One of her brothers, Michael, had allegedly warned her that if she didn't tell the truth, he would testify against her. On cross-examination she maintained, "They said in English but I didn't understand it exactly. Right now I don't understand it." Asked if she had replied, "I have already told the police the story, I don't want to change it for fear they would put a charge against ... [me] for leaving a sick woman alone." When the family had warned her her statement was false, she would not answer with a definite "yes" or "no."

Norma's animosity towards Annie was clearly apparent at the trial. Her statement to the police would be read into the record and in it she claimed, "I did not know that Annie Rubletz was expecting a child, she being of a fat nature did not show any signs of being in the family way." Only two weeks after the baby's birth, when she noticed Annie out of bed, pale and thin, had she suspected that Annie might have given birth.

It might have seemed to an interested spectator that Annie's lawyer, McGregor, had done little to this point. But McGregor began to show his hand with his cross-examination of Bretherton, centred on Annie's confession of August 27, which was about to be entered into the court as Exhibit B. Would the sergeant say the words in the statement were a paraphrase, he asked. Bretherton answered that the words were Annie's and that she "has got a pretty fair command of English, that girl." McGregor pressed the point. The words in the statement were in the first person singular and in the narrative form, he continued, asking if Annie had actually began her statement with the words: "I have been told by Sergeant Bretherton in the presence of Constable Fitzgerald that I do not have to make a statement to the police but what I do say will be taken down in writing and may be used as evidence against me at my trial. I make the following statement of my own will and accord."

"Certainly not," snapped Bretherton. "That is the way we start all our statements if they are given voluntarily."

Finally, he admitted that Annie had not used any of the words McGregor had read aloud, but continued to claim that she had said, "The party responsible [for impregnating her] is my brother-in-law, Leslie B. Tetlock." When an unsatisfied McGregor seemed prepared to carry the language questions further, Judge H. Y. MacDonald testily threatened to exclude the jury if McGregor maintained his detailed analysis. McGregor explained he was merely setting up his objection to the statement of August 27; he continued his attack on its wording by suggesting that Annie had answered questions with either a "yes" or "no" and that Bretherton had subsequently translated them into "policese." McGregor gave various examples, such as "that the police unearthed today." Finally he asked if there was "one word there that she said except the word 'yes.'" Bretheron stuck to his guns: "I say she did."

Constable Fitzgerald was the next to come under McGregor's attack. He corroborated Bretherton's evidence, but when asked if he had "put meaning into the words that ... [he] thought suitable," he admitted, "sure, quite a lot." McGregor continued to hammer away at his theme that the police themselves had put language and sentence structure into Annie's mouth: "And in the usual way the question and answer were condensed and written down in the first person singular, as if it were the words of the accused." He followed this by asking, "In no sense can you say this girl volunteered all this information? It was dragged by question and answer?"

Fitzgerald answered there had been "no dragging at all. I am not saying that she was not assisted in some respects. She was assisted in some respects but the contents of that statement is her statement." On re-direct he modified this by explaining that "assisted" meant they had explained the meanings of words to Annie.

Mr. Justice MacDonald, obviously fearing that the jurors' sympathy for Annie might lead it to nullification, warned that it was their duty "to accept the law as stated ... by the presiding judge." In his charge he counselled that "the case really hinges on her own statement" made when "she had no counsel and no near relative present." But, he continued, there was no doubt that the baby had been born alive and that Annie had smothered it. "If the child was born alive," as Annie had admitted in both statements, the jurors had to decide whether Annie had "killed it with the intention of killing it." If they decided so, then she was guilty of murder. But, if after considering all the evidence, they felt "reasonable doubt ... and find her not guilty," Macdonald asked that they consider two written questions.

The first question was "On or about the 8th day of June 1940, had a child been recently born to the accused, Annie Rubletz?" Of course there could be no doubt on that point. The second question, then, was "If your answer to the first question is 'Yes,' ... did she ... by some secret disposition of such child, or of the dead body of such child, endeavour to conceal the birth thereof?" The offence, he advised, was "not in hiding the body, it is trying to hide the fact that she had given birth to the child and hiding the body is only a means of doing it."

Naturally enough the questions confused the jury. After two hours deliberation the foreman returned to court with questions of his own. Had Annie received legal counselling before making the statement of August 27? His lordship replied that there was no evidence pointing to such counselling. Next, the foreman asked whether the jury had to "accept the statement of August 27th as voluntarily given?"

"Oh, yes," answered MacDonald, "you have to accept that it was given voluntarily but what weight you will give to it, whether you accept it as truth or not, is entirely for you."

"Can we reduce the charge?" the foreman next asked.

"No."

Well, then, he continued, "in the event that a verdict of guilty is brought in on the charge, do we have to answer the questions that you have submitted to us?" Only if they found Annie not guilty of murder would the jury have to answer the questions. The debate lasted less than an hour before the jury returned to announce: "We find the accused guilty of murder as charged, but due to the circumstances surrounding the case we are bringing in a strong recommendation for mercy." The following day, September 26, Annie Rubletz was condemned to death, receiving "the sentence with the same calmness that ... predominated her attitude during the trial."[3] It was, the *Prairie Farmer* noted, the first time Judge MacDonald had so sentenced a woman in his entire thirty-eight year career on the bench.[4]

In several cases jury nullification has made shadowy appearances. The judge who presided in the *Hawkes* trial warned if the largely "American" jury had realized the death sentence was mandatory and that the mercy recommendation might not be followed, "they would have returned a different verdict" despite the evidence. The jurors unsuccessfully tried to nullify the law so as to protect Annie Robinson. In *Rubletz*, Justice Macdonald stressed in his charge that it was "the *duty* of the jury to accept the law as stated to them by the presiding judge." This was fairly unusual, at least in capital cases involving women since 1867. Such remarks, for example, did not appear in the reported charges for Workman, Robinson, Coward or Hawkes. Macdonald's statement hinted that he feared jury nullification and the obvious desire, as expressed by the foreman, to acquit (without however disobeying judicial instructions) shows his fear was justified. Public reaction to the Rubletz sentence was extremely hostile. This kind of response had been reflected by juries in infanticide cases for over two hundred years, with many perverse verdicts or lack of confidence in the prosecution. It would continue until the law was radically changed in 1948. To gain a perspective, the history of jury nullification in general and, specifically, in infanticide cases must be studied.

The law in England and Canada is fairly easily stated. In the 1660s, English jurors were regularly fined or imprisoned for ignoring judges' instructions on law. This was done most dangerously in ordinary criminal proceedings but, more explosively, in trials of Protestant dissenters. The issue was resolved in the momentous *Bushel* case in 1670, following the prosecution of Quakers William Penn and William Mead for seditious preaching to an unlawful assembly. The prevailing statute law was exceedingly harsh, prohibiting any religious meetings of non-Anglicans of five or more people. After deliberation, eight jurors expressed their readiness to convict. The Recorder threatened the recalcitrant four; if they persisted, "you shall be locked up, without meat, drink, fire, and tobacco ... we will have a [guilty] verdict by the help of God or you shall starve for it." After another abortive attempt, the jury finally returned a verdict of not guilty. The court fined the jurors with imprisonment, until the fine was paid.[5] The imprisoned, Edward Bushel and his fellow jurors, sought a writ of *habeas corpus* to release them from unlawful detention. The case was heard by the Court of Common Pleas, with Chief Justice Vaughan presiding.[6] Vaughan discharged the petitioners.

Then and now some commentators have claimed his decision sanctified jury nullification; but, as specialist scholars note, Vaughan's reasoning was based on the more conservative position that the judge, if able to punish, would inevitably encroach on the jury's exclusive fact-finding role and that he could never know absolutely whether the jury was making law rather than applying it to their view of the facts.[7]

In any event, sanctions from the Bench for "unlawful" verdicts were thereafter illegal. The law was well summarized by Lord Mansfield over a century later in *Dean of St Asaph* (1783-4). Juries had the raw power to nullify, simply because they were uncontrolled; but they had no "right" to do so: "the jury who usurp the judicature of the law ... are ... wrong ... It is the duty of the judge, in all cases of general justice, to tell the jury how to do right, though they have it *in their power* to do wrong."[8] This power-but-no-right distinction has ever since remained the law.[9] In Canada, it was reaffirmed by the Ontario Court of Appeal in *R v. Morgentaler et al.* (1985) and the Supreme Court of Canada.[10] In the United Kingdom and Canada the law has not created more than the most minimal controversy.

The legal path in the United States is quite different.[11]

In practice, jury nullification has had an enormous impact. In the late eighteenth century, English juries battled with judges in seditious libel cases. The end result was Charles James Fox's famous Libel Act of 1792, which allowed the jury, following the judge's instructions, to deliver a general verdict, which included application of sedition law to the facts.[12] More importantly for everyday life, juries often undermined the "bloody code" by "pious perjury." Goods stolen in a dwelling house worth dozens of pounds were, for example, valued at thirty-five, even thirty-nine shillings because a valuation of one more shilling made the crime a capital offence. Pickpocketers, who by definition stole *privily* from the victim, were often acquitted on the capital charge because the jury "assumed" the victim must have known what was happening, and so on.[13] In many of these cases the judges winked at the nullifications, either because they agreed the penalty was outrageous or wanted to ensure some conviction, even if not capital, or both. The ultimate effect was the radical reduction of death offences by Parliament from more than two hundred to four in the years 1808-41. These achievements, fostering freedom of the press and eliminating capital punishment in many, many dubious areas, have been generally applauded then and now.

In the United States, northern juries generally refused to convict, in the face of the evidence, persons charged under the Fugitive Slave law, designed to prevent Afro-American slaves from reaching freedom in British North America, especially Upper Canada. In the 1920s, liquor prohibition cases taken to the jury, with compelling proof, often failed. There was, of course, the down side of white juries occasionally acquitting white murderers of blacks and people of colour, but the primary fault there was the reluctance to prosecute, the laxity of prosecution when done, as well as the unwillingness of witnesses of a lynching to testify. But even if well-prosecuted cases had occurred, it is almost certain, acquittals would have been high and this knowledge discouraged prosecutors.[14] Jury nullification has had costs to justice.

Canada has had its "perverse" verdicts, which were afterwards applauded. Pious perjury was common in the late eighteenth and early nineteenth centuries.[15] One Montreal woman, Charlotte Hamelin, seems to have been an inveterate thief. Convicted of dwelling house larceny in 1795, her death sentence was commuted to banishment. At the March assizes of 1796 she was charged with the capital offence of breaking into a house during day time and stealing £5 or more. The jury reduced the charge to non-capital larceny on the ground there was no convincing proof of breaking in. This verdict seems certainly motivated by a desire to protect a not-so-clever, poor recidivist — who had failed to remain banished — from the possibility of hanging.[16]

Before the Morgentaler abortions trials, the clearest case of jury nullification was the political trial in Montreal, in 1838, of four alleged rebel-murderers of government informer Joseph Chartrand. The killing occurred after all military activity southeast of Montreal had ceased following the 1837 rebellion. The evidence against the four accused was overwhelming. But their defence lawyer, Charles Mondelet, proved brilliant — in one of the first full defences by counsel allowed by law in British North America. He argued that the area in revolt had reverted to a state of nature when the government lost control of it. The only semblance of rule was provided by the rebel *patriotes* under Louis-Joseph Papineau. Despite the judge's explicit denial of such a defence, the all-*Canadien* jury acquitted.[17]

As was the case with a pious perjury and *Chartrand*, Canadian examples of jury nullification usually involved revulsion to the death penalty. In 1877, Justice Minister Edward Blake justified his successful bill to remove that penalty in cases of intercourse with a girl of ten or under and attempted murder by stating that because executions might "take place, convictions were more difficult to obtain than otherwise would be the case."[18]

The same difficulty in obtaining convictions was true in Great Britain and Canada in infanticide prosecutions. From the eighteenth century to the mid-twentieth, in both areas, the crown seldom prosecuted, judges were sympathetic, grand juries failed to indict and trial juries tended to acquit, even when the evidence was conclusive. Constance Backhouse shows that in Upper Canada and Ontario, from 1840 to 1900, there were twenty-seven murder trials for hundreds of discovered infanticides. Of these twenty-seven, eighteen accused were discharged by juries, six were found guilty of the lesser offence of concealing the birth and only two women were convicted; one verdict is not known.[19] In the few cases of conviction, there was usually a mercy recommendation, as in the Rubletz trial. No women appear to have been executed for infanticide.

For most of this period, children were often thought to be the property of their parents. High infant mortality made infanticide seem less heinous than other forms of killing and the death of the newly born was deemed not to be painful to the victim nor harmful to society — particularly upper income society. Throughout the period, juries usually sympathized with the desperation involved in the crimes: such as a poor servant girl who would lose her job and any chance of good references. In some quarters, as Professor Backhouse notes, it was thought that such desperate women might otherwise react violently against society at large or the fathers, who were indeed long thought at least equally to blame, as in the case of Rubletz.

By the 1940s, prosecution for infanticide had become almost hopeless. As explained to the Commons in 1948 by Justice Minister J.L. Ilsley:

> there are cases where the mother kills her newborn child, and that in the normal case of that kind it is useless to lay a charge of murder against the woman, because invariably juries will not bring in a verdict of guilty. They have sympathy with the mother because of the situation in which she has found herself. Therefore crown prosecutors ... lay [much easier] charges of concealment of birth [with a maximum penalty of two years].[20]

In the same year, Parliament enacted a provision, following English precedent, making infanticide a special crime, dependent on the mother's disturbed mental balance and punishable up to three years in prison, raised to five in the new code.[21] Problems soon arose. The term "newly born child" was not defined; one of four and a half months in age was excluded by a trial judge. The problem was solved in the 1955 code by arbitrarily setting the age as under one year.[22] This in turn required further medicalization of infanticide — which scholars have found was mainly mythical.[23] After these changes, it was believed that either the woman had not mentally recovered from giving birth or that she continued to be irrational because of the effect of lactation.[24]

The sentence on Rubletz, as could be predicted, prompted widespread comment and concern. Judge Macdonald wrote to the Secretary of State on September 30 that "in view of the youthfulness of the accused and of the sordid circumstances surrounding her life and the immoral atmosphere in which she was evidently brought up, I wish strongly to join with the jury in recommending mercy." The Cara Amica Club, composed primarily of young business women, petitioned for clemency because "there had to be communal responsibility for the conditions in which this girl lived after her moral frailty had been exposed previously."[25] Arthur L. Davis, in a letter dated October 10, commented that he'd want the father punished and then offered his opinion that the act of childbirth may have unbalanced Annie: "There are times in the life of a woman when, while not actually insane, her reasoning power is temporarily unbalanced." "A Business Girl," after agreeing with the sentiments of other petitioners for clemency, advised "Of course, there will probably be the odd frozen mitt who thinks she deserves it ... why should the girl always have to bear the brunt of it while the man's name is never mentioned." Then, after everything's over, "he ventures out again as large as life ... a heck of a fellow with the ladies."

"A Father and a Parent" supported these sentiments. "The man having first broken one of the ten commandments found in Exodus 2:14," he reasoned, "should be the one to receive the severe sentence." Surely this meant "that we in Canada, should not let women suffer for the beastly acts of men, who have no respect for the grandeur of a woman's soul." Mercy should be given to Annie, "Another Mother" wrote, "as there is enough bloodshed going on in the world now, without any hangings of girls." A confused Mrs. E. Eaton of Regina agreed. "Canada should not coddle criminals and in my opinion justice should take its course. Many hysterical writers blame the men, but why not put the blame where it belongs. Prostitution is rife in small towns in Sask. as young girls are seen soliciting men on the streets." However, it seemed Mrs. Eaton would allow clemency for Annie but advised sternly "sterilization would be the [better] answer" as she'd previously had another illegitimate child. She threw her support behind "Another Mother," calling it the "most sensible thing I have read for some time. Girls are afforded good protection in Sask if they can name the man, but so many girls are prostitutes themselves that the father is unknown."[26]

But, of course, there were the "odd frozen mitts" as "a Business Girl" would have said. "Another Mother"[27] thought it disgusting the way immodesty was flaunted. Why throw so much blame on the men when so many girls are willing to sink to the lowest ebbs? Women should be the moral uplifters of the human race while men are the breadwinners.

As petition after petition reached Ottawa, McGregor appealed the sentence on October 22. A month later the Saskatchewan Court of Appeal quashed the conviction and ordered a new trial.[28] The question and answer method of the police that had produced the "confession" was certainly an issue. Other grounds for the appeal were that the judge had erred in not allowing three witnesses to appear for the defence to discredit crown witness Helen Skwarchuk. Nor had he allowed the jury to find on a reduced charge, and he had not explained or instructed the jury on the point of non-culpable homicide.[29] Found guilty of concealing her baby's birth at this new trial, Annie Rubletz was released from prison on the grounds that she'd already spent the equivalent time of her sentence (one year) in the Battleford jail.

Aged twenty-three, Mary Paulette lived with her "Treaty" parents in what was then the Northwest Territories.[30] The police considered them "quite superior to the average Indian" and although they were "not well to do," they had "always made a fair living with hunting and trapping" to the point where they had "never known want." Nor were they prepared to do so.

Mary's life, for a while, seemed a success story. At eighteen, she had married Magloire Paulette, a special constable with the R.C.M.P. Fort Smith detachment and they had one child. Then Mary's life began to fall apart when Magloire Paulette committed suicide in June 1948. Besides dealing with that trauma, she had to worry about her own future for she was pregnant with their second child at the time. Her parents took her in and she lived quietly with them, developing a reputation for good behaviour as a moderate drinker who liked to play poker. As the R.C.M.P. report would say: "She has always been very well behaved in the Settlement and there has never been the slightest suspicion of her having been mixed up in any rowdy drinking parties." Gambling, the report would go on to say, was "quite prevalent amongst Indians and Halfbreeds of both sexes" in Fort Smith; Mary, therefore, was distinguished by her moderation. She was "a very shy, quiet type of woman, quite intelligent and extremely polite at all times." Furthermore, Sergeant G. Abraham of the Fort Smith R.C.M.P. held a nearly universal opinion when he, having known Mary since childhood, declared she was the last person he expected to get into trouble.

But trouble found Mary. In 1950 she strained her parents' resources and tolerance to the limit when she had an illegitimate child. The father, "Signalman" Gibson, a serviceman stationed at Fort Smith, could offer neither marriage nor help with the raising of the child. Matters escalated when he was transferred out of the area and left Mary, again pregnant, to fend for herself. Other than her parents, her only support was "relief" rations from the Department of Resources and Development.

In May 1951, she found herself alone in her parents' house. Her father, Jeremy Tourangeau, was away hunting and her mother and Bernadette Tourangeau, her sister, had gone to church. At 8:00 p.m. the contractions began while she was bathing her children. She put them to bed and went to the outdoor toilet. As the pains became more frequent, she thought about "how hard it would be to bring up four children." Her mother had made it extremely obvious that the fourth child would not be welcome; eventually, Mary Paulette's thoughts turned and she began to wish the baby would be still-born. But that was not to be. The little girl was born alive.

Mary later claimed she thought about a recent Alberta case where a mother had killed a newly born child and received a sentence of two years. Maybe this would be the solution to the problems a fourth child presented. Despair and worry about her situation warred with the temptation to copy the actions of the mother from Alberta: "this kept going through her mind and ... [she began] thinking that she would never be found out." In this frame of mind, Mary Paulette took pieces of paper and stuffed her newly born infant's mouth full. After the baby's movements ceased, and without looking at her child again, she dropped it "down the hole of the toilet and then covered it with sand that she brought from behind their house with a pail."

Almost immediately, she had second thoughts. Overcome by remorse, she stayed in the outhouse, too frightened to move. Evidence that she'd given birth was obvious. Although she had covered the toilet floor with paper, it was stained with blood, as was the toilet seat. But after giving birth and after choking her baby, Mary was too weak to do anything about the blood stained outhouse. About an hour after she had entered the outhouse, she left it and went to bed. Her mother and sister came home, and remained only briefly, before leaving again to play cards. When Mary got up early the next morning, she was able to clean up the toilet and throw the incriminating evidence down the hole.

Mary's mother and sister were obviously relieved and accepted the ridiculous story Mary told on May 14 — that she had miscarried her five-month old fetus and disposed of it down the toilet. Another sister,

Ernestine Burke, warned Mary that she would be caught. The matter began to unravel the very next day when the police began investigating.

The first suspicion that all was not right with Mary's story originated out of friendliness; one of the R.C.M.P. detachment, seeing that Mary was clearly "unpregnant," had asked how the baby was doing. To his surprise, she denied giving birth; then, faced with increasing pressure, consented to have a medical examination. Only after a doctor confirmed she had given birth recently did she change her story.

In her ensuing trial on September 19, 1951, Mary, perhaps rashly, elected to be tried without a jury as was her right under the Northwest Territories Act.[31] The facts regarding the baby's birth were uncontested and her court-appointed defence counsel, D.J. Hagel, attempted unsuccessfully to prove that "she may have been temporarily mentally unsound." But there were no witnesses to Mary's mental state at the time of the birth to support this contention; consequently, Mr. Justice J.F. Gibben, according to Hagel, "felt he could not find for the lesser offence of infanticide."[32] Mary Paulette was convicted of murder and sentenced to death, September 20, 1951.

The fight for her life came from the Northwest Territory officials associated with her case. John Parker, the crown prosecutor for the Mackenzie District, N.W.T., offered the best explanation of her feelings at the time of her child's birth. In a letter to General Young, Commissioner for the Northwest Territories, Parker wrote:

> There is little doubt in my own mind why she killed this child. She had no husband; she was dependent almost entirely upon rations given to her through the R.C.M.P., and she already had three children and probably thought she would have the greatest difficulty in supporting another one. She lived with her father and mother, and although the evidence was that they knew nothing about her condition, I have the greatest difficulty in believing that they could have been unaware that she was going to have a child. The evidence was conclusive that this was a full-term baby, and I cannot believe that the girl's mother did not know that a baby was on the way. The Police investigated the matter thoroughly but the girl's mother, Mrs. Tourangeau, insisted that it was all a

> surprise to her. ... She ... probably made it clear to the girl
> that another child in the household was not required.

My own view is that Mary Paulette found herself in an impossible position.

Although Parker agreed with the verdict, he felt "very strongly" that "the penalty should be very sharply reduced. Had she been convicted of infanticide the maximum sentence would have been three years." As Mary had already spent four months in jail, he pointed out, "the appropriate penalty would be a year or eighteen months." To buttress his plea and impress the bureaucrats in Ottawa, he added that as a crown prosecutor he had never before asked for such a "drastic reduction" but "given the circumstances of the case" felt it "should be made and be made as soon as conveniently possible."[33] In a follow-up letter to F.P. Varcoe, the Deputy Minister of Justice, Parker again argued for commutation saying that he felt "justice would be served and the woman adequately punished if she received a sentence of ... one year."[34]

Mary Paulette's sentence was commuted, but Parker's suggestion of a one year sentence was disregarded. In January 1954, R.G. Robertson, of the Office of the Commissioner of the Northwest Territories, took up the fight. In a letter to Varcoe, he reminded the Department of Justice that in February 1953 it had promised to review Mary's case. Life in Kingston Penitentiary had severely affected Mary, bringing back tuberculosis that had been in remission. The Territories' administration had arranged for her to be transferred from penitentiary to the Ongwanada Sanatorium, also in Kingston, on a temporary ticket of leave. He enclosed supporting medical evidence and reiterated his plea that she be sent home.

A.J. McLeod of the Remission Service advised in reply that only when Mary was well enough to be released from hospital would an "exercise of clemency" be contemplated.[35] On February 24, 1954, Parker intervened again, reminding the Remission officials that he had "tried several times in the past to have the sentence reduced." To drive his feelings home to the distant bureaucracy in Ottawa, he said no one had pressured him to help Mary, nor did he know "her friends or any member of her family." Again he asked that the matter be reviewed and once more the Remission Service replied that she could not be considered for clemency until her health was better. Rubbish, snapped Parker. "It seems to me," he wrote back on March 8, 1954, "that there is not much incentive for Mary Paulette to get well quickly if the only prospect she faces is return to the peniten-tiary for the rest of her life."

Mary Paulette's case did not fit the medical guidelines that defined infanticide. She had acted out of economic need and, as Parker had written shortly after her conviction, "Infanticide, as defined in the Code, would ... cover only a comparatively few of the cases in which a mother kills her new-born infant... [T]he definition of infanticide should be broadened to include all those cases where a mother, under stress of circumstances, kills her new-born child. I think, in fact, juries probably usually apply more liberal interpretation[s] than is strictly justified by the definition."[36]

His was but one of many voices asking that Paulette's case be treated as one of infanticide, not murder. There seems to have been causal connection between this leniency, Parker's statement on continuing jury nullification and the new provision in the 1955 Criminal Code, which permitted infanticide convictions even if the medical proof could not be made.[37] Baby killing by the mother ceased for all practical purposes to be murder and the creation of a new homicide, subtracted from murder, set a major precedent. In 1961 it was followed when capital murder was restricted to planned killings, homicides committed in the course of certain other violent offences, and the killing of police officers and prison guards.

There is another slightly later set of jury nullifications that had a profound effect on women. In Canada the present freedom to choose abortion owes a great deal to jury nullification in the various Morgentaler cases. In the 1970s he was tried three times by Quebec juries for illegal abortion (no accredited hospital, no certificate of a therapeutic abortion committee) and thrice acquitted, although one acquittal was reversed. On March 10, 1982, the Quebec government threw in the towel. Attorney General Marc-André Bédard told the National Assembly that it was almost impossible to get a jury to convict a qualified physician for illegal abortion; henceforth, his ministry and the police would concentrate, not on *bona fide* clinics operating outside the law, but on abortions performed in unhygienic conditions or by unqualified persons.[38]

A similar development took place in Ontario. Morgantaler and two co-accused were acquitted in the Ontario High Court of Justice in 1984.[39] Counsel for the defence, Morris Manning, took the highly unusual step, in Canada, of telling the jury it was their right to find that section 251 of the Criminal Code, dealing with abortion, was "bad law" because it was unfair to women who wished to abort. If so, they had "a right to say it shouldn't be applied."[40] The jury complied but nullification was declared entirely against the law by the Ontario Court of Appeal, which ordered a new trial.[41] That new trial never took place, as an appeal was launched to the Supreme Court of Canada, which in 1988 held section 251 unconstitutional.[42] All judges there decided against jury nullification, Chief Justice Brian Dickson's comments being the most comprehensive.[43] Besides quoting from *Dean of St. Asaph* (1783-4) and a mid-twentieth century Judicial Committee precedent,[44] Dickson referred to inequality among accused based merely on personal sympathy or antipathy and gave some of the United States' experience as telling: "a jury fueled by the passions of racism could be told they need not apply the law against murder to a white man who had killed a black man. Such a possibility need only be stated to reveal the potentially frightening implications of Mr. Manning's assertions." Justice Beetz agreed, stating that the strong condemnation of the Court of Appeal in Ontario was "required for the benefit of counsel who in other proceedings may be tempted to follow this unacceptable practice."[45]

But whatever the proper role of the jury, as indicated by the Supreme Court, it is ironic that jury nullification in Canada's two largest provinces must have inclined the court in the very same case towards its momentous decision holding section 251 *ultra vires* (beyond the power of) Parliament and the latter's reluctance to do anything about it.[46]

As Mary languished in the sanitarium MacLeod announced on March 11, 1954 that a review of her case had been launched. On hearing the news, Northwest Territories' Commissioner Robertson responded with an offer that her hospital treatment would be continued at his office's expense in the N.W.T. if needed and "regardless of whether she is under sentence or not." Armed with this reassurance the mills of the Remission Service began to grind slowly; in its discussion the issue of infanticide was raised as it had been apparently in all previous talk on the case. In his letter of

May 18, recommending ticket of leave status for Mary Paulette, MacLeod advised the solicitor general: "You will recall that following a lengthy discussion [in 1952], particularly with respect to the possibility that infanticide, rather than murder, might have been the proper charge in this case." To add weight to his recommendation, MacLeod pointed out that the former and present Commissioners and "defence" counsel remained actively interested in the case. On the same day, MacLeod advised "that ... Mary Paulette be now granted a Ticket of Leave" conditional upon the Commissioner of the Northwest Territories being satisfied with "all arrangements for her return to the community."

It was fortunate for Mary Paulette that the condition was not that the Ongwanada Sanatorium be satisfied. On June 24, 1954, more than a month after MacLeod's instruction, its medical director wrote the warden of Kingston Penitentiary that his institution had "been having a little trouble with this patient and as [a] result I have not told her you have her ticket of leave." Further surgery was necessary but, in any case, Hopkins had "told her [that] her ticket of leave is pending and ... also ... that unless she stopped breaking Sanatorium rules I would have her leave cancelled."

Warden W.F. Johnstone was puzzled. In his subsequent letter to the Remission Service he said that the suggested time limit proposed by Dr. Hopkins was six months. Then he asked, "In view of the time limit of thirty days from the date of issuance of Ticket of Leave in which this inmate must be set at liberty," what should he do?

Remission wrote back that Mary now had the status of a discharged prisoner who happened to be undergoing medical treatment. But that was not quite how the sanatorium viewed it. Dr. Hopkins obstinately refused to release Mary into the care of the Territories Commission. Only after he was sharply rebuked and reminded that his was not a penal institute and that he had no power to block her release did Mary enter into the care of N.W.T. officials.

Philosopher Jean-Paul Sartre wrote that human life began on the "far side of despair." Unfortunately, the opposite seems true when evaluating the cases of Annie Rubletz and Mary Paulette. Alone at the time of their children's births, they made desperate decisions resulting in the end of life, not its beginning, for their children.

Conclusion

A long line of scholars has described the patriarchal values attached to past criminal law when applied to women. This book has extended that line of study to many new areas, such as eligibility for and equality in jury duty, husband killing, female spectators at public executions and the male response thereto, the doctrine of spousal coercion, jury recommendations to mercy and, in part, infanticide. These additional illustrations reveal how all-encompassing such values were. Changes in societal attitudes as reflected especially in the law have been given where relevant.

The term "patriarchal" refers to the attitudes and powers of the father of a family, a male ruler or the male elders of a tribe, corporation, private club, polity and so on. In certain areas of female behaviour, patriarchal rule can be harsh; in others, lenient. So it was in the male dominated criminal law of Canada and in England during the the period before capital punishment was abolished.

Harshness appeared in the substantive law related to female servants killing their employers and wives their husbands. These crimes were classified as treasons and punished by burning alive. This penalty (after strangulation for some decades) lasted in England until the 1780s. Men were never liable to be treated as traitors for murdering their wives, despite this being an obvious betrayal of the marriage vow. In actual practice, husband-murders were dealt with much more severely than wife-killers in the United Kingdom during the 1800s and other female murders in Canada, from 1867 to 1962. Women who played a man-like leadership role in capital offences (such as Eleanor Power, Margaret Whippy, Mary Aylward) or merely participated in "public" murders committed by men (such as Florence Lassandro, Elizabeth Popovitch, Marguerite Pitre) were hanged much more often than not.

Patriarchal attitudes towards women frequently inclined to leniency. Although the idea that such a practice was "chivalrous" has been denied by some historians and criminologists, especially American ones, the majority of scholars have accepted it.[1] For Canada, the publications of Carolyn Strange in the 1990s solidly ground lenience in male chivalry; that is, protecting those perceived as defenceless, although she quite properly points out that most manifestations were demeaning and perpetuated harmful stereotypes.[2] Only a very few women benefited from this lenience and the material in this book supports Strange's conclusions.

Not all such chivalry was demeaning. The very marked tolerance of infanticide by nineteenth century Canadian males running the judicial process (crown prosecutors, grand jurors, judges, trial jurors and advisers on the exercise of mercy) for instance, reflected a general empathy for the desperate plight of poor and unmarried mothers. But most of the chivalric protection of women in the criminal law was indeed demeaning and truly a "sham chivalry."

Chivalrous attitudes, usually based on stereotyping, viewed most women as frail but pure of mind. Women were seen as passive in general, submissive to husbands in particular, and emotional — indeed, easily disturbed mentally rather than rational. Such stereotypes are thought by the large majority of scholars today to have been demeaning in making women both less and more than human, and wrong in fact, as the passage of time has now shown.

That most wives lacked the mental toughness to disobey spousal orders to commit crimes was probably never true and, in supposing that, the law was indeed as Dickens described in *Oliver Twist* (1837-8): "a ass" and "a bachelor." By the late nineteenth century, such presumption had become something of a joke in legal circles, being finally abolished as unreal in Canada in 1892 and in the United Kingdom in 1925. The twinned assumptions that women offenders, almost invariably, could not control their emotions and could easily became dupes of men often justified the marked tendency of juries to recommend mercy and Ottawa to commute death sentences, after Confederation. The incredible delays in making Canadian women eligible for and then equally obliged to do criminal jury duty, not finally realized until 1972, was based on the false assumption that female psyches were so frail that they had to be sheltered from hearing or seeing unseemly things. At the time, this assumption was belied by "respectable" women attending sensational trials and public executions — without notable harm. The modern era, where women sit on criminal juries, has led to no visible spawning of female monsters or babbling imbeciles.

The patronizing assumption of mental frailty seems to have lain behind the 1948 infanticide amendment, which removed that offence from the murder category. Specialist scholars have concluded that mothers killing their babies because of mental instability due to giving birth were always a minority.[3] Historians like Malcolmson and Backhouse make it very clear that in the eighteenth and nineteenth centuries infanticides were overwhelmingly the result of economic desperation.[4] The cases of Annie Rubletz and Mary Paulette suggest that motive remained strong in Canada at least to the middle the last century, and Parliament accommodated it in the 1955 Code. In the 1980s the assumption of mental disturbance under stress was also applied in the United Kingdom to violent female criminals, significantly reducing their sentences compared to those given comparable men; women were in fact portrayed as irresponsible victims of life rather than actively dangerous people.[5] This helped a few women at the expense of most.

It is also clear that chivalry was aimed at the chaste and the passive. Women who were at all promiscuous or aggressive were usually not considered worth protecting. They fared badly in the administration of both capital and non-capital criminal justice. Wives who showed criminal initiative, for example, fell outside the sheltering umbrella of spousal coercion. Proof or even suspicion of adultery was usually fatal, as the love triangle husband murders committed by Catherine Snow, Marie-Anne Crispin and Cordelia Viau (Quebec, 1898-9) attest. Elizabeth Workman, undoubtedly perceived by federal authorities as a violent drunk and adulteress, was the only woman after Confederation to be hanged in the face of a jury's recommendation to mercy and despite being a battered wife.

The same was true of non-capital offences. Battered women were often unprotected by existing law and welfare agencies, because of assumptions they deserved a beating for provoking their husbands or ignoring orders. Until the recommendations of the Royal Commission on the Status of Women (1970) led to reform, a woman was protected from men's sexual attacks only if she was "of previously chaste character."[6] This limitation applied to seduction of: girls fourteen or fifteen; those sixteen or seventeen by males of eighteen or more; women younger than twenty-one under promise of marriage; and female employees.[7]

Until fairly recently, most victims of rape had to prove their chaste character on cross-examination in order to obtain convictions. Carolyn

Strange offers a shocking but believable statistic and explanation: "from 1880 to 1930, not a single Toronto domestic who laid a complaint of indecent assault or rape against her master saw him punished. At the root of the justice system's dismissal of female claims lay the belief that only an unchaste woman could induce a man to make a sexual advance."[8]

The "respectable" women who watched Julia Murdock's death illustrated two tendencies present at the time. First, of course, was the fact that public executions drew huge crowds of spectators, including many women. This was especially so when there was a sexual angle to the crime or criminals. Second, "holier-than-thou" males condemned their presence.

Even after the abolition of public executions, trials with a sexual theme also drew crowds to the court room. When that Toronto jury acquitted Carrie Davies, the front page story in the *Daily News* complained that "Many of the women [spectators] were well-dressed and evidently of the 'upper' stratum, but they pushed and jostled with the rest, intent on satisfying a more or less morbid curiosity."[9] In fact, the newspaper could almost have been writing about crowds rushing into the Toronto court house to watch the recent trial of Paul Bernardo. While women received rebuke, there was almost none given to the male spectators.

The high attendance of women, including those of the "upper stratum" at public executions can obviously be traced to the relative lack of entertainment for females outside their homes, particularly the more "bloody" forms of entertainment. But Carrie Davies' trial and studies of other jurisdictions hint that many deeper motives may have existed.

Arlette Farge writes about spectators at executions in eighteenth century Paris: "At the heart of that slow ritualization of agony and the prolonged gaze of the crowd upon it there resided without a doubt, the desire to taste and see, to penetrate the mystery of what it was to lose one's life."[10] Farge writes brilliantly about female spectators, which she clearly proves were legion at many executions and usually the last to avert their eyes. She explains this obsession as arising from the intimacy of women with both life and death. "This strange amalgamation between her reproductive nature and the significant level of infant mortality ... gave her a direct hold on the permanent mysteries of life and death."[11]

Therefore, according to Farge, the curiosity wasn't morbid, but natural. Judith Knelman writes of the gathering of the clan at the execution of women in nineteenth century England: "For ... [them], a hanging ... was the thrill of seeing what happened to those of their sex who transgressed."[12] As for male condemnations, Farge concludes, most expressed guilt by portraying the women as being after what they were — cruel and barbaric as well as indulging in "a very freaky kind of pleasure."[13] Thus the argument can be made that male censuring of female attendance at public executions is one more example of patriarchy.

Some of the cases studied herein raise current issues, such as the fate of battered women. The use of expert psychological or psychiatric testimony to right the balance against those finding themselves in situations such as Elizabeth Workman cannot be denied. But some scholars have concluded that the "battered woman syndrome" has been treated by the courts as evidence of mental disorder, suggesting those recurrently beaten are not rational. By perpetuating the old myth, this shows that lingering patriarchy is yet a part of the criminal justice system. The most persuasive critique of the "battered woman syndrome" is the 1997 article by Patricia Kazan.[14]

Kazan's foremost point is that "heightened sensitivity" and "learned helplessness" are often incompatible with *reasonable* action in pre-emptive self-defence. A "woman's heightened sensitivity may make her hypersensitive to her batterer's behaviour, causing her to fear grave danger at the slightest change in this behaviour," but the change triggering her pre-emptive strike may well not be one which "actually corresponds to a real and present danger." Furthermore, a woman who has learned helplessness, "might not be able to perceive alternatives to the use of deadly force even if such options were readily available." Indeed, learned helplessness would seem to sit very badly with the forceful act of killing. Thus, legal logic tells against the syndrome and to allow dozens of special, subjective versions of reasonable self-defence would produce a nightmare in law enforcement.

Kazan's second point is that while expert evidence of the three-part cycle of violence and the unfriendly context in which a battered woman operates remains necessary, evidence related to the psychological results of the syndrome will often not be. In cases like *Lavallee*, acquittals can be obtained on the basis of rational self-defence unaided by proof of mental aberration. In that case it could be easily argued that simple experience of beatings made Lyn Lavallee aware that Kevin Rust was close to an extremely violent attack on her, especially when he actually loaded a gun and handed it to her. Unlike actions accompanying previous death threats, this was a major change signalling that the coming attack would probably threaten her life. At the time — and on many occasions before she had sought assistance — without success. Proof could also probably have been made that she had nowhere to go safely and no prospect of earning a decent living. If so, Lavallee had engaged in a perfectly rational act of self-defence when not mentally "sick."

Kazan does, however, reserve a role for the battered woman syndrome. It would come into play when rationality could not be proved, but the accused's mental disturbance fell short of insanity. The verdict where the syndrome was linked to the act would be an acquittal on the grounds that the victim-accused's mental condition negated *mens rea*, that is the specific intent to commit murder. Depending on her danger to society, the convicted woman would either be discharged or institutionalized as a patient.

These suggestions provide a promising start to making battered women's cases less often self-contradictory or contrary to important legal logic. They are less likely to perpetuate the irrational stereotype, but able to protect many battered women who kill or attempt to kill their batterers, whether the former have acted irrationally or with perfect reason. Thus, the focus will also be shifted away from treating battered women as easily "understandable" deviants, to the need for socio-economic protection and the political will to provide such.[15]

It is easy to portray jury nullification in a sympathetic way as democratic and/or humanitarian. Many were outraged when the jury in the Latimer case was not permitted to find manslaughter instead of second degree murder for the killing of Tracy, Robert Latimer's daughter, who had been suffering from a form of cerebral palsy. Latimer's actions carried a life sentence by law, with no parole before ten years. Had the jury been told of a right to nullification, it seems likely the verdict would have been manslaughter.[16]

There is Texan folklore — and that of other places, including the Ottawa valley — of a sharecropper, with eleven mouths to feed, who stole a pig from one of his employers. It was found in the cropper's pigpen and he was charged with larceny. The jury returned a verdict of "not guilty, but he should give back the pig." An irate judge forced further deliberation to return a "true verdict." A few minutes later the jury pronounced its "true verdict": "not guilty and he can keep the pig."[17] But things aren't really that one-sided.

In modern times, the concept has excited a great deal of interest in academic circles, the interested public and courts in the United States — for example, the Michigan acquittals and ultimate conviction of Dr. Jack Kevorkian on charges of assisting suicide.[18] In the international index to Legal Periodicals from August 1981 to September 1998, there are sixty-one articles listed relating to American affairs and none relating to Canada. With respect to Canada, there is only a two page article, which is for nullification, on the Robert Latimer euthanasia case listed in the index to Canadian legal periodicals, from 1987 to November 1998.[19] In the United States, the "Fully Informed Jury Association," of some 6,000 members, uses all available information channels, including the internet, to convince the public that jurors should vote their own morality regardless of instructions from the Bench on the law. This campaign appears to be succeeding. A recent nationwide poll had three of four Americans in agreement and there is a definite increase lately in jury defiance, although it cannot be quantified.[20] Canada has no equivalent organization. This movement has reached the point in the United States that judges are often reluctant to appear to be against juror independence.[21] In the last Kevorkian trial (the conviction), in which the doctor defended himself, he asked the jury to disregard the law. The prosecution thereupon requested the judge to issue an explicit instruction declaring jury nullification to be illegal. She refused, a stance almost impossible to imagine in Canada.[22]

Before evaluating jury nullification, two recent developments should be noted. In the United States there have been calls for black jurors to nullify in favour of black defendants because of the systemic police and prosecutorial bias against them and their generally impoverished backgrounds. This goes further than encouraging black jurors to maintain their healthy suspicion of police work and that of the District Attorneys' offices. Its principal advocate, Paul D. Butler, restricts the idea to "passive" crimes such as drug possession and even non-violent distribution of marijuana to adults.[23] But once told their rights, will jurors thus confine themselves?

The second development of note is the late 1970s polling conducted under the auspices of the Law Reform Commission of Canada. Members of the general public, jurors and judges were asked to respond to this hypothetical instruction from the Bench: "It is difficult to write laws that are just for all conceivable circumstances. Therefore, you are entitled to follow your own conscience instead of strictly applying the law if it is necessary to do so to reach a just result." The extremity of contrast between the public, including jurors, on the one hand and Canadian judges is startling: 76.4% of the public thought the instruction should definitely or probably be given. The comparable percentage for jurors after serving was 60.4%. That for judges was a hostile 4.5%. Whatever the lack of present controversy, the seeds exist for a future one.[24]

In the past, jury nullification has affected both genders and in the future it will continue to do so. In Canada, while a jury has the power to nullify, it has no right to do so. This status should be maintained. That is, jurors should not be instructed they have such a power, much less a right, nor should defence counsel be allowed to urge them on. Canada, as opposed to the United States, has no constitutional or historical warrant for doing otherwise. Juries, while a useful popular counterweight to legal and parliamentary elites, are not as representative as Parliament and should not usurp the latter's prerogatives. But, more importantly, any change giving juries the right to determine law might result in its widespread use, with deleterious effect. The right to jury nullification is not necessary to protect Canadians against executive or legislative tyranny as things now stand.

Jury nullification has certain defects and is unlikely to further specified social values. As Greenwood wrote in 1984:

> If from a law-and-order orientation one believes ... that state necessity should be a defence to crimes committed by police ... or security operatives [e.g. the R.C.M.P. Security Service in Quebec during the 1970s; Oliver North more recently in the Iran-Contra affair] one might welcome jury nullification, at least until one

reflected that ... civil disobedience activists [of a leftist persuasion] might go free [on the same basis].

Today, someone zealous for the protection of human life might applaud a jury's perverse verdict of acquittal where the accused had damaged a clinic that performed abortions, but exhibit hostility to like verdicts in cases of assisted suicide or especially non-voluntary euthanasia (such as in Latimer case).

Other problems remain, including the fading, even further, of the ideal of equality before the law on a personal basis or on a geographical basis. Would assisted suicide be treated differently by juries in small town Canada as opposed to the metropolitan centres? Again, juries told they are superior to judges might not stop at acquittals in the face of the law and evidence as presented, but proceed to convict perversely. Whenever these convictions occurred, the accused would be punished retroactively, a gross breach of the rule of law. In addition, if racial nullification overflowed into Canada, pitting aboriginals, blacks, and Asians against Caucasians or against each other, retaliation would be inevitable and justice would be lost in a racist morass. Finally, the almost inevitable large increase of "hung juries" might place intolerable strains on an already overburdened system. In the United States, a generation ago, juries unable to reach a unanimous verdict in criminal cases ran at about 5%. Coincident with the growth of jury nullification sentiments in recent years, that rate has often doubled, rising to 15% and 20% in Washington, D.C. and California respectively.[25]

This does not mean that jury nullification should never occur, only that the right should not be granted. There certainly should not be sanctions against or investigations of perverse verdicts. Indeed, *de facto* jury nullification is one strong bastion against tyrannical law. This was agreed to by the Law Reform Commission of Canada in 1980, the words of which were quoted with moderate approval by none other than Chief Justice Dickson: "It may even be true that in some limited circumstances, the private decision of a jury to refuse to apply the law will constitute ... 'the citizen's ultimate protections against oppressive laws and oppressive enforcement of the law.'" The Commission gave several examples of the latter, even in non-political cases — for example, being badly treated by the police and/or wrongfully singled out for prosecution.[26] Dickson also approved Leventhal J. in the United

States Court of Appeals, Columbia District case of *Dougherty* (1972) when he referred to the "marvellous balance" of the existing system with the "jury acting as a 'safety valve' for exceptional cases, without being a wildcat or runaway institution." Lord Devlin graphically wrote about the reality of the system even without a right to nullify in his book *Trial by Jury* (1966), "the first object of any tyrant in Whitehall would be to make Parliament utterly subservient to his will; and the next to overthrow or diminish trial by jury, for no tyrant could afford to leave a subject's freedom in the hands of twelve of his countrymen. So that trial by jury ... is the lamp that shows that freedom lives."[27]

Whenever a strong public consensus — national or regional — appears, Canadian juries will today nullify laws they think oppressive as they have done in the past. Furthermore, past nullifications, in Canada and Britain at least, have generally been on the wave of the future: with regard, for example, to seditious libel, the "bloody code," infanticide, and abortion. One great exception concerns the rights of unions and leftist ideologues.[28] Juries should be encouraged to accompany recommendations to mercy, where appropriate, with reflections on the fairness of the law in question or its enforcement in the particular case. This is not entirely unprecedented in Canada and in the one instance we know of, helped save the man's life.[29]

We don't wish to rehash the arguments against capital punishment, even though its revival in Canada is certainly possible, given its prevalence in the United States, western Canadian opinion, and the position of Her Majesty's Loyal Opposition in 2000. Suffice it to say we agree with the three abolition arguments which have dominated that side of the parliamentary debate since its beginning in 1914: the absence of any discernible effect of general deterrence, the degrading moral example set by the state in taking lives during peace time and the possibility of putting innocent persons to death.[30] We concentrate on the third argument.

Chapter 5 told of Canadians who were capitally-convicted with some executed, due to distortions of the law: Power, Hawkes, and Maloney. To these, could be added the case of Louis Riel whose lawyers' plea of insanity was rejected in court and by Ottawa. Riel, a self-proclaimed prophet, believed himself ordered by his God to rebel.[31] James Hadfield, defended by the brilliant Thomas Erskine on the grounds of the accused's conviction he had been divinely commanded to attempt George III's murder by shooting, was acquitted of treason in 1800.[32] In such circumstances of religious extremity how could either Hadfield or Riel have known right from wrong? If capital punishment is ever reintroduced, these legal distortions could again prove fatal in murder or especially treason trials.[33]

In the cases previously discussed, where serious doubts have arisen about factual guilt, Snow was probably guilty but three others may have been innocent — Julia Murdock, Mary Aylward and Marguerite Pitre, all of whom were hanged. Elizabeth Coward, though not executed, was probably not guilty. A cursory examination of English cases revealed three persons convicted, in two cases hanged, who were almost certainly innocent — Fenning, the man transported to Australia in 1835 and Evans. As well, former Attorney General Kelly claimed that between 1802 and 1840 there had been at least twenty-two wrongful convictions for capital offences. Seven of these were executed. Arthur Koestler proved the point by adding nine more English cases from the late nineteenth and twentieth centuries where the accused was probably innocent.[34] As Kelly, Koestler, and criminologist Neil Boyd note, the known miscarriages of justice, whether probable, possible or virtually certain, are but the beginning. Late in July 1998 the British Court of Appeal virtually proclaimed the innocence of Derek Bentley, hanged in 1953 for the shooting of a police officer, when it quashed the conviction because of a totally biassed trial.[35]

Canada in recent years has exonerated several convicted murderers: Donald Marshall, in Nova Scotia; Guy Paul Morin, in Ontario; David Milgaard, in Saskatchewan; and Gregory Parsons, in Newfoundland. The process of possible exoneration under the Criminal Code has begun for Clayton Johnson in Nova Scotia, convicted in 1993 of killing his wife, and Robert Baltovitch in Ontario, convicted a year earlier of murdering his lover.[36] These cases were often marked by the tunnel vision and/or incompetence of prosecutors, police, and forensic scientists.[37] Parsons was convicted largely on the basis of hearsay.[38]

Undoubtedly, the numbers of persons known to have been wrongfully convicted for murder will only grow in the future. Decades ago, these people might well have been executed. An energetic and effective Association in Defence of the Wrongfully Convicted has been pressing for all kinds of reviews and the federal ministry of justice has initiated about sixty-five, as of early 1999.[39] Another factor almost guaranteeing the growth of these numbers is the forensic use of DNA, which proved the innocence of Morin, Milgaard, and Parsons. In the United States, to 1997, the use of DNA exonerated thirty-six prisoners, including one who had spent eleven years on death row.[40] As late as March 1999, investigations of over-zealous prosecutors there were still uncovering wrongful death sentence convictions.[41] In one Texas case a man on death row recently had his sentence commuted when it was proved conclusively he had been in another state at the time of the murder.[42] Indeed, the Republican governor of Illinois, who favours capital punishment, suspended executions in January 2000 after revelations that since 1976 twelve executed persons and thirteen released from death row had been wrongfully convicted.[43] President Clinton has asked all relevant states to review their death penalty procedures and there is no doubt that in the United States, at the beginning of the third millennium, execution of the innocent is the most important argument against capital punishment.[44]

Koestler wisely teaches that with actual execution, the exoneration of a convict becomes even harder — much much harder.[45] The executed convict is no longer around to stimulate, suggest leads, profess innocence, confirm or deny "new" facts and so on. Supporters can easily lose interest. Anything like the dedication shown by Bentley's sister and later his niece, who worked forty-six years for justice, or by Joyce Milgaard who spent more than twenty-eight years of tireless sacrifice to clear her son's name is very, very rare.[46]

The reintroduction of hanging or other lethal penalties for murder and treason would also certainly involve unfair singling out for execution of certain people. Many have written that such selections amount to a lottery and thus help negate any deterrent value of capital punishment. It is easy to make the case against capital punishment when the politics of mercy are considered. Interventions by the influential have almost always been important as in the cases of Pilotte, McManus, Napolitano, Hawkes, and Coward. Those without them, such as Julia Murdock, have usually fared less well in obtaining clemency. The ability to pay for a highly competent lawyer can be also an important factor as in the case of Elizabeth Workman.

Past experience also indicates that in situations of rebellion, which today would also include multiple terrorist acts by Canadian residents, those singled out from the many for the ultimate punishment were not necessarily the ones most active in committing treason. Following the second rebellion in Lower Canada in 1838, men were hanged or spared for reasons not clearly indicated from the trial.[47]

The incidence of execution has of course varied with the attitudes of ministers of justice and the influence of public opinion on cabinets. From Confederation to 1962, over 40% of men capitally-convicted were hanged. During John Diefenbaker's tenure, the rate of commutation reached 80% and no one was executed after the Liberals regained power in 1962. In the twentieth century no woman — of the thirteen sentenced to death — was sent to the gallows until 1923.[48] In the 1930s three of seven females for whom cabinet decisions were made underwent execution.[49]

In the cases of men condemned to death, the government ignored almost 25% of juries' recommendations to mercy. Future comparative studies will doubtless confirm this to be "authoritarian." Will such a rate decline significantly in a future era if capital punishment is re-instated? This is by no means certain. Canada's history has emphasized a deference to political authority; indeed, a very obvious one when compared to the United States.[50]

And it is so in the present criminal law. Using the override clause in the Charter (s. 33), Parliament alone can suspend the tyranny-defeating writ of habeas corpus, designed to test illegal detention or imprisonment, for any reason whatever or even none at all. In the United States, Congress can constitutionally suspend only during actual war or insurrection, and not always even then.[51] It is so also with respect to the law and public attitudes relating to trial by jury. In the land of our southern neighbour, there is a large academic lobby for jury nullification, another very powerful propaganda lobby and it is legally practised in two states — Indiana and Maryland. Few well-read Canadians know about it and it is illegal everywhere in this country. In the States, the double jeopardy provision of the constitution prevents any appeal of an acquittal. Here the crown can appeal not guilty verdicts for error in law.[52]

An American study demonstrates that statutes in the various states make "predatory" murder (e.g. effected during another crime such as rape or robbery and contract killings) liable to the death penalty. The same statutes do not make the most heinous of pure (non-monetary) "domestic" homicides equally liable, even though they arise from spousal battering or cold-blooded love triangle murder schemes. This is a very debatable ranking of opprobrium and works to protect more men than women from appearing on death row.[53]

A final question: would the reimposition of the death penalty revive the sham chivalry involved in protecting women as less rational than men, whether in capital prosecutions, acquittals, jury pleas for clemency and commutations? Such would deny equal treatment of similar guilt because of gender and might also give a boost to such stereotypes as being emotionally driven and dupes of men which are gradually fading. That such a result is not impossible results from female executions rates in the United States where the lobby for equal rights is much more vocal than in Canada. Since 1608 only about 500 of approximately 19,000 executions have been women, some 3%. The lethal injection given Karla Faye Tucker in early February 1999 for a double slaying by pickaxe was the first Texas execution of a female since 1863 although there were hundreds of death sentences between the two dates, and the second in the United States as a whole from 1976. Perhaps things are changing. Tucker, followed by another woman in February 2000, was in fact executed and many thought only because the Texas authorities felt obliged to show respect for gender equality on death row.[54] But two swallows do not make a summer.

The numbers of possible, probable and almost certain innocents executed rebut the common retentionist argument that fatal miscarriages of justice are almost as rare as the Dodo.[55] How fortunate it has been and will be for convicted but innocent "murderers," male and female, and society in general, that death penalties, the politics of reprieve and the demeaning "sham chivalry" of capital justice are gone.

And gone forever — we hope.

Endnotes

ENDNOTES TO THE INTRODUCTION

1 Details from the *Montreal Gazette*, 10, 12, 14, 27, 30 Sept. 1949.

2 The number has to be inexact because of the problem with pre-Confederation records. For example, Julia Murdock (Chapter 4) was unknown to scholars working in the field before our study. A case by case search of the benchbooks would have revealed her fate but such a study awaits publication. We came across a reference to her by chance when studying the Rebellions of 1837-38. We apologize to francophone readers for the fact there are no pre-Conquest studies. The reason is simple — we lacked the expertise and the resources to do the subject justice.

3 For details on earnings and prices in 1790s Lower Canada, as an example, see F. Murray Greenwood, *Legacies of Fear: Law and Politics in Quebec in the Era of the French Revolution* (Toronto: The Osgoode Society/University of Toronto Press 1993), xv.

4 See on this Leon Radzinowicz, *A History of English Criminal Law and its Administration from 1750*, vol. 1 (London: Stevens & sons 1948); Douglas Hay, "Property, Authority and the Criminal Law," in *Albion's Fatal Tree: Crime and Society in Eighteenth Century England*, ed. Douglas Hay *et al.* (London: Allen Lane 1975), 17.

5 The classic myth is of a jury who valued a £2 note as being worth thirty-nine shillings, thus making the theft non-capital.

6 For the types of cases dealt with in this paragraph, see Jerome Hall, *Theft, Law and Society* 2nd ed. (Indianapolis: Bobbs-Merritt 1952), 118-30.

7 Radzinowicz, *English Criminal Law*, 147.

8 James C. Oldham, "On Pleading the Belly: A History of the Jury of Matrons," *Criminal Justice History: An International Annual*, 6 (1985), 1-36 at 10.

9 Ibid., 33-6.

10 Ibid., 22.

11 Ibid., 19-21.

12 Judith Knelman, *Twisting in the Wind: The English Murderess and the English Press* (Toronto: University of Toronto Press 1998), 260-1, 305 nn. 13-4.

13 In *Persons Sentenced to Death in Canada, 1867-1976: An Inventory of Case Files in the Records of the Department of Justice,* eds. Lorraine Gadoury and Antonio LeChasseur (Ottawa: National Archives 1992 — hereafter ICF), the three women who successfully pled pregnancy had their death sentences commuted (nos. 0604, 0989, 1117). For a fourth case see Frank Anderson, *A Dance with Death: Canadian Women on the Gallows 1754-1954* (Calgary: Fifth House 1996), 1-6 (Sophie Boisclair).

14 Jim Phillips, "Women, Crime, and Criminal Justice in Early Halifax, 1750-1800," in Phillips, Tina Loo and Susan Lewthwaite, eds., *Essays in the History of Canadian Law (volume V): Crime and Criminal Justice* (Toronto: The Osgoode Society for Canadian Legal History 1994), 174 at 178-81. In general see also ibid., 199 n. 22.

15 J. Douglas Borthwick, *A History of the Montreal Prison from A.D. 1784 to A.D. 1886* (Montreal: A. Periard 1886), 257-66. Slightly more than half of Borthwick's list of convicts (over 250) cannot be identified by gender, mainly because of the use of initials or the omission of first names.

16 "The Lottery of Death: Capital Punishment, 1867-1976," *Manitoba Law Journal,* 23 (1996), 594 at 607.

17 For a useful synthesis of the secondary sources, see Robert B. Shoemaker, *Gender in English Society 1650-1850: The Emergence of Separate Spheres?* (London: Longman 1998), 296-304.

18 See the Supreme Court, Easter Term Rolls 1 and 3 for 8, 9 April 1768, RG 39 'J', vol. 1, pp. 52, 55 and Belcher's sentence in MG 1, vol. 1738, #111, all in the Public Archives of Nova Scotia [PANS] and the *Nova Scotia Gazette,* April 21 1768. See also Jim Phillips, "The Operation of the Royal Pardon in Nova Scotia, 1749-1815," *University of Toronto Law Journal,* 42 (1992), 401 at 437-8.

19 "Register of the Court of Quarter Session of the Peace holden in and for the District of Montreal," TL, S1, S11/00003, Archives du Québec, Montreal (Jan. 9-12 1793, 42-50); Civil Secretary Thomas A Coffin to Sheriff E.W. Gray, March 24 1794, Civil Secretary's Letter Books,

1788-1829, RG 7, G 15 C, vol. 2, National Archives of Canada [NA]; draft pardon for Campbell, Pardons, 1766-1858, RG 4, B 20, vol. 1 (341-3), NA.

20 We were unable to categorize two murders and the statistics were based on the ICF.

21 See Anderson, *Dance with Death*, 58-62.

22 See Chapter 5.

23 Transcript of Evidence, RG 13, vol. 1533.

24 Anderson, *Dance with Death*, 176-81. See also Aritha Van Herk, 'Driving Towards Death,' in Elspeth Cameron & Janice Dickin, eds., *Great Dames* (Toronto; University of Toronto Press 1997), 55-71.

25 For the United Kingdom in the nineteenth century see Knelman, *Twisting in the Wind*, ch. 7. For the eighteenth century (e.g. a girl of 16 burnt at the stake, 1738, for murdering her mistress) see Radzinowicz, *English Criminal Law*, I: 209-19; Ruth Campbell, "Sentence of Death by Burning for Women," *The Journal of Legal History*, 5 (1984), 44 at 46; Shelling A.M. Gavigan, "Petit Treason in Eighteenth Century England: Women's Inequality Before the Law," *Canadian Journal of Women and the Law*, 3 (1989-90), 335.

26 This sad tale is well told by Tom Mitchell in his "'Blood with the Taint of Cain': Immigrant Labouring Children, Manitoba Politics and the Execution of Emily Hilda Blake," *Journal of Canadian Studies*, 28 (1993-4), 49.

27 Judith A. Osborn, "The Crime of Infanticide: Throwing out the Baby with the Bathwater," *Canadian Journal of Family Law* 6 (1987) 47 at 50-1 and references therein cited; Knelman, *Twisting in the Wind*, 154-6.

28 See e.g. Constance Backhouse, "Desperate Women and Compassionate Courts: Infanticide in 19th Century Canada," *University of Toronto Law Journal*, 34 (1984), 447 at 450-3, 464; Phillips, "Royal Pardon," 436-8. Backhouse deals with four convictions in Upper Canada/Ontario. Pardons were issued in two cases; one convict escaped and the result in another case is unknown.

29 One was the case of infanticide by a grandmother (see Chapter 8): ICF, 0383, 0569, 0865, 1058, 1173, 1190, 1381.

30 For the artificial criterion of a year, see Chapter 10 and for evidence of the insanity presumption in the United Kingdom see Knelman, *Twisting in the Wind*, 70-1.

31 Borthwick, *Montreal Prison*, 261.

32 See "Memorandum for the Minister of Justice" in the case of *R v. McGee*, Sept. 9 1912 and supporting documents: RG 13, vol. 1547. See also Phillips, "Royal Pardon," 436-8; ICF, 0604 (stepdaughter).

33 *R v. Poiré, Quebec Gazette*, 2 April 1801.

34 30 Geo. III, c. 48.

35 9 Geo. IV, c. 31.

36 Thomas Laquer, "Crowds, Carnival and the State in English Executions, 1604-1868," in *The First Modern Society: Essays in English History in Honor of Lawrence Stone*, ed. A.L. Beier *et al.* (Cambridge: Cambridge University Press 1989); Louis P. Masur, *Rites of Execution: Capital Punishment and the Transformation of American Culture, 1776-1865* (Oxford: Oxford University Press 1989), ch. 2. See also the following note.

37 Arthur Koestler, *Reflections on Hanging* (London: Victor Gollancz 1956), 16.

38 *Crime and Punishment in Canada: A History* (Toronto: McClelland & Stewart 1991), 444, 523 n. 17. For a savage critique of this thinly researched and generally antiquarian book see Jim Phillips, "Recent Publications in Canadian Legal History," *Canadian Historical Review* [CHR], 78 (1997), 236 at 248-51.

39 Letter to Murray Greenwood, March 18 1996, in the author's possession.

40 At 105-11; quotation, 110.

41 *Montreal Transcript*, June 26 1858; *Montreal Weekly Gazette*, 28 June 1858; *Le Courier de Saint-Hyacinthe*, July 1 1858; Father H. Beaudry, *Précis historique de l'execution de Jean- Bapt. Desforges et de Marie-Anne Crispin*, 2nd ed. (Montreal: Louis Perrault c. 1858).

ENDNOTES TO CHAPTER ONE

1 See below for a definition and description of the rule by fishing admirals. We are deeply indebted to Jerry Banister for information in this chapter. He generously gave us his typescript of the "Proceedings of the Court of Oyer and Terminer, held on October 8 1754 by adjournment," [hereafter Keen murder trial] 1754 Assizes, GN2/1/1, pp. 171-80, Public Archives of Newfoundland [hereafter PANL]; his notes on documents in the Colonial Secretary's Letterbook

(GN2/1/A, vol. 2, 170-83); together with his article 'Surgeons and Criminal Justice in Eighteenth Century Newfoundland,' in Greg T. Smith, Allyson N. May and Simon Devereaux, eds., *Criminal Justice in the Old World and the New: Essays in Honour of J.M. Beattie* (Toronto: Centre of Criminology 1998), 104-34.

2   Anecdote based on evidence given by Dennis Hawkins, Keen Murder Trial. The story of Eleanor Power is relatively well known and varies enormously in accuracy. See, for example, Rev. Charles Pedley, *The History of Newfoundland from the Earliest Times to the Year 1860* (London: Longman et al. 1863); Paul O'Neill, *The Story of St. John's Newfoundland* 2 vols. (Erin. Ont.: Press Porcepic 1976) and "Jezebels and The Just," *Newfoundland Quarterly*. 12 (1980), 25-30, although O'Neill has Governor Bonfoy administering the island in 1705. Other accounts include M.J. McCarthy, "The Irish in Early Newfoundland," *Newfoundland Quarterly*, 83 (1988), 43-8. By far the most inaccurate is the latest (1996), Anderson's *Dance with Death*, 33-7. Anderson, as usual, has told a great story but it is, unfortunately, more legal fiction than history. As he does not document his 'facts,' it is difficult to know where he has taken them from. For example, not only has he mistaken the date of the murder, he has a supposed brother-in-law of Eleanor Power as the chief prosecution witness ("Richard Power told a hushed courtroom" ... p. 35) — a total fabrication according to the trial record.

3   See Keen's biography in *Dictionary of Canadian Biography* [DCB], III: 323-4 by Keith Matthews.

4   See O'Neill, *Seaport Legacy*, II: 553.

5   Biography of Christopher Aldridge, jr., DCB, III: 9-10.

6   *Journal of the Commissioners for Trade and Plantations from January 1754 to December 1758* (London: His Majesty's Stationery Office 1913), 44-5.

7   Pedley, *History of Newfoundland*, 87-8.

8   Evidence of Nicholas Tobin, Keen Murder Trial. Unless otherwise indicated all details of the crime are from Tobin's testimony.

9   This particular detail has fascinated all who have written on the subject. Probably Eleanor chose male clothing for ease of movement as much as camouflage. There are other examples of women donning male clothes when doing 'male' work: see, for example,

women in Upper Canada during the War of 1812 wearing buckskin trousers when taking over farming responsibilities: Robina and Kathleen Macfarlane Lizars, *Humours of '37, Grave, Gay and Grim: Rebellion Times in the Canadas* (Toronto/Montreal: W. Briggs/C.W. Coates 1897).

10 In his rather inaccurate accounting of the story in 1988, M. J. McCarthy ("The Irish in Early Newfoundland," p. 44) alleges that Eleanor "had gone off for a romp with one of the Irish soldiers," i.e. Lumley. We could find no historical basis for this claim.

11 See O'Neill, "Jezebels and the Just," p. 29. Transportation meant that a convicted person would be taken (transported) to a penal colony for a set term: usually seven or fourteen years, or for the remainder of his or her natural life.

12 O'Neill asserts that three buckles were stolen but Tobin specifically says "one single buckle": ibid. and Tobin evidence, Keen Murder Trial.

13 For further reading see Pedley, *History of Newfoundland*, Janet Paterson, 'The History of Newfoundland 1713-1763,' unpublished M.A. thesis (University of London,1931); Lounsbury, *Fishery*; C. Grant Head, *Eighteenth Century Newfoundland: A Geographer's Perspective* (Toronto: Carleton Library/McClelland & Stewart 1976); W. Gordon Handcock, *Soe longe as there comes noe women: Origins of English Settlement in Newfoundland* (St. John's: Breakwater Books 1989).

14 See references in above note and Keith Mathews, *Lectures on the History of Newfoundland 1500-1830* (St. John's: Breakwater Books 1988), 132. By far the most thorough published study of mid-eighteenth century Newfoundland population is Handcock's *Noe Women*. See especially 95-104.

15 10 & 11 Wm. III (1699), c. 25. (The charters had been issued in 1634, 1661, 1676). For further reading on the evolution of Newfoundland justice see in particular Reeves, *History of the Government of Newfoundland*; Christopher English and Christopher Curran, *Silk Robes & Sou'westers: a Cautiooooous Beginning, the Court of Civil Jurisdiction* (npp. Newfoundland Law Commission 1991); Bannister, "Surgeons and Criminal Justice."

16 Reeves, *History of the Government of the Island of Newfoundland*, 52-3, (London: J. Sewell, J Debrett, & J. Downes [1793] Johnson Reprint Corporation 1967) emphasis added.

17 See Henry Osborn's instructions, 3 June 1729, CO 5/195195, 1A-6, Public Record Office, Kew, U.K..

18 See Osborn's commission, 31 May 1729, Great Britain. Privy Council. Judicial Committee. *In the Matter of the Boundary between the Dominion of Canada and the Colony of Newfoundland on the Labrador Peninsula* (1927), Appendices, IV: 1838-40.

19 Eleven constables were also appointed for six judicial districts stretching from Bonavista to Placentia.

20 Francis Fane, counsel to the Board of Trade, to that Board, 26 April 1730, MG 11, CO 194, vol. 8, 307v-18, NA; Attorney General Philip Yorke to same, 27 April 1730, ibid., 295- 307.

21 Mathews, *Lectures*, 137.

22 Ibid.

23 English and Curran, *Silk Robes*, 25-6. In England and the Canadas defence counsel could appear with the consent of the court (seldom refused). They could argue points of law and examine/cross examine witnesses, but could not (until 1836) address the jury.

24 See e.g. the examples related to petty treason in ch. 2.

25 SN 1837, c. 4.

26 Colonial Secretaries Letterbook, vol. 2, fol. 170, GN2/1/A, PANL.

27 Keen murder trial. Unless otherwise noted all further quotations are from this source.

28 24 Geo. II, c. 37.

29 We have relied primarily on Albert Hartshorne, *Hanging in Chains*. (London: T. Fisher Unwin 1891), 15-23, 52-3, 72-81; Radzinowicz, *History of the English Criminal Law*, I: 213-20.

30 The practice was not authorized by Parliament until 1752 and then only for murder: 25 Geo. II, c. 37.

31 Quoted from Radzinowicz, *History of the English Criminal Law*, I: 218 n. 59.

32 Ibid.

33 4 & 5 Wm. IV, c. 26, ss. 1, 2.

34 Court of King's Bench (U.C.), Termbook, 1803, Archives of Ontario (AO).

35 Pedley, *History of Newfoundland*, 90.

36 *Newfoundlander*, 9 Jan. 1834; ch. 5 below; O'Neill, *Seaport Legacy*, II: 581-3.

37 Ibid.

38 Colonial Secretaries Letterbook, op. cit.

39 Frank Anderson claims this distinction for Mary and Richard Aylward of Belleville in 1862: *Dance with Death*, 214.

40 Colonial Secretaries Letterbook, op. cit. Emphasis added.

41 See text below and Bonfoy's biography, op. cit.

42 Quoted in ibid.

43 Ryder to the Duke of Bedford, 30 Jan. 1749/50, MG 11, CO 194, vol. 12, 170-5, NA.

44 Reeves, *History of the Government of Newfoundland*, pp. 115-6. Reeves (1793) refers to the past widespread assumption among Newfoundlanders that the commission was void.

45 Murray was a jurist who definitely favoured upholding the prerogative wherever possible. Lloyd's views are unknown.

46 (1697), Foster, 353; Edward Hyde East, *Pleas of the Crown* 2 vols. (London: A. Strahan 1803) I: 257.

47 Radzinowicz, *History of English Criminal Law*, I: 146 n. 26.

48 Phillips, "Royal Pardon in Nova Scotia," 430-1.

49 It is quite possible, of course, the governor might have looked upon her case in the same light as Nova Scotia's Chief Justice Jonathan Belcher viewed Margaret Whippy who had led a gang of burglars. She was condemned to the gallows for straying from the submissive roles required of women (see Introduction). But, in this case, Eleanor Power, although a leader, was not *the* leader of the first break-in. Halluran was.

50 According to M. J. McCarthy there were 2498 English inhabitants in 1627: "The Irish in Early Newfoundland," 44.

51 See references in Bonfoy's biography.

52 See his biography, DCB, III: 189. The material in this paragraph is based on McCarthy, "The Irish in Early Newfoundland."

53 See ibid., 45.

54 14 Geo. III, c. 83. It did retain the king's supremacy, allowing him to appoint bishops, for example.

55 As had Margaret Whippy, treated in the Introduction.

ENDNOTES TO CHAPTER TWO

1 Following Quebec custom, the women in this chapter are referred to by their given or "maiden" names, not those of their husbands.

2   Details on the Corriveau family are from the court martial record
    mentioned in the succeeding note and from three articles by Luc
    Lacourcière: Marie's biography in DCB, III: 142-3; "Le triple destin de
    Marie-Josephte Corriveau (1733-1763)," and "Le destin postume de
    la Corriveau," in *Les Cahiers des Dix*, 33 (1968), 239-71 and XXXIV
    (1969), 213-42 respectively.

3   To this point the musings of Father Thomas Blondeau have been
    extrapolated from the record of the trial of Joseph Corriveau for
    murder: "Copy of the Proceedings of a General Court Martial held
    at Quebec the 29th March 1763," microfilm C-12585, NA, copied
    in 1948 from the original record found in the papers of the Judge
    Advocate General, Court Martial Proceedings, WO 71/137, PRO
    (also examined). The NA copy has no pagination and all
    quotations are from it unless otherwise documented.

4   Lieutenant Governor Ralph Burton to Secretary of State Lord
    Egremont, May 21, 1763, MG 11, CO 42, vol 1, NA.

5   Unless otherwise specified, details concerning the administration
    of justice under military government are taken from Frederick
    Bernays Wiener, *Civilians Under Military Justice: The British
    Practice since 1689 Especially in North America* (Chicago/London:
    University of Chicago Press 1967), ch 2, particularly.

6   For further details see Wiener, *Civilians Under Military
    Government*, 49.

7   Amherst to Murray, Sept 23, 1760, WO 34/3/25, cited by Wiener,
    Civilians Under Military Government, 40-1.

8   Crahamé, a former army officer at the conquest of Quebec, would
    become civil secretary to Murray and General Carleton after him.
    He would become Administrator then Lieutenant Governor and
    for four years (1770-4) ran the colony. He was also responsible for
    efficiently organizing the defence of Quebec in 1775. The well born
    Saillant's clientele included many among New France's elite,
    include the Intendant Bigot. Murray continued him in the office. A
    royal notary was not restricted to practising in a single judicial
    district. For Crahamé's biography see DCB, IV: 789-83.

9   The main sources for this section are Radzinowicz, *History of English
    Criminal Law*, 209-13; Gavigan, 'Petit Treason in Eighteenth Century
    England: Women's Inequality Before the Law.'

10 See Kinda K. Kerber, *No Constitutional Right to be Ladies: Women*

and the Obligations of Citizenship (New York: Hill & Wang 1998), 13, 315 n. 30.

11 By 1790 the penalty had been reduced to forfeitures; being drawn to the place of execution on a sledge (hurdle), rather than riding on a cart; and dissection followed hanging: 30 Geo. III, c. 48. Although we know of no Canadian cases of petty treason, the following are noteworthy. In 1804, Newfoundlander Catherine Brown was charged with murdering her husband, not with the more technically correct petty treason (see Anderson, *A Dance with Death*, 146-9). It is barely conceivable the prosecutor chose murder for some reason other than ignorance. Proof, by two witnesses, as required in treason cases was available and the harsh penalty of burning had been abolished. In the 1834 trial of Catherine Snow in St. John's, Newfoundland, for killing her spouse (chapter 5), the attorney general informed the jury that Catherine and a co-accused, who had been the deceased's servant, would, if convicted, be guilty of petty treason. This was nonsense. In the United Kingdom petty treason had been entirely abolished in 1828 (9 Geo. IV. c. 31) and that abolition was part of Newfoundland's law. The attorney general probably realized his error, since neither the servant nor Snow was drawn to the place of execution on a sledge: *The Public Ledger*, 14 Jan. 1834; *The Newfoundlander*, 24 July 1834; F. Murray Greenwood and Barry Wright eds., *Canadian State Trials* (Toronto: The Osgoode Society for Canadian Legal History/University of Toronto Press 1996), 11-22, particularly 14-5.

12 Quoted in Radzinowicz, *History of English Criminal Law*, I: 211 See also 212 n. 33.

13 Quoted in Campbell's "Sentence of Death by Burning for Women," 217.

14 Although American historian Frederick Bernays Wiener, *Civilians Under Military Justice*, ch. 2 *passim.*, dealt with the issue as early as 1967, English Canadian and Quebec historians ignored this part of the saga under 1996. See Douglas Hay, "Civilians Tried in Military Courts: Quebec, 1759-64," Greenwood and Wright eds., *Canadian State Trials*, I: 4.

15 WO 71/68 136 as cited in Wiener, *Civilians Under Military Justice*, 45.

16 See Wiener, *Civilians Under Military Justice*, ch. 2.

17 For a 1990s example of this malicious falsehood being promulgated see Carrigan, *Crime and Punishment in Canada*, 249.

ENDNOTES TO CHAPTER THREE

1 C.R. Fairbanks & A.W. Cochran, *Report of the Trial of Edward Jordan and Margaret Jordan his Wife for Piracy & Murder at Halifax on the 15th Day of November 1809, together with Edward Jordan's Dying Confession: To Which is Added the Trial of John Kelly for Piracy and Murder on the 8th Day of December, 1809* (Halifax: James Bagnall at the *Novator* Office 1810) - [hereafter Jordan trial], iii. We thank Jim Phillips of the University of Toronto for suggesting this case to us and Barry Cahill of the Provincial Archives of Nova Scotia (PANS) for his considerable help with the documents.
2 Jordan Trial, iii.
3 MG 9, vol. 78, *Occasional Scrapbook*, 1: 75, PANS.
4 Particulars extrapolated from various descriptions of Jordan's appearance. See, e.g., *Nova Scotia Royal Gazette*, 10 Oct. 1809. For information on Jordan's life before the events leading to his trial, see his confession, Jordan trial, 34-6.
5 Ibid., 34.
6 We have been unable to corroborate this story from a search of available printed sources such as Daniel Gahan, *The People's Rising: Wexford 1798* (Dublin: Gill & Macmillan 1995) and Sir Richard Musgrave, *Memoir of the Irish Rebellion of 1798* 4th ed. [(eds. Steven W. Myers and Delores E. McKnight) Fort Wayne, Ind.: Round Tower 1995]. A search or the name index in the Rebellion Papers (Series 620) held by the National Archives of Ireland, Dublin, proved equally fruitless. Maybe Jordan's command was not considered noteworthy or it's conceivable (given his general veracity) that he changed his name after emigrating.
7 Margaret Jordan's statement to the court, Jordan trial, 30-1.
8 A quintal is generally reckoned as 120 fish; see ch. 1 above.
9 Evidence of John Pigot, Jordan trial, 16.
10 From this point, unless otherwise identified, quotations are from Power's testimony, Jordan trial, 20-8.
11 The sum mentioned in the trial record is £.11 (p.20), with the

contract running for slightly more than six months.

12 Pigot's testimony, Jordan trial, 16.

13 *Nova Scotia Royal Gazette*, Oct 17, Nov. 7, 1809.

14 Ibid., Nov. 7, 1809.

15 H. Gerald Stairs, *The Stairs of Halifax* (unpublished typescript 1962), 32, PANS.

16 He was tried in a court of vice-admiralty, December 8, 1809, found guilty but recommended to mercy and later pardoned: Prevost to Cecil Jenkinson, June 23, 1810, R.G. 1, vol. 58, doc. 112, PANS.

17 As authorized in 11 & 12 Wm. III, c. 7.

18 "Accounts of the Expenses attending the trial and Execution of Edward Jordan (December 15, 1809)," R.G. 5, Series A, vol. 16, doc. 81, PANS.

19 Kelly's defence statement at his trial indicated that Jordan had shot Mathews prior to the fray on the stairs, that he had later hit him on the head with a boat hook handle and that Jordan had thrown Heath and Mathews overboard. There was no suggestion that Margaret had been present then and she stated in evidence that she didn't know whether her husband had thrown them into the sea or they had fallen overboard.

20 *R v. Elizabeth Archer et al.* (1826) 1 Moody 143 (hereafter *Archer*); *R v. Thomas Cruse and Mary, his Wife* (1838) 2 Moody 53 (hereafter *Cruse*).

21 *R v. Caroubi* (1912) 76 J.P. 262 (hereafter *Caroubi*); *R v. Peel and Wife, The Times*, March 14, 15 1922 (hereafter *Peel*).

22 *A History of the Criminal Law of England*, 3 vols. (London: Macmillan & Co. 1883), II: 105- 6. See also, e.g., *Peel*.

23 See Darling J.'s judgment in *Peel*.

24 See particularly *Kenny's Outline of Criminal Law*, 18th ed. by J.W. Cecil Turner (Cambridge: Cambridge University Press 1952), 63-5.

25 See Darling J.'s judgment in *Peel* citing Robert Brooke's *Abridgement*, originally published in 1568.

26 U.K., H.L. *Parliamentary Debates*, 5th ser., vol. 50, cols. 697-706 (21 March 1922), hereafter *Parl. Deb.*, 1922.

27 Ibid., 1922, 1838.

28 *Oliver Twist*, ch. 15.

29 *History*, II: 105-6.

30 See Darling's judgment in *Peel*.

31 Canada, House of Commons, *Debates*, vol. 35, col. 2711 (May 17, 1892).

32 *Caroubi.*

33 See n. 21 above. To understand fast-posting scams see the movie *The Sting.*

34 *Parl. Deb.*, 1922. See also, e.g., case comment in *Peel* by T.C.H. in the *Cambridge Law Journal* 1 (1923), 336.

35 Criminal Justice Act, 15 & 16 Geo. V., c. 86, s. 47.

36 This paragraph is based on the jurists mentioned in the text below and the following cases: *R v. Simpson* (16 Chas. 2) Kel. 31; *R v. Ingram* (10 Anne) 1 Salk 384 (hereafter *Ingram*); *Archer*; *R v. Price* (1837) 8 C & P 10; *Cruse*; *Peel.*

37 Blackstone, *Commentaries*, IV: 28-9.

38 *History of the Pleas of the Crown*, vol. 1 (c. 1670), ed. by S. Emlyn (London: E. & R. Nutt & R. Gosling 1736), 45-7, 434, 516.

39 *Commentaries*, IV: 28-9; *A Treatise on Crimes and Indictable Misdemeanors*, 2nd ed., 2 vols (London: Joseph Butterworth and Son 1826), I: 15-6. The only example of adoption we have found is Arthur Rockman Cleveland, *Women under the English Law from the Landing of the Saxons to the Present Time* [1896] (reprint - Littleton, Colorado: Fred B. Rothman & Co. 1987), 113-4.

40 *A Treatise of the Pleas of the Crown*, vol. 1 [1716] (reprint - London: Professional Books 1973), ch. 1, ss. 9-12.

41 Russell adopted it. The court in *R v. Mary Buncombe* (1845) 1 Cox C.C. 183 thought it an open question, but did not decide the point. Stephen, *History*, II: 105-6, suggested robbery was "probably" exempted. Robbery as an exemption was explicitly denied by the recorder of London in a robbery with violence case, *R. v. Martha Torpey* (1871) 12 Cox C.C. 45 and by Cleveland, *Women under the English Law*, 113-4.

42 *Commentaries*, IV: 28-9. The only adoption we found was by Russell (n. 39 above).

43 *Cruse* at 57; *Peel*; case comment on *Peel*, n. 35 above.

44 There is an ambiguous judicial statement in *R v. Samuel Smith and Sarah Smith* (1858) Dears & Bell 553, which could be used as an argument to the contrary. However, acquittals of a wife proved to have personally used violence were gained in *Ingram* (assault), a century before the *Jordans'* case.

45   Nov. 20, 1809.

ENDNOTES TO CHAPTER FOUR

1   Details of the crime are taken from the *Toronto Patriot*, Aug 18., 21, 24, Nov. 28, 1837; John Beverley Robinson's Benchbook (Home District, March-April, October-November 1837), Supreme Court of Ontario Judges Benchbooks, Assizes 1835-1842, RG 22-390, Box 23, AO. Unless otherwise stated, all quotations concerning the crime and trial are from the November 24 issue of the *Patriot*.

2   Details of the inquest are from the *Chronicle & Gazette and the Kingston Commercial Advertiser*, Aug. 23, 1837, copying or paraphrasing a story from the *Toronto Commercial Herald*.

3   *York Commercial Directory, Street Guide and Register, 1833/4* (York, U.C.: Thomas Dalton 1834). We found in this and other directories no mention of Mrs. Dunlop or the Henrys. However it seems she lived close to Nathan Phillip Square. Upper George Street ran from Newgate Street (nearly opposite the jail) to Richmond Street and is now Victoria Street.

4   *Toronto Patriot*, Aug. 18, 1837.

5   Assize Minutebooks, Criminal, 1832-1837, RG 22-134-6, AO.

6   For further information see Sherwood's biography in DCB, VIII: 796-801. How Murdock managed to afford Sherwood or if he represented her free of charge has to be a matter of conjecture.

7   *Twisting in the Wind: The Murderess and the English Press* (Toronto, Buffalo and London: University of Toronto Press 1998). Details about arsenic and quotation are from 51.

8   This list is taken from Paul Romney's biography of Widmer in DCB, VIII: 931-5. Unless otherwise cited, all details about Widmer are from this source.

9   Unfortunately the *Patriot*, while devoting columns to the medical evidence, did not cite this legal evidence.

10 George W. Spragge, ed., "A Letter from Government House, Toronto, December 1837," *Ontario History*, 51 (1959), 234-5. For identification of the writer see Ged Martin, "Sir Francis Bond Head: The Private Side of a Lieutenant-Governor," *Ontario History* 73 (1981), 155, 168 n. 55.

11 An intriguing connection though can be made from the 1894

recollections of a Thomas Anderson concerning the 1837 rebellion published by J. Ross Robertson (*Robertson's Landmarks of Toronto: A Collection of Historical Sketches of the Old Town of York...* [Toronto: J. Ross Robertson 1894]). He reportedly stated (228-9): "The rebels were to meet over my store on the Monday before the fight at Montgomery's, but there was a girl hanged in front of the jail on Toronto street that day and there was such a crowd in town that the arrangement fell through." While Anderson was clearly wrong on dates, the connection of Mackenzie's rising and Murdock's execution was firmly implanted in his mind more than half a century after the event. Anderson claimed credit for digging up the bodies of Lount and Mathews to put a marble in Lount's coffin for the purpose of later identification (229).

12 William Kilbourn, *The Firebrand: William Lyon Mackenzie and the Rebellion in Upper Canada* (Toronto: Clarke, Irwin 1956), ch. 13.

13 See Knelman, *Twisting in the Wind, passim.*

14 Dec. 20, 1837, as paraphrased or quoted in the *Montreal Gazette*, Jan. 2, 1838.

15 Two other much less inflammatory accounts claimed Henry had died, "the victim of disease, caused by intemperance." See the *Patriot*, Dec. 19, 1837; *Kingston Chronicle and Gazette*, Dec. 23, 1839.

16 Dec. 20, 1837. The *Patriot* (Dec. 19, 1837) reported that in her last moments, Murdock was attended "by a British Wesleyan Minister."

17 See n. 14 above.

18 *Les Anciens Canadiens* [1863] (Quebec: Librairie Beauchemin 1899), 216-8, translation Greenwood. The assumption about the past was more than folkloric myth.

19 Arlette Farge (trans. Carol Shelton), *Fragile Lives: Violence, Power and Solidarity in Eighteenth-Century Paris* (Oxford/Cambridge: Polity Press/Blackwell Publishers 1993), 186.

20 Dec. 12, 1862.

21 Dec. 10, 1862. The *Chronicle* was a decided advocate of abolishing public executions.

22 Aug. 3, 1838. Psychological factors affecting female spectators and male censurers will be dealt with in the Conclusion.

23 The leading scholarly work on the early English criminal jury is no help here, stating only that "juries sometimes convicted with a recommendation for mercy": Thomas Andrew Green, *Verdict*

According to Conscience: Perspectives on the English Criminal Trial Jury 1200- 1800 (Chicago: University of Chicago Press 1985), 282.

24 *St. Catherine's Journal*, Aug. 16, 1838.

25 Green, *Verdict According to Conscience*, 282, nn. 48-9 cites three instances from 1750-1, but makes no mention of the judges' all important sentiments nor of the results. For two cases of English women being executed despite jury pleas (1848, 1849), see Knelman, *Twisting in the Wind*, 134-6, 192.

26 J. Douglas Borthwick, *A History of the Montreal Prison from A.D. 1784 to A.D. 1886* (Montreal: A Periard 1886), 257-62. There were only one dwelling house theft, one definite pickpocketing and three shoplifting executions, 1812-38 in the Montreal District, but sixteen for cattle/horse stealing and eleven for burglary. Robbery and forgery were the other serious property crimes.

27 Constance Backhouse, *Petticoats and Prejudice: Women and Law in Nineteenth Century Canada* (Toronto: The Osgoode Society for Canadian History History/University of Toronto Press 1991), 112-24.

28 Arthur to Durham, Sept. 29, 1838, as paraphrased in *Report of the Public Archives of Canada*, 1923, 120. The original seems to have disappeared or been misplaced in the Durham Papers held by the NA.

29 *R v. Despard et al.* (1803) 28 St. Tr. 345 at 524, 528.

30 See reference in n.1 above.

31 Anderson, *Dance with Death*, 211-14. The couple had been convicted of fatally shooting an armed and threatening neighbour on their farm. See ch. 5 below.

32 Knelman, *Twisting in the Wind*, 181-2.

33 Ibid.

34 Ibid., *passim.*, but particularly 93-101, 111-20.

35 7 & 8 Geo. IV, c. 29; 2 & 3 Wm. IV, c. 62. Dwelling house larceny ceased to be capital for Upper Canada in 1833: SUC 1833, c. 3.

36 In almost all cases the executioner strangled the convict to death before the burning began. In 1790 (30 Geo. III, c. 48) the penalty was changed to being drawn on a hurdle (prescribed for traitors, rather than a cart) to the place of execution, hanging and dissection. For petit treason see ch. 2 and Radzinowicz, *History of England Criminal Law*, I: 209-13.

37 9 Geo. IV, c. 31, s. 2; SUC 1833, c. 4, s. 3.

ENDNOTES TO CHAPTER FIVE

1   See Carolyn Strange, "Wounded Womanhood and Dead Men: Chivalry and the Trials of Clara Ford and Carrie Davies," in Franca Iacovetta and Mariana Valverde, eds., *Gender Conflicts: New Essays in Women's History* (Toronto: University of Toronto Press 1992).

2   Our principal sources are the comprehensive report of Judge Galt to the Secretary of State, Jan.8, 1917, R.G. 13, vol. 1472, file 584A/CC4, 1916-24, NA, and the office report of the Department of Justice, Jan. 31, 1917, ibid.

3   Harold Maulson to Judge Galt, Dec. 16, 1916, ibid. According to this letter Hamilton told Maulson that he had once told Teenie "that he had no intention to marry at least while his mother lived." This strengthening of motive did not affect Galt's lenient report on the trial.

4   Chief of Remissions Branch to Governor General Byng, Jan. 22, 1924, ibid.

5   Quoted in Koestler, *Reflections on Hanging*, 111.

6   Ibid., 113.

7   *Twisting in the Wind*, 182-8.

8   Ibid., 131-2; R.T. Paget & S.S. Silverman, *Hanged - and Innocent?* (London: Victor Gollancz 1953), 115-253; Syd Dernley with David Newman, *The Hangman's Tale: Memoirs of a Public Executioner* (London: Pan Books 1989), 70-82.

9   *Dance with Death*, 100-5; 211-4

10 Our principal source is the multi-columned trial report in the *Newfoundlander* of Jan. 23, 1834. Other sources are given in the notes. The two secondary accounts are riddled with errors. Anderson, for example, has Snow escape hanging in chains only because of a quick burial by her priests, while O'Neill (*A Seaport Legacy*, II: 583-5) gets the execution date wrong, among other facts.

11 *The Public Ledger*, Jan. 14, 1834; *Newfoundlander*, Jan. 16, 1834.

12 Sept. 12, 1833.

13 Jan. 16, 1834.

14 *Newfoundlander*, July 24, 1834; *The Public Ledger*, July 11, 22, 1834.

15 *A Seaport Legacy*, 571.

16 The issue of Oct. 31, 1862 contains the trial report. That of December 12, 1862, the execution and ancillary related material.

17 For the report see Oct. 29, 1862; for the execution, Dec. 10, 1862.

18 *Chronicle*, Dec. 10, 1862; *Intelligencer*, Dec. 12, 1862. Richard Aylward concurred with the letter written only to the eldest daughter signed before four witnesses. The letter to all the daughters is much more detailed. Both were written in jail, Dec. 6, 1862.

19 10 Cl. And F. 200.

20 Rev. 4th ed. (St. Paul, Minn.: West Publishing Co. 1968), 934-5.

21 *Intelligencer*, Dec. 12, 1862.

22 See Boyd, *Last Dance*, 3; 61-2. See also pp. 498-506 of the trial report, RG 13, vol. 1566-7, file CC 337, NA; judgment of the Supreme Court of Canada, ibid; Judge Nicol Jeffrey's report to the Minister of Justice, March 3, 1931, ibid., 3, 6-7, 10; and J. Phillips Jones (General secretary of the Social Service Council of Canada) to the Minister of Justice, June 16, 1931, Steinberg Capital Case File; William P. Krug (Mayor of Chesley, where Steinberg lived for many years as a respectable merchant) to the Minister of Justice, June 29, 1931, ibid. Steinberg was probably executed because of anti-Semitism, not proof of guilt. Other cases studied are at pp. 32-9 (Wilbert Coffin, 1956); 107-11 (John Davidoff, 1951); 111-21 (Bobby Cook, 1960).

23 NW 2397 R 5, file #116208, Pre-Emption Record, GR 112, vol. 217, Archives of B.C. Unless otherwise indicated, all information on Elizabeth Coward comes from her capital case file, R.G. 13, vol. 1485 (1.1, 1.2), vol. 1486 (2.1, 2.2), file 555A/C56, NA.

24 Again her belief was based simply on a piece of paper shown to her by Coward.

25 There was never any doubt Elizabeth loved her children. When she and James left for B.C., they placed the younger ones into the care of the local equivalent of the children's aid society, planning to bring them to Canada as money became available.

26 The matter was only settled when the Hudson's Bay storekeeper paid the men in August to rid himself of the problem.

27 Evidence of John Roberts.

28 At the post-mortem Dr. William Stone from Vanderhoof found that the bullet had gone "in at the left nostril, penetrating the base of the brain and severing the upper part of the brain from the lower" (from his evidence at the Coward trial).

29 Raynor had been with the Provincial Police Force a mere eighteen months.

30 Such testing should have been possible. Scotland Yard had virtually perfected fingerprinting during the first decade of the century and ballistic testing had played a huge role in a Canadian trial twenty years earlier. See Carolyn Strange, "Wounded Womanhood and Dead Men," 149-88 at 165 on the Clara Ford trial.

31 In interviews long after the completion of the case, Dunwoody would gloat at his own cleverness, embellishing the story to appear a hero. See for example, Cecil Carl, *Tales of the British Columbia Provincial Police* (Sidney, B.C.: Gray's 1971), 109-116. Due to freedom of information practice of the Archives of B.C. I was unable to examine any police records, including such innocuous files as those for car maintenance in 1916. Any self-respecting researcher should be outraged at the interpretation this holder of public records has placed on the Freedom of Information Act.

32 Thanks to Patricia Kennedy of the National Archives for pointing this out.

33 Bird had previously represented the would-be Punjabi immigrants on the *Komagata-Moru* and would unsuccessfully sponsor an Asian for admittance to the B.C. bar in 1918. On the latter see Joan Brockman, "Exclusionary Tactics: Women and Visible Minorities in the Legal Profession in British Columbia," in Hamar Foster & John McLaren, eds., *Essays in the History of Canadian Law (vol. V): British Columbia and the Yukon* (Toronto: The Osgoode Society for Canadian Legal History/University of Toronto Press 1995), 520-1.

34 Rose Thibault to the Minister of Justice, May 21, 1918. After the death sentence was passed, Elizabeth claimed to have been pregnant. An examination was ordered but it became obvious before one could be made that she was not "in the family way."

35 The sources for the Pitre case are the trial judge's report (n.d.); the judgments in appeal; Department of Justice memoranda (for the minister, Dec. 27, 1952; solicitor general, Dec. 31 1952 and a "Condensed Summary" of the proof in court, n.d.) from R.G. 13, C-1, vol. 1695, 1.1, 2.1.

36 Montreal *Herald*, Jan. 9 1953.

37 *Kingston Chronicle*, Dec. 23, 1837.

38 Sherwood's biography, DCB, VIII: 796-801.

39 On Front Street: *York Commercial Directory*.

40 Nov. 22, 1837.

ENDNOTES TO CHAPTER SIX

1 Carolyn Strange, *Qualities of Mercy: Justice, Punishment and Discretion* (Vancouver: UBC Press c. 1996).

2 Karen Dubinsky and Franca Iacovetta,"Murder, Womanly Virtue, and Motherhood: The Case of Angelina Napolitano, 1911-1922," *CHR*, 72 (1991), 505; Constance Backhouse, *Petticoats and Prejudice: Woman and Law in Nineteenth-Century Canada* (Toronto: The Osgoode Society/Women's Press 1992), 112-24; Tom Mitchell, "'Blood with the Taint of Cain': Immigrant Labouring Children, Manitoba Politics, and the Execution of Emily Hilda Blake," *Journal of Canadian Studies*, 30 (1993), 30.

3 Phillips, "Women, Crime and Criminal Justice in Early Halifax" and "The Operation of the Royal Pardon in Nova Scotia, 1749-1815," 401; Strange, "Lottery of Death;" Strange, "Discretionary Justice: Political Culture and the Death Penalty in New South Wales and Ontario, 1890-1920," in her *Qualities of Mercy*, 130. The four remaining studies are: Jonathan Swainger, "A Distant Edge of Authority: Capital Punishment and the Prerogative of Mercy in British Columbia, 1872-1880," in Hamar Foster & John McLaren, *Essays in the History of Canadian Law: British Columbia and the Yukon* (Toronto: The Osgoode Society/University of Toronto Press 1995); Tina Loo, "Savage Mercy: Native Culture and the Modification of Capital Punishment in Nineteenth-Century British Columbia," in *Qualities of Mercy*, 104; Strange, "Introduction," ibid., 3; Barry Wright, "'Harshness and Forbearance': The Politics of Pardons and the Upper Canada Rebellion," ibid., 77.

4 Phillips, "Operation of the Royal Pardon," 436-9; Strange, "Lottery of Death;" Strange, "Discretionary Justice," 151-3.

5 "Lottery of Death."

6 Basing ourselves on the carefully compiled inventory to the capital case files (see Introduction), we find that only 11 of the 57 convicted women were hanged, a rate of 19.3%.

7 "The Royal Pardon and Criminal Procedure in Early Modern England," *Historical Papers*, 9 (1987), 21. See also Phillips's comments (nn. 3 and 4 above).

8 The only woman in Canada known to have been even arrested for treason was Mrs. Thomas Walker in 1775.

9 Radzinowicz, *A History of English Criminal Law*, I: 150-7.

10 U.K., House of Commons, *Parliamentary Debates*, 5th series, vol. 117 (hereafter Parl. Deb., 1919), col. 387 (Captain Elliott, 25 Oct. 1919).

11 She also quoted the proponent of the motion to abolish capital punishment (Mr. Robert Bickerdike, M.P. for Montreal, St. Lawrence) to this effect: "I cannot believe it possible that a man who is a man would stand for hanging a woman or a child, and I do not think that any of those who have spoken today would do so." Not everyone shared the chivalrous sentiments of Bickerdike and Laurier. The M.P. for West Peterborough, J.H. Burnham, stressed the new ideal of sexual equality: "since men and women are [soon] to be the same electoral entities, they must appear before the law on an equal footing without distinction in every possible case. This is one of them. If I am liable to be hanged, my wife, if I have one, must be liable also": Canada, House of Commons, *Debates* (19 April 1917), 626. Even Laurier would not change the law on point, since he recalled a Quebec case where an "awful murder" had been committed by a woman and a young boy, with the woman being "the more guilty": ibid., (s.d.), 622.

12 *English History 1914-1945* (Oxford: Clarendon Press 1965), 38.

13 Ibid. Taylor notes that such miscellaneous jobs as tramway and bus conductors and Y.M.C.A. workers were largely taken over by women. The number of domestic servants, mainly women, dropped by 400,000.

14 For two good examples, of countless ones, see ibid., 94; Parl. Deb., 1919, col. 1293 (Mr. Spoor, July 4, 1919).

15 The Representation of the People Act (1918), 7 & 8 Geo. V, c. 64, s. 4; Parliament (Qualification of Women Act), 8 & 9 Geo. V, c. 47, s. 1.

16 See Chapter 3 on Margaret Jordan, who probably would have been convicted in Halifax of piracy (1809) except for the presumption.

17 9 & 10 Geo. V, c. 71.

18 For examples, women were already able to practise as doctors and solicitors.

19 Parl. Deb. 1919, cols. 382-90.

20 Ibid., cols. 343-4.

21 SA 1921, c. 8, ss. 3, 5, 17; SA 1966, c. 45, s.5.

22 David Ricardo Williams. *Just Lawyers: Seven Portraits* (Toronto: The Osgoode Society 1995), 179. Macgill was named to the juvenile court.

23 Elsie Gregory Macgill, *My Mother the Judge: A Biography of Judge Helen Gregory Macgill* (Toronto: Ryerson Press 1955). For her influence with Farris see 155-7.

24 *The Daily Colonist* (Victoria), 15 Dec. 1922. The statute is SBC 1922, c. 38.

25 This and the next paragraph are based on Catherine Cleverdon, *The Woman Suffrage Movement in Canada* 2nd ed. (Toronto: University of Toronto Press 1974), *passim*. but particularly 58, 60, 93, 111-5, 133.

26 *Daily Colonist*, Dec. 15, 1922.

27 University Women's Club, Add. Mss. 872, vol. 1-2, Minutes, Vancouver City Archives. Vol. 8, file 100, Misc, notes that "Judge Helen Greg. MacGill [sic] made Convenor of Better Laws for Women & Children — at that time laws passed in the reign of Chas. II were in force. With her leadership and co-operation with other women's organization the following Acts were passed" — Equal Guardianship; Minimum wage; Mother's Pension; Family Maintenance; and the age of marriage was raised from 12 and 14 to 16 and 18 for females and males respectively. The Vancouver Council of Women's minutes are preserved in U.B.C.'s Special Collections, box 6, nos. 6-8.

28 Dec. 15, 1922; Dec 16,. 1922.

29 Dec. 17, 1922.

30 Among those pages four were devoted specifically to B.C. legislation: 853, 858-61.

31 See e.g., RSNS 1884, c. 106, ss. 1-5.

32 *Edwards et al. v. AG Canada et al.* (1930) A.C. 124 (Lord Sankey for the Board).

33 Canada, House of Commons, *Debates*, vol. 2, 1972, col. 1723 (Grace MacInnes, April 28, 1972).

34 The provinces had been empowered by the BNA Act [s. 92 (14)] to legislate regarding the constitution of provincial courts with Parliament empowered to regulate "Procedure in criminal matters." In case of conflict federal law would prevail.

35 Cleverdon, *Suffrage Movement*, 56.

36 Ibid., 212.

37 Canada, Senate, *Debates*, 1970-2, I: 465.

38 Canada, House of Commons, *Debates*, 1948, IV: 3829-37, quotation at 3830.

39 Appeals to the decentralizing Judicial Committee of the Privy

Council were abolished in 1947; Newfoundland joined Canada in 1949 without consultation with the provinces; and public hospital insurance was instituted in 1951.

40 SS 1950, c. 23, ss. 3, 4.
41 SS 1947, c. 35. The same province, three years earlier, enacted the first Bill of Rights in Canada, although it did not deal with gender equity.
42 Ontario's "Newspaper Hansard," 1951, microfilm reel 25, A-5 to A-10; reel 26 (March 21) B- 1 to D-1, National Library of Canada.
43 SO 1951, c. 41, ss. 1, 3, 4, 8.
44 SM 1952, c. 37, ss. 2, 4; SNB 1954, c. 50, s. 1.
45 SPEI, 1966, c. 22, ss. 1, 2; OY 1961, c. 1, s. 1; ONWT, 1965, c. 6, s.1. For Alberta see n. 21 above.
46 "Women on Juries," *Alberta Law Review*, 12 (1979), 321.
47 (1915), 47 S.C. 131. Like Quebec and Nova Scotia, the two territories went at once from ineligibility to equality. It must also be said that for one halcyon period (1791 to 1834, perhaps even to 1849) Quebec's women meeting property criteria arguably possessed the right to vote and did actually vote, occasionally in large numbers. Ironically, it was the so-called "democrat" Louis-Joseph Papineau who in 1834 attempted to reduce these women to the status of non-persons.
48 SBC 1964, c. 26, s. 5. For the territories see references in n. 46 above.
49 Canada, Senate, *Debates*, 1970-1972, II: 1007-8 (19 May 1971). For the American experience see reference in Linda K. Kerber, *No Constitutional Right to be Ladies: Women and the Obligations of Citizenship* (New York: Hill & Wang 1998), 124-220. In Tennessee, for example, virtually all women in the 1960s and early 1970s opted out (pp. 207, 359 nn. 266-7).
50 *Report of the Royal Commission on The Status of Women in Canada* (Ottawa: Information Canada 1970), 343-4.
51 SA 1971, c. 56, s. 2; SO 1972, c. 112, s. 3.
52 Canada, Senate, *Debates*, 1970-1972, I: 465-6 (3 Feb. 1971, Thérèse Casgrain).
53 SQ 1971, c. 15, s. 2.
54 SN 1971, c. 76, ss. 13, 14.
55 Canada, Senate, *Debates*, 1970-1972, I: 465-6.
56 Ibid., I: 742-6 (March 23, 1971).
57 Ibid., 1963, 294-5 (July 18, 1963). See also pp. 391-2.
58 Ibid., 1970-1972, I: 804-7 (March 30, 1971).

59 Ibid., II: 990-2; 1002 (May 18, 1971); 1007-8 (May 19, 1971); 1010-1 (May 25, 1971); 1241 (June 30, 1971; 1254-5 (Sept. 15, 1971).

60 Canada, House of Commons, *Debates*, 1971-2, VIII, Sept. 21, 1971.

61 Ibid., 1972, II: 1698-1819, *passim*; III: 2328-34.

62 SC 1972, c. 13, s. 46.

63 SM 1972, c. 56, s. 1; SNB 1972, c. 40, s. 1A; SS 1973, c. 50, s. 2.

64 SPEI 1980, c. 30, s. 4; SN 1980, c. 47, ss. 4, 7, 41 (took effect in 1981).

65 Kerber, *No Constitutional Right*, 124-220.

66 See Chapter 9 for a full treatment of this case.

67 Loo, "Savage Mercy," 108, 112; Strange, "Discretionary Justice," 151; *Sarnia Observer*, April 18, 1873 and CCF, vol. 1410, passim. (both re Elizabeth Workman's case); Boyd, *Last Dance*, 27.

68 See e.g. CCF for Napolitano.

69 See e.g. PC 3007 in the Elizabeth Coward CCF file.

70 R.G. 13, vol. 1638 (1.1, 1.2, 2), file CC 548. The prisoner was executed.

71 See below for a brief description.

72 R.G. 13, vol. 1411, file 81A. For a clear English example see Koestler, *Reflections on Hanging*, 122.

73 We ignored rape, piracy and attempted murder as no one was executed for these crimes in the period. There were 38 convictions (all male) for the "minor" capital crimes, but no executions. It is clear juries found the death penalty excessive for these offences. In the thirty-four cases where we know the recommendation, fully twenty-two were recommended to mercy, a rate just under 65%. Rape had ceased to be *mandatorily* capital in 1873. The presiding judge could sentence to death or to life imprisonment or a jail term of seven years or more: SC 1873, c. 94. During the period specified, there were twenty-six men capitally convicted of rape, only three of them after 1873 and one in 1873. We also excluded cases where the accused died in jail, had his/her conviction quashed on appeal and/or was granted a new trial resulting in no capital conviction or where the penal result was not established and numerous cases where the compilers of the inventory were unable to determine one way or the other whether the jury had recommended mercy. Carnal knowledge of a girl under ten years was capital until 1877: SC 1877, c. 28, ss. 1-2. No one was convicted of this crime in the Dominion when it carried the death penalty. The sentence for attempted murder and carnal knowledge were set at two to life and five to life respectively. Burglary had ceased

to be capital for the United Canada in 1865 (SPC 1865, c. 13) and for the whole Dominion in 1869 (SC 1868, c. 21, s. 51). Why the compilers included three convictions for burglary in P.E.I., 1876 (nos. 896-7, 910) remains a mystery.

74 This is not at all to minimize the judge's position, as a full investigation would undoubtedly show. In Annie Robinson's case, Chapter 8 below, the Justice Department's recommendation of mercy relied on the judge's recommendation, not that of the jury or its manifest reluctance to convict.

75 Before beginning our research we knew about the Despard and Louis Riel (1885) precedents and that was it. Riel appears to have been the only convicted traitor felon or traitor executed in Canada despite a jury recommendation for mercy.

76 *Sarnia Observer*, April 18, 1873; CCF, vol. 1410; Chapter 7 below.

77 For Gallien, see n. 73 above; and for Poulin, R.G. 13, vol. 1411, file 83A. At the time of the trial, though, Poulin was pregnant.

78 Oct. 23, 1915.

79 Letters dated 30 May, 6 June 1911 respectively: R.G. 13, vol. 2698 (1, 2, 3, 4, 5) file 446A/CC22. Napolitano was also pregnant at the time of the trial.

80 Nov. 23, 1915, Coward CCF.

81 Oct. 8, 1915, ibid.

82 Ibid.

ENDNOTES TO CHAPTER SEVEN

1 Quotations taken from Lee Stuesser, "The 'Defence' of 'Battered Woman Syndrome' in Canada," (1990) 19 Man. L.J., 195 at 196.

2 *R v. Lavellee* (1988), 52 Man. R. (2d); 274 (Man. C.A.); *R. v. Lavallee* [1990] 1 S.C.R. 852, 55 C.C.C. (3d) 97. For readings on the case and further comment see below at nn. 47-8.

3 Details as to the Workman case are taken from her Capital Case file, R.G. 13, vol. 1410, file 64A, 1873. The quotation in this sentence comes from Mr. Justice Adam Wilson in his letter to the Secretary of State, Toronto, May 8, 1873. Unless otherwise acknowledged, all further quotations and references are from this file.

4 *Twisting in the Wind*, 42, 105-7, 122.

5   *Principles of Punishment,* quoted from by Nancy Tomes, "A 'Torrent of Abuse': Crimes of Violence between Working-class Men and Women in London, 1840-1875," *Journal of Social History,* 11 (1977-8), 328 at 339.

6   Elizabeth Pleck, *Domestic Tyranny: The Making of Social Policy against Family Violence from Colonial Times to the Present* (New York/Oxford: Oxford UP 1987), 84.

7   Linda Gordon, *Heroes of their Own Times: The Politics and History of Family Violence, Boston 1880-1960* (New York: Viking 1988), 257.

8   Harvey, "Wife-battering in Montreal," 134, 137-8. See n. 36 below for full reference.

9   Terry L. Chapman, "'Till Death do us Part': Wife Beating in Alberta, 1905-1920," *Alberta History,* 36 (1988), 13 at 18-20.

10 16 Vict. c. 30.

11 41 Vict. c. 19, s. 4.

12 Tomes, "Torrent of Abuse," 339-40.

13 Elizabeth Pleck, "Wife Beating in Nineteenth-Century America," *Victimology: An International Journal,* 4 (1979), 60, *passim.* but particularly 64-72.

14 *Heroes of their Own Times,* 254-5.

15 See references in nn. 5-9 above.

16 Harvey, "Wife Battering in Montreal," 135-6. See n. 36 below for full reference.

17 Judith Fingard. *The Dark Side of Life in Victorian Halifax* (Porter's Lake, Nova Scotia: Pottersfield Press 1989), 171-85, particularly at 175-7.

18 Ibid.

19 SC 1909, c. 9, "Schedule." This became paragraph c) to s. 292 of the Criminal Code dealing with indecent assaults, originally enacted in 1890 (c. 37, s. 12).

20 Criminal Code of 1892, s. 262; Offences Against the Person Act, SC 1869, c. 20, s. 14; RSC 1886, c. 162, s. 35.

21 See Chapman, *op. cit.,* 20.

22 Quoted in Stoddard, *op. cit.,* 23-4.

23 Ibid., 28-30.

24 See references in nn. 5-9 above.

25 Jan. 4, 1999.

26 Details on the murder taken from the trial record, Workman Capital Case file, ibid.

27 For his biography see DCB, XII: 1107-8. As a notable politician, Wilson had a long Liberal history. From the two criminal trials we studied (Mary Aylward and Elizabeth Workman) we suspect he had little sympathy for poor, rather distasteful female defendants.

28 See n. 33 below, ch. 1.

29 Dubinsky and Iacovetta, "The Case of Angelina Napolitano," 165-8.

30 Quoted in ibid., 167.

31 On the day of his death, Pietro tried to force his pregnant wife into prostitution, threatening that if she did not hand over her earnings from the bed, he would kill her and take the children. Britton completely ignored this: ibid., 165-6.

32 See ch. 9.

33 Edward Stoddard, *Conflicting Images: the Murderess and the English Canadian mind, 1870-1915* [(M.A. thesis, Dalhousie University) Ottawa: National Library of Canada 1991], 25-8.

34 Unless otherwise specified, the following analysis of the evidence is based on material found in Workman's Capital Case file.

35 Such as a crown attorney, four barristers (including Mackenzie), four solicitors, a doctor, the M.P.P., the mayor of Sarnia, various clergymen and merchants.

36 On the basis of "reliable information from people living in St. Mary's," the *Sarnia Observer* (Apr. 18, 1873) reported him "often coming home [there] in a state of intoxication, and dragging his wife out of bed, and forcing her to give him the pittance she had earned by washing during the day, so that he might spend it in liquor." In her study, "To Love, Honour and Obey: Wife-battering in Working-Class Montreal, 1869-79," *Urban History Review* 19 (1990-1) 128] Kathryn Harvey speculated (p. 131) that it likely "enraged wives to be excluded from sharing in the all important decision on how a husband's wage was to be spent." How much more might they have been seething mad if their own earnings were forcibly taken for drink, when the family was in want?

37 May 8, 1873.

38 After all, Butler was often asked in for drinks and leaving at 4:00 a.m. is not necessarily damning.

39 The *Sarnia Observer* reported (Nov. 1, 1872) that "according to

common report, an intimacy at once sprang up between him [Butler] and Mrs. Workman, which was the subject of free comment among the neighbors."

40 7, 16-7, 88-9, quotation at 89.

41 These are taken from the ICF. In the last century (1867-1900) three of six women who murdered their husbands were hanged, well over the general execution rate for females. But fourteen of the twenty-three convicted wife killers (60.87%) also suffered execution. Taking the sample down to 1962, the last year when capital punishment was used, the executed were: i) husband killers, eight out of twenty (40%); ii) wife killers, sixty-four out of 126 (50.8%). Such numbers give no warrant for transference. When the six nineteenth century convicted husband killers are compared with other female murderers, however, a different picture emerges. Only two of these had juries urging clemency while five of the eight 'others' received recommendations of clemency. Overall, 1867-1962, nine of twenty-one husband killers (47.37%) received jury pleas; fully fourteen of twenty-two of the others (63.63%) were so favoured. Half of the six husband killers prior to 1900 were executed; only one of the eight other females capitally convicted met that fate. In total, the first group (husband killers) was hanged at a rate of 40% (eight of twenty); the second, that is, other female murderers, at a rate of a mere 17.39% (4 of 23).

42 This contrast obviously suggests further research needs to be undertaken, but such is outside the compass of this book.

43 See e.g. Knelman, *Twisting in the Wind*, 260.

44 See *Prosper* v. *R.* (1994) 92 C.C.C. (3d) 353; *R* v. *Matheson* (1994) ibid., 545. These cases held that the provinces did not have to provide free counsel service for persons detained outside regular business hours. Chief Justice Lamer, for the majority in *Prosper* (p. 373) stated: "To be absolutely clear, the issue of whether the Charter guarantees a right to state-funded counsel *at trial* and *on appeal* does not arise here."

45 Alexander Mackenzie to Sir John A. Macdonald, May 28, 1873, CCF for Elizabeth Workman,

46 See e.g. Knelman, *Twisting in the Wind*, 238-9.

47 (1990) 55 C.C.C. (3d) 97. The decision written by Madame Justice Bertha Wilson was entirely concurred with by five of the seven judges and in substance by Sopinka J. The decision followed the lead of the

American courts beginning about a decade earlier. For useful commentary on the case see particularly Martha Shaffer, "R. v. Lavallee: a Review Essay," *Ottawa Law Review*, 22 (1990), 607; Donna Martinson *et al.*, "A Forum on Lavallee v. R.: Women and Self-defence," *University of British Columbia Law Review*, 25 (1991), 23; Patricia Kazan, "Reasonableness, Gender Difference, and Self-defence Law," *Manitoba Law Journal*, 24 (1997), 549.

48 *The Battered Woman* (New York: Harper & Row 1979) and especially *The Battered Woman Syndrome* (New York: Springer Publishing Co. 1984). See the case report at 117-24.

49 Ibid. at 103.

50 *Sarnia Observer*, June 23, 1873.

ENDNOTES TO CHAPTER EIGHT

1 Testimony of Ernest Albert Wright, Robinson Capital Case file, RG 13, vol. 1484, CC 49. This chapter is based almost exclusively on this file and unless otherwise indicated all information and quotations are from it. Wright's testimony is from part 2.

2 In 1909 John was the oldest at twenty; then Jessie aged nineteen; Ellen, seventeen; Tom, sixteen, Maggie, fourteen; Katie, twelve, Annie, nine; William Henry, eight, Martha, six and George, four. George was Ellen's child born in 1906.

3 The girls slept in a combination bedroom-kitchen-living room the youngest sons and the older boys slept outside.

4 Crown Attorney J.H. Clary to Minister of Justice, October 11, 1909.

5 Ibid.

6 Although Jessie and Ellen would also simultaneously produce three sets of children: the first set in 1905-6; the second in March 1908; the third in August and October 1909. A doctor was present only in 1909.

7 Wright's explanation for her collapse is that she thought he might have been her husband. But pencilled in the transcript near this remark is the word "Dogsberry."

8 Although all four men denied they were under the influence of alcohol, there can be little doubt that it factored into the situation in some way. The quotation comes from the testimony of Constable Boyd in the second trial (for the murder of Ellen's baby).

9 And again the child died.

10 October 16, 1909, emphasis original.

11 Details of the McManus case taken from RG 4, B 20, vol. 15, pp 5613-6168, NA; King's Bench judges' correspondence 1830-39, TL 19, S1, SS 777, ANQ, Montreal.

12 To Lieut.-Col. Yorke, Sept. 22, 1830, ibid. at 5613.

13 The restrictions are extremely strange. Other pardons banned returning to Lower Canada. Some prohibited all British North America or British territory in its entirety. And why Vermont should be excluded but not New York must be left as a matter of conjecture.

14 This vignette is based on RG 5, B 3, vol. 10, pp. 1341-9; RG 1 E 3, vol. 86, pp. 14-27, 102, 223-4; Inspectors' Minutes, RG 73, vol. 347, NA.

15 (Toronto: McClelland & Stewart 1996). This vignette is based on Atwood's book and RG 73, vols. 347, 365, 417; RG 13, D-1, vol. 1050, NA.

16 RG 5, A 1, pp. 98343-93.

17 Our research was exhaustive in both the National Archives and the Archives of Ontario.

18 B.C. resident Florence Lassandro was hanged in Alberta though.

19 Emphasis in the original.

20 Emphasis in the original.

ENDNOTES TO CHAPTER NINE

1 Letter from Mrs J.C. Ellis to Mamie Rosser, Sept. 1, 1915, Washington, Indiana, Hawkes Capital Case file, RG 13, vols. 1479 (1.11, 1.2), 1480 (2.33, 4.1, 4.2, 5.1, 5.2), vol. 2699 (6.1, 6.2), file 560A/CC33, Hawkes capital case file. Throughout the file, Jennie's surname is spelled variously: Hawkes (the name on many official documents), or Hawks.

2 Mamie Rosser to the Bishop of Alberta, Nov. 18, 1915, Hawkes CC.

3 Mrs. Margaret Baye to same, Nov. 17, 1915, ibid.

4 Evidence of Henry Stoley, Hawkes transcript, Hawkes CC. The land was described as 'open land and brush with some breaking on it.' Unless otherwise identified the following information is from the transcript of Jennie Hawkes' trial.

5 It's easy to read the medical evidence and deplore the long delay in

treatment through eyes accustomed to emergency response teams. Given the fact that the hospital was only in its third year at that site, that it was really a converted house, Robertson and Dixon probably did a good job for the times.

6   See John A. Yogis, *Canadian Law Dictionary* (Woodbury, N.Y.: Barrows 1983), p. 59 and *C.T. Gogstad & Co. v. The S.S. "Camosun"'* (1941), 56 B.C.R. 156 at 157 (Admiralty).

7   For a short biography of Ives see the description of the Ives papers, Legal Archives of Aberta, Archives Network of Alberta.

8   Ives' charge to the jury; Judgments in the Court of Appeal, Hawkes file.

9   W. 229, paras. 1-3.

10 Ed. J.W. Cecil Turner, 136.

11 Ibid., n. 1.

12 *Pleas of the Crown*, I: 260.

13 *Lowther* v. *R.* (1957) 26 C.R. 150.

14 3 Nov. 1915.

15 21, 23 Oct. 1915.

16 *The Fernie Free Press*, Sept. 17, 22 Oct. 1915.

17 Hawkes file.

18 To the acting solicitor general.

19 Ibid.

ENDNOTES TO CHAPTER TEN

1   *Economy of Writings*, vol. 2 as found in Angela Partington, ed., *The Concise Oxford Dictionary of Quotations* (Oxford/New York: Oxford University Press 1993).

2   The story of Annie Rubletz is reconstructed from her capital case file, RG 13, vol. 1190, CC 522, NA.

3   *Regina Leader-Post*, Sept. 25, 1940.

4   Quotation taken from press clippings in ibid.

5   Phillip B. Scott, "Jury Nullification: An Historical Perspective on a Modern Debate," *West Virginia L.R.*, (1988-9), 389 at 394-408.

6   6 St. Tr. 999.

7   Gary J. Simson, "Jury Nullification in the American System: A Skeptical View," *Texas L.R.*, 54 (1975-6), 488 AT 491-4; Green, *Verdict According to Conscience*, 249; Scott, "Historical Perspective," 407-8.

8   21 St. Tr. 847 at 1039-40 (emphasis original).

9   See e.g. *Joshua v. R* (1955) AC 121 at 130 (JCPC, Lord Oaksey).

10 52 O.R. (2d) 353 at 432-5; *Morgentaler* v. *R.* (1988), 37 C.C.C. (3d) 449 (S.C.C.).

11 See Scott, "Historical Perspective," 409-16; Clay S. Conrad, "Scapegoating the Jury," *Cornell Journal of Law and Public Policy*, 7 (1997-8), 7 at 13; *U.S. v Battise* (1835) 24 F. Cas. 1042; *Sparf & Hansen v. U.S.*, (1895) 156 U.S. 51; *U.S. v Dougherty*, (1972) 473 F. 2d 1113 (D.C.); and the Conclusion.

12 Green, *Verdict According to Conscience*, 32, ch. 8; Michael Lobban, "From Seditious Libel to Unlawful Assembly: Peterloo and the Changing Face of Political Crime c. 1770-1820," *Oxford Journal of Legal Studies*, 10 (1990), 307 at 310-22; 30 Geo. III, c. 60.

13 See particularly Hall, *Theft, Law and Society*, 118-30.

14 See Conrad, "Scapegoating the Jury," *passim* but particularly 21-9.

15 For the years 1792-1811 see R.G. 4, B 16, vol. 11 ("Records of Criminal Offences in the Courts of King's Bench, 1765-1827"); RG 4, B20 ("Pardons, 1766-1858"), vols. 1 and 2, NA; "Court of King's Bench Termbooks" for Upper Canada, Archives of Ontario (e.g. cases of Christopher and Sarah Van Licklin-1799, dwelling house); *Montreal* and *Quebec Gazettes*.

16 *Montreal Gazette*, Sept. 14, 1795, Sept. 12, 1796; draft pardon, Oct. 24, 1794, R.G. 4, B 20, vol. 1, pp. 406-9. See also the pickpocketing case of Joseph Faries, ibid., 334-6. A search was made for the cases in the Archives nationales du Québec, TL 19, S1, S11/00001, "King's Bench Minutes/Proceedings," but the registers and records of that court were virtually destroyed by a 1844 fire in the Montreal court house.

17 F. Murray Greenwood, "The Chartrand Murder Trial: Rebellion and Repression in Lower Canada, 1837-1839," *Criminal Justice History: An International Annual*, 5 (1984), 129 at 135-46.

18 Canada, *Debates*, House of Commons, 1877, vol. 3, 318-9 (27 Feb. 1877).

19 The principal sources used are R. W. Malcolmson, "Infanticide in the Eighteenth Century" in J.S. Cockburn, ed., *Crime in England 1550-1800* (London: Methuen 1977); Backhouse, "Nineteenth Century Infanticide in Canada," 456, 461-4, 475-8; P.C. Hoffer and N.E.H. Hull, *Murdering Mothers: Infanticide in England and New*

England 1558-1803 (New York: New York University Press 1984); Lionel Rose, *Massacre of the Innocents: Infanticide in Great Britain, 1830-1939* (London: Routledge & Kegan Paul 1986); Osborne, "The Crime of Infanticide."

20 Canada, *Debates*, House of Commons, 1948, vol. 5, 5184-5 (14 June 1948).

21 SC 1948, c. 39, s. 7. The new code, enacted by SC 1953-4, c. 51, came into force, April 1, 1955.

22 S. 2(27).

23 See the Conclusion.

24 S. 204.

25 Letter dated October 7, 1940.

26 The reply to this letter by the Department of Justice was returned as "unclaimed and unknown."

27 A different person from "Another Mother."

28 R. Charlton, Registrar, Court of Appeal Saskatchew to Dep. Minister of Justice, Nov. 22, 1942.

29 *Montreal Standard*, Feb. 22, 1941.

30 Details for this portion of the chapter are from the Mary Paulette capital case file, RG 13, vol. 1699, CC 728, part 1.

31 She had that right under s. 44 of the Northwest Territories act: Parker to General Young, Commissioner of the Northwest Territories, Sept. 24, 1941.

32 Hagel to Deputy Minister of Justice, Sept. 22, 1941.

33 Op. cit., Sept. 24, 1951.

34 Sept. 29, 1951.

35 Jan. 15, 1954.

36 To the Deputy Minister of Justice, Sept. 29, 1951, R.G. 13, C 1, vol. 1699, file CC 728.

37 S. 570.

38 *R. v. Morgentaler et al.* (1984), 14 C.C.C. 258 at 274-5 (O.H.C.J.). Abortion, originally capital, carried a sentence of imprisonment for up to life.

39 Ibid.

40 *R. v. Morgentaler et al.* (1985), 52 O.R. (2d) 353 at 432-6.

41 Ibid.

42 *Morgantaler v. R.* (1988), 37 C.C.C. (3d) 449 (S.C.C.).

43 At 481-3 (Lamer J. concurred).

44 *Joshua* v. *The Queen* (1955) AC 121. See above for the *Dean of St. Asaph*.

45 At 522-3 (Estey J. concurred). Beetz also cited McIntyre J. on the principle: *R* v. *Mezzo* (1986), 1 S.C.R. 802 at 836. For McIntyre J., with whom La Forest J. concurred, and Wilson J. see pp. 543, 565.

46 For a similar conclusion see Geroge N. Carter, "The Latimer Trial: The Case for Jury Nullification," *Law Times*, December 21, 1997, 5.

ENDNOTES TO THE CONCLUSION

1 See particularly Etta Anderson, "The 'Chivalrous' Treatment of the Female Offender in the Arms of the Criminal Justice System: A Review of the Literature," *Social Problems*, 23 (1976) 350 (it's a myth). See also n. 53 below and Strange, "Wounded Womanhood," 181 nn. 10, 11, 12.

2 Ibid.; "Lottery of Death"; "Political Culture and the Death Penalty in New South Wales and Ontario, 1890-1920."

3 See Osborne, "Crime of Infanticide," and the authorities therein cited. How significant the minority is, even today, remains unclear. See story on p. A12 in the *Globe and Mail*, June 29, 1999.

4 Malcolmson, "Infanticide in the Eighteenth Century"; Backhouse, "Infanticide in Nineteenth-century Canada."

5 Hilary Allen, "Rendering Them Harmless: The Professional Portrayal of Women Charged with Serious Violent Crimes," in Pat Carlen and Anne Worrall, eds., *Gender, Crime and Justice* (Philadelphia: Open University Press 1987), 81.

6 Report, 372-3.

7 Ss. 138(2), 143, 144, 145(1)(b).

8 "Wounded Womanhood," 197.

9 Ibid., 164. For a British example (1886) see Knelman, *Twisting in the Wind*, 234-7.

10 *Fragile Lives*, 188-90.

11 Ibid., 189.

12 *Twisting in the Wind*, 261-2.

13 *Fragile Lives*, 189.

14 "Reasonableness, Gender Difference and Self-Defence Law," *Manitoba Law Journal*, 24 (1997), 549.

15 See ch. 7, text at nn. 47-9 and references therein.

16 George N. Carter, "The Latimer Trial: The Case for Jury Nullification," *Law Times*, Dec. 21, 1997, 4-5.

17 Described and quoted in ibid., 4.

18 Kevorkian has been present at more than 130 assisted deaths (as of late March 1999). He has been tried five times, with three acquittals, a mistrial and finally, a conviction: *Globe and Mail*, March 24, 27, 1999. The conviction was for second degree murder (the others for assisting suicide) and the doctor was sentenced to 10-25 years in prison: ibid., April 14, 1999.

19 See Carter, "The Latimer Trial," 4-5. There may also be a handful of others. See e.g. Grant Huscroft, "The Right [n.b.] to Seek and Return Perverse Verdicts," *Criminal Reports*, 3rd Series, vol. 62, 1988, 123-6. Carter and Huscroft repay reading.

20 *Guardian Weekly*, March 7, 1999 (story taken from the *Washington Post*). We thank George Tuttle for this reference.

21 Ibid.

22 *Globe and Mail*, March 27, 1999.

23 See e.g. his "Race-based Jury Nullification: Case-in-Chief," *The John Marshall L.R.*, 30 (1997), 911.

24 The Law Reform Commission of Canada, *Studies on the Jury* (n.p.p.: n.p. 1979), 17, 66, 138 (polling done by Anthony N. Doob).

25 *Guardian Weekly*, March 7, 1999.

26 Law Reform Commission of Canada, *The Jury in Criminal Trials* (Ottawa: Minister of Supply and Services Canada 1980), 8-11. The Commission avoided the question whether the jury should have a right to nullify.

27 Quoted in Huscroft, "Perverse Verdicts," 125.

28 For Britain see E.P. Thompson, "Subduing the Jury," *The London Review of Books*, Dec. 4, 1986. We thank Barry Wright for this reference. Highlight cases in Canada are the Winnipeg General Strike Trials, 1919-1920 and the trial of the Toronto Communist leaders, 1931-2.

29 In April 1838 a patriot raider into Upper Canada, Edward Theller, was found guilty of high treason in Toronto. Theller, born in Ireland, had emigrated to the United States at the age of nine and had become an American citizen. Chief Justice John Beverley Robinson took pains to instruct the jury that however severe it might seem, anyone born in the British Dominions owed allegiance to the Crown

for life, such being unaffected by any acquisition of new citizenship. This doctrine of perpetual allegiance, although undoubtedly the law (until 1870), had been viewed by many as archaic as early as the first half of the eighteenth century [*Aeneas Macdonald* case (1747), 18 St. Tr. 857]. In *Theller* the jury found the accused guilty but added a disapproving note: "on the ground that his birth makes him a subject." Robinson interpreted this to be a recommendation for mercy and convinced Lieutenant Governor Arthur and the executive council to commute Theller's sentence of death partly on this ground: Robinson to Arthur, April 11, 1838, Q Series, vol. 404, NA; proceedings of the Council, April 23, 1838, enclosed with Arthur's dispatch to Colonial Secretary Glenelg, April 25, 1838, ibid.

30 See in general, Chandler, *Capital Punishment in Canada*, ch. 1, 2. For deterrence, see Ezzat Abdel Fattah, *A Study of the Deterrent Effect of Capital Punishment with Special Reference to the Canadian Situation* (Ottawa: Information Canada 1972).

31 For Riel's controversial trial and aftermath see George F.G. Stanley, *Louis Riel* (Toronto: Ryerson Press 1963), ch. 16-9; L.H. Thomas, 'A Judicial Murder - The Trial of Louis Riel,' in Howard Palmer, ed., *The Settlement of the West* (Calgary: Comprint Publishing 1977), 37; *Louis Riel: Justice Must be Done* (Winnipeg: Manitoba Métis Federation Press 1979); Thomas Flanagan, *Riel and the Rebellion Reconsidered* (Saskatoon: Western Producer Prairie Books 1983). For the trial report and a useful introduction see Desmond Morton, ed., *The Queen v. Louis Riel* (Toronto: University of Toronto Press 1974).

32 *R. v. Hadfield* (1800) 27 St. Tr. 1281.

33 Riel and his counsel were of course fighting very strong political forces arrayed against them. But if his lawyers had given emphasis to *Hadfield* the result might have been different.

34 See Chapter 5.

35 *Vancouver Sun*, July 31, 1998.

36 Ibid., April 1, 1998; *Globe and Mail*, March 16, 2000.

37 See e.g. reference in n. 41 below and Fred Kaufman [sole Ontario commissioner on the conviction of Guy Paul Morin (1998)], "The Anatomy of a Murder," *Bishop's University Alumni Newsletter*, April 1999.

38 *Globe and Mail*, Nov. 5, 1998. See also the editorial in the *Vancouver Sun*, June 29, 1998 (re Ontario case of Peter Frumusa

who was released on the grounds of innocence after spending eight years in prison for first degree murder).

39 *Vancouver Sun*, Jan. 4, 1999.

40 Sigrid Macdonald, "David Milgaard," www.philsmith.com/ JusticeDenied/html/features/david-milgaard.html.

41 "Prosecutions out of control," editorial page, *Globe and Mail*, March 19, 1999.

42 *Vancouver Sun*, Feb. 18, 2000.

43 *Globe and Mail*, Feb. 1, 2000.

44 Ibid., *Vancouver Sun*, Feb. 18, 2000.

45 *Reflections on Hanging*, 112-3.

46 Macdonald, "David Milgaard."

47 Greenwood, "The General Court Martial of 1838-39 in Lower Canada," 263-5; Boissery, *A Deep Sense of Wrong*, ch. 7. One major object of the executions was to terrify men of the Canadien middle class, to whom the English governing elite from the 1790s on had tended to attribute almost magical influence over the demographically crucial farmers. Minor participant at Chateauguay, twenty-two year old notarial student (articling solicitor) Joseph Duquette was hanged because Colborne found out he managed a tavern and must have been "an influential man among the rural population." Wheelwright Toussaint Rochon was described by the Deputy Judge Advocates as a "conspicuously guilty" leader at Beauharnois but was spared the rope by the governor because he was perceived as "a habitan [sic] of no influence." One man of subordinate rank was executed for being a bailiff and hence part of a "class of men [who] command a peculiar influence among the lower order of Canadian peasantry." There are many more such examples in Canadian and British history.

48 Based on the ICF, nos. 314, 383, 568, 569, 604, 631, 830, 884, 989, 1173, 1190, 1244, 1381.

49 Ibid., nos. 276, 313, 1101, 1357, 1365, 1384. Strange ("Lottery of Death"), bases the reintroduction of female executions from 1923 partly on the waning of feminism in the 1920s and the achievement of greater equality for women with the granting of the right to vote.

50 See e.g. S.M. Lipset, 'National Values: Canada and the United States,' in J.W. Berry & G.J.S. Wilde, eds., *Social Psychology: The Canadian Context* (Toronto: McClelland & Stewart 1972), 13; Edgar Z.

Friedenburg, *Deference to Authority: The Case of Canada* (White Plains, N.Y.: M.E. Sharpe 1980).

51 See Jean-Marie Fecteau, F. Murray Greenwood and Jean-Pierre Wallot, "Sir James Craig's 'Reign of Terror' and Its Impact on Emergency Powers in Lower Canada, 1810-13," in Greenwood and Wright, *Canadian State Trials*, I: 323 at 331-6.

52 *Globe and Mail*, Feb. 26, 27, March 1,2, 1999.

53 Elizabeth Rapaport, "The Death Penalty and Gender Discrimination," *Law and Society Review*, 25 (1991), 367, *passim.* but particularly at 374-82. Rapaport argues convincingly that the structure of the state capital statutes and the violent crimes women usually commit (domestic, assisting a man etc.), account much more than chivalry for the gross under-representation of convicted women murderers on death row — .1% compared with 2%.

54 *Vancouver Sun*, Jan. 29, Feb. 3, 4, 5, 1998.

55 It is true that legal reforms, such as the likely restriction of jail informants' testimony (editorial, *Globe and Mail*, Jan. 5, 1999) and the use of DNA would probably reduce the number of innocents executed if capital punishment were reintroduced. But previous reforms (rights to full defence by counsel, appeal and to testify) and forensic breakthroughs in ballistics and fingerprinting (c. 1880-1910) failed to eliminate the problem or even reduce it to a rarity. Many murder cases can't be solved by DNA testing and this number will grow as perpetrators adjust, as they did with finger-printing and ballistics.

Selected Bibliography

MANUSCRIPT SOURCES
Archives nationales du Québec, Montreal [ANQM]
King's Bench Judges' Correspondence 1830-39
King's Bench Minutes/Proceedings
Register of the Court of Quarter Sessions
Archives of British Columbia
GR 112: Pre-Emption Records
Archives of Ontario [AO]
Assize Minutebooks, Criminal, 1832-37
Court of King's Bench Termbooks for Upper Canada
Supreme Court of Ontario Judges Benchbooks
National Archives of Canada [NA]
MG 11: Colonial Office Papers
5: North America
42: Canada
194: Newfoundland
Q Series
RG 1: Executive Council: Quebec, Lower Canada, Upper Canada, Canada, 1764-1867
E 3: Upper Canada. Submissions to the Executive Council
RG 4: Provincial and Civil Secretaries' offices, Lower Canada
B 16: Records of Criminal Offences in the Courts of King's Bench, 1765-1827
B 20: Applications for Pardons and Clemency, 1766-1858
RG 5: Provincial and Civil Secretaries Offices: Upper Canada and Canada West, 1791-1867
A 1: Secretaries' Correspondence, Upper Canada, Sundries
B 3: Petitions and Addresses
RG 7: Canada, Governor General's office
G: 15C: Civil Secretary's Letter Books
RG 13: Department of Justice

B: Legal Branch
1: Capital Case Files [CCF] — over 250 items examined (trial transcripts, Appeal and judges' reports, correspondence, newspaper clippings etc.)
RG 73: Corrections Branch, Inspectors' Minutes
Public Archives of Newfoundland [PANL]
Colonial Secretary's Letterbook
Proceedings of the Court of Oyer and Terminer
Public Archives of Nova Scotia [PANS]
Supreme Court, Easter Term Rolls
MG 9: Scrapbooks
RG 1: Bound volumes of Nova Scotia records, 1624-1867
RG 5: series A, expenses
Public Record Office, Kew, U.K. [PRO]
Colonial Office Papers
42: Canada. Original Correspondence
War Office Papers
71: Proceedings of General Courts Martial
81: Judge Advocates General Letterbooks
University of British Columbia
Special Collections
Vancouver Council of Women Minutes
Vancouver City Archives
Additional Manuscripts: University Women's Club Minutes

CONTEMPORARY PRINTED SOURCES

Beaudry, Father H. *Précis historique de l'execution de Jean-Baptiste Desforges et de Marie-Anne Crispin.* Montreal: Louis Perrault c. 1858.
Blackstone, Sir William. *Commentaries on the Laws of England* [1765-70], ed. George Sharswood. Philadelphia: J.B. Lippincott 1859.
Borthwick, J. Douglas. *A History of the Montreal Prison from A.D. 1784 to A.D. 1886.* Montreal: A Periard 1886.
Canada. House of Commons. Debates.
Canada. Senate. Debates.
East, Edward Hyde. *Pleas of the Crown.* London: A Strahan 1803.
Fairbanks, C.R. & A.W. Cochran. Report of the Trial of Edward Jordan and Margaret his wife for Piracy & Murder at Halifax on the 15th

Day of November 1809, together with Edward Jordan's Dying Confession: To Which is Added the Trial of John Kelly for Piracy and Murder on the 8th Day of December, 1809. Halifax: James Bagnall at the Novator Office 1810.

Gaspé, Philippe-Joseph Aubert de. *Les Anciens Canadiens.* [1863]. Quebec: Librairie Beauchemin 1899.

Great Britain. Privy Council. Judicial Committee. In the Matter of the Boundary between the Dominion of Canada and the Colony of Newfoundland on the Labrador Peninsula. London: His Majesty's Stationery Office 1927.

Hale, Sir Mathew. *Historia Placitorum Coronae — The History of the Pleas of the Crown* [c. 1670], ed. S. Emlyn. London: E. & R. Nutt & R. Gosling 1736.

Hawkins, William. *A Treatise of the Pleas of the Crown.* [1716]. Reprint. London: Professional Books 1973.

Journal of the Commissioners for Trade and Plantations from January 1754 to December 1758. London: His Majesty's Stationery Office 1913.

Kyte, E.C., ed. *Old Toronto: A Selection of Excerpts from Landmarks of Toronto by John Ross Robertson.* Toronto: Macmillan 1954.

Lizars, Robina & Kathleen Macfarlane. *Humours of 37: Grave, Gay and Grim: Rebellion Times in the Canadas.* Toronto/Montreal: W. Briggs & C.W. Coates 1897.

Ontario. Newspaper Hansard. National Library of Canada microfilm.

Pedley, Rev. Charles. The History of Newfoundland from the Earliest Times to the Year 1860. London: Longman et al. 1863.

Report of the Public Archives of Canada.

Report of the Royal Commission on The Status of Women in Canada. Ottawa: Information Canada 1970.

Russell, William Oldnall. *A Treatise on Crimes and Indictable Misdemeanours.* 2nd ed. London: Joseph Butterworth & Son 1826.

Spragge, George W. ed., "A Letter from Government House, Toronto, December 1837," *Ontario History* 73 (1981).

Stephen, Sir James Fitzjames. *A History of the Criminal Law of England.* London: Macmillan & Co. 1883.

U.K. House of Commons, Parliamentary Debates.

U.K., House of Lords. Parliamentary Debates.

York Commercial Directory, Street Guide and Register, 1833/4. York, U.C.: Thomas Dalton 1834.

NEWSPAPERS

Calgary Herald
Chronicle & Gazette and the *Kingston Commercial Advertiser*
Daily Colonist
Fernie Free Press
Globe and Mail
Guardian Weekly
Hastings Chronicle (Belleville, U.C.)
Intelligencer (Belleville, U.C.)
Le Courier de Saint-Hyacinthe
Montreal Gazette
Montreal Herald
Montreal Standard
Montreal Weekly Gazette
Morning Albertan
Newfoundlander
Nova Scotia Royal Gazette
Nova Scotia Gazette
Novator (Halifax)
Public Ledger (St. John's)
Quebec Gazette
Regina Leader Post
Sarnia Observer
St. Catherine's Journal
Toronto Commercial Herald
Toronto Patriot
Vancouver Daily Province
Vancouver Sun

SECONDARY PRINTED SOURCES
1. BOOKS

Anderson, Frank. *A Dance with Death: Canadian Women on the Gallows 1754-1954.* Calgary: Fifth House 1996.

____. *Hanging in Canada: A Concise History of Capital Punishment.* Calgary: Frontier Publishing 1973.

Atwood, Margaret. *Alias Grace.* Toronto: McClelland & Stewart 1996.

Backhouse, Constance. *Petticoats and Prejudice: Women and Law in*

Nineteenth Century Canada. Toronto: The Osgoode Society/ University of Toronto Press 1991.

Black's Law Dictionary.

Boissery, Beverley. *A Deep Sense of Wrong: The Treason, Trials, and Transportation to New South Wales of Lower Canadian Rebels after the 1838 Rebellion.* Toronto: The Osgoode Society/Dundurn Press 1995; St. Leonard's, N.S.W.: Allen & Unwin 1996.

Boyd, Neil. *The Last Dance: Murder in Canada.* Scarborough, Ont.: Prentice-Hall c. 1988.

Cameron, Elspeth & Janice Dickin, eds. *Great Dames.* Toronto: University of Toronto Press 1997.

Carl, Cecil. *Tales of the British Columbia Provincial Police.* Sidney, B.C. Gray's 1971.

Carrigan, D. Owen. *Crime and Punishment in Canada: A History.* Toronto: McClelland & Stewart 1991.

Chandler, David. *Capital Punishment in Canada.* Toronto: Carleton Library/McClelland & Stewart 1976.

Cleveland, Arthur Rockman. *Women under the English Law from the Landing of the Saxons to the Present Time.* [1896]. Reprint. Littleton, Colo.: Fred B. Rothman & Co. 1987.

Cleverdon, Catherine. *The Woman Suffrage Movement in Canada.* 2nd ed. Toronto: University of Toronto Press 1974.

Cockburn, J.S., ed. *Crime in England 1550-1800.* London: Methuen 1977.

Dernley, Syd with David Newman. *The Hangman's Tale: Memoirs of a Public Executioner.* London: Pan Books 1989.

English, Christopher & Christopher Curran. *Silk Robes & Sou'westers: a Cautious Beginning, the Court of Civil Jurisdiction 1791.* npp. Newfoundland Law Reform Commission 1991.

Farge, Arlette (trans. Carol Shelton). *Fragile Lives: Violence, Power and Solidarity in Eighteenth-Century Paris.* Oxford/Cambridge: Polity Press/Blackwell Publishers 1993.

Fattah, Abdel. *A Study of the Deterrent Effect of Capital Punishment with Special Reference to the Canadian Situation.* Ottawa: Information Canada 1972.

Fecteau, Jean-Marie, F. Murray Greenwood & Jean-Pierre Wallot, "Sir James Craig's 'Reign of Terror' and Its Impact on Emergency Powers in Lower Canada, 1810-13," in Greenwood & Wright's *Canadian State Trials - I.*

Fingard, Judith. *The Dark Side of Life in Victorian Halifax.* Porter's Lake, N.S.: Pottersfield Press 1989.

Friedenburg, Edgar Z. *Deference to Authority: The Case of Canada.* White Plains, N.Y.: M.E. Sharpe 1980.

Gordon, Linda. *Heroes of their Own Times: The Politics and History of Family Violence, Boston 1880-1960.* New York: Viking 1988.

Green, Thomas Andrew. *Verdict According to Conscience: Perspectives on the English Criminal Trial Jury 1200-1800.* Chicago: University of Chicago Press 1985.

Greenwood, F. Murray. Legacies of Fear: *Law and Politics in Quebec in the Era of the French Revolution.* Toronto: The Osgoode Society/University of Toronto Press 1993.

___ & Barry Wright, eds. *Canadian State Trials: I- Law, Politics and Security Measures, 1608-1837.* Toronto: The Osgoode Society/ University of Toronto Press 1996.

Hall, Jerome. *Theft, Law and Society.* Indianapolis: Bobbs-Merrill 1952.

Handcock, W. Gordon. *Soe longe as there comes noe women: Origins of English Settlement in Newfoundland.* St. John's: Breakwater Books 1989.

Hartshorne, Albert. *Hanging in Chains.* London: T. Fisher Unwin 1891.

Hay, Douglas et al. *Albion's Fatal Tree: Crime and Society in Eighteenth Century England.* London: Allen Lane 1975.

Head, C. Grant. *Eighteenth Century Newfoundland: A Geographer's Perspective.* Toronto: Carleton Library/McClelland & Stewart 1976.

Hoffer, P.C. & N.E.H. Hull, *Murdering Mothers: Infanticide in England and New England 1558-1803.* New York: New York University Press 1984.

Hustack, Alan. *They Were Hanged.* Toronto: James Lorimer 1987.

Kerber, Linda K. *No Constitutional Right to be Ladies: Women and the Obligations of Citizenship.* New York: Hill & Wang 1998.

Kilbourn, William. *The Firebrand: William Lyon Mackenzie and the Rebellion in Upper Canada.* Toronto: Clarke, Irwin 1956.

Knelman, Judith. *Twisting in the Wind: The English Murderess and the English Press.* Toronto: University of Toronto Press 1998

Koestler, Arthur. *Reflections on Hanging.* London: Victor Gollancz 1956.

Law Reform Commission of Canada. *Studies on the Jury.* n.p.p.: n.p. 1979.

____. *The Jury in Criminal Trials.* Ottawa: Minister of Supply and Services Canada 1980.

Lounsbury, Ralph Greenlee. *The British Fishery of Newfoundland 1634-1763*. New Haven, Conn.: Yale University Press 1934.

Macgill, Elsie Gregory. *My Mother the Judge: A Biography of Judge Helen Gregory Macgill*. Toronto: Ryerson Press 1955.

Masur, Louis P. Rites of Execution: *Capital Punishment and the Transformation of American Culture, 1776-1865*. Oxford: Oxford University Press 1989.

Mathews, Keith. *Lectures on the History of Newfoundland 1500-1830*. St. John's: Breakwater Books 1988.

O'Neill, Paul. *The Story of St. John's Newfoundland*. Erin, Ont.: Press Porcepic 1976.

Paget, R.T. & S.S. Silvermann. *Hanged — and Innocent?* London: Victor Gollancz 1953.

Pleck, Elizabeth. *Tyranny: The Making of Social Policy against Family Violence from Colonial Times to the Present*. New York/Oxford: Oxford University Press 1987.

Strange, Carolyn. *Qualities of Mercy: Justice, Punishment and Discretion*. Vancouver: UBC Press c. 1996.

Radzinowicz, Leon. *A History of English Criminal Law and its Administration from 1750*. London: Stevens & Sons 1948.

Rose, Lionel. *Massacre of the Innocents: Infanticide in Great Britain, 1830-1939*. London: Routledge & Kegan Paul 1986.

Taylor, A.J.P. *English History 1914-1945*. Oxford: Clarendon Press 1965.

Turner, J.W. Cecil, ed. *Kenny's Outline of Criminal Law*. 16th ed. Cambridge: University Press 1952.

Walker, Lenore. *The Battered Woman*. New York: Harper & Row 1979.

____. *The Battered Woman Syndrome*. New York: Springer Publishing Co., 1984.

Williams, David Ricardo. *Just Lawyers: Seven Portraits*. Toronto: The Osgoode Society 1995.

Yogis, John A. *Canadian Law Dictionary*. Woodbury, N.Y.: Barrows 1983.

2. ARTICLES

Allen, Hilary. "Rendering Them Harmless: The Professional Portrayal of Women Charged with Serious Violent Crimes," in Pat Carlen and Anne Worrall, eds., *Gender, Crime and Justice*. Philadelphia: Open University Press 1987.

Anderson, Etta. "The 'Chivalrous' Treatment of the Female Offender in the Arms of the Criminal Justice System: A Review of the Literature," *Social Problems* 23 (1976).

Avio, Kenneth. "The Quality of Mercy: Exercise of the Royal Prerogative in Canada," *Canadian Public Policy* 13 (1987).

Backhouse, Constance. "Desperate women and Compassionate Courts: Infanticide in 19th Century Canada," *University of Toronto Law Journal* 34 (1984).

Bannister, Jerry. "Surgeons and Criminal Justice in Eighteenth Century Newfoundland," in Greg T. Smith, Allyson N. May & Simon Devereaux, eds. *Criminal Justice in the Old World and the New: Essays in Honour of J.M. Beattie.* Toronto: Centre of Criminology 1998.

Briggs, S.C. "Treason and the Trial of William Joyce," *University of Toronto Law Journal* 7 (1947).

Beattie, John M. "The Royal Pardon and Criminal Procedure in Early Modern England," *Historical Papers* 9 (1987).

Brockman, Joan. "Exclusionary Tactics: Women and Visible Minorities in the Legal Profession in British Columbia," in Hamar Foster & John McLaren, eds. *Essays in the History of Canadian Law: VI - British Columbia and the Yukon.* Toronto: The Osgoode Society/University of Toronto Press 1995.

Butler, Paul D. "Race-based Jury Nullification: Case-in-Chief," *The John Marshall Law Review* 30 (1997).

Campbell, Ruth. "Sentence of Death by Burning for Women," *The Journal of Legal History* 5 (1984).

Carter, George N. "The Latimer Trial: The Case for Jury Nullifcation," *Law Times,* Dec. 21, 1997.

Chapman, Terry L. "'Till Death do us Part': Wife Beating in Alberta, 1905-1920," *Alberta History* 36 (1988).

Conrad, Clay S. "Scapegoating the Jury," *Cornell Journal of Law and Public Policy* 7 (1997-8).

Dictionary of Canadian Biography [DCB]. Toronto: University of Toronto Press 1966-. Several volumes; several articles.

Dubinsky, Karen and Franca Iacovetta. "Murder, Womanly Virtue, and Motherhood: The Case of Angelina Napolitano, 1911-1922," *Canadian Historical Review* 72 (1991).

Gavigan, A.V. "Petit Treason in Eighteenth Century England: Women's

Inequality Before the Law," *Canadian Journal of Women and the Law* 3 (1989-90).

Greenwood, F. Murray. "The Chartrand Murder Trial: Rebellion and Repression in Lower Canada, 1837-1839," *Criminal Justice History: An International Annual* 5 (1984).

___. "The General Court Martial of 1838-39 in Lower Canada: an Abuse of Justice," in W. Wesley Pue and Barry Wright, eds., *Canadian Perspectives on Law and Society: Issues in Legal History*. Ottawa: Carleton University Press 1988.

Harvey, Kathryn. "To Love, Honour and Obey: Wife-battering in Working-Class Montreal, 1869-79," *Urban History Review* 19 (1990).

Hay, Douglas."Property, Authority and the Criminal Law," in Douglas Hay et al., *Albion's Fatal Tree: Crime and Society in Eighteenth Century England*. London: Allen Lane 1975.

Huscroft, Grant. "The Right to Seek and Return Perverse Verdicts," *Criminal Reports* 62 (1988).

Kaufman, Fred. "The Anatomy of a Murder," *Bishop's University Alumni Newsletter*, April 1999.

Kazan, Patricia. "Reasonableness, Gender Difference, and Self-Defence Law," *Manitoba Law Journal* 24 (1997).

Lacourcière, Luc. "Le destin postume de la Corriveau," *Les Cahiers des Dix* 34 (1969).

____. "Le triple destin de Marie-Josephte Corriveau (1733-1763)," *Les Cahiers des Dix* 33 (1968).

Laquer, Thomas. "Crowds, Carnival and the State in English Executions, 1604-1868," in A.L. Beier et al. *The First Modern Society: Essays in English History in Honor of Lawrence Stone*. Cambridge: Cambridge University Press 1989.

Lipset, S.M., "National Values: Canada and the United States," in J.W. Berry & G.J.S. Wilde, eds. *Social Psychology: The Canadian Context*. Toronto: McClelland & Stewart 1972.

Lobban, Michael, "From Seditious Libel to Unlawful Assembly: Peterloo and the Changing Face of Political Crime c. 1770-1820," *Oxford Journal of Legal Studies* 10 (1990).

Loo, Tina. "Savage Mercy: Native Culture and the Modification of Capital Punishment in Nineteenth-Century British Columbia," in Carolyn Strange's *Qualities of Mercy*.

Martinson, Donna et al., "A Forum on Lavallee v. R.: Women and Self-

Defence," *University of British Columbia Law Review* 25 (1991).

McCarthy, M.J. "The Irish in Early Newfoundland," *Newfoundland Quarterly* 83 (1988).

Martin, Ged. "Sir Francis Bond Head: The Private Side of a Lieutenant-Governor," *Ontario History* 73 (1981).

Mitchell, Tom. "'Blood with the Taint of Cain': Immigrant Labouring Children, Manitoba Police and the Execution of Emily Hilda Blake," *Journal of Canadian Studies* 28 (1993-4).

Morrow, W.G. "Women on Juries." *Alberta Law Review* 12 (1979).

Oldham, James C. "On Pleading the Belly: A History of the Jury of Matrons," *Criminal Justice History: An International Journal* 6 (1985).

O'Neill, Paul. "Jezebels and the Just," *Newfoundland Quarterly* 12 (1980).

Osborn, Judith A. "The Crime of Infanticide: Throwing out the Baby with the Bathwater," *Canadian Journal of Family Law* 6 (1987).

Phillips, Jim. "Women, Crime and Criminal Justice in Early Halifax, 1750-1800," in Phillips, Tina Loo and Susan Lewthwaite, eds., *Essays in the History of Canadian Law: V - Crime and Criminal Justice*. Toronto: The Osgoode Society for Legal History 1994.

_____. "The Operation of the Royal Pardon in Nova Scotia," *University of Toronto* Law Journal 42 (1992).

_____. "Recent Publications in Canadian Legal History," *Canadian Historical Review* 78 (1997).

Pleck, Elizabeth. "Wife Beating in Nineteenth-Century America," *Victimology: An International Journal* 4 (1979).

Rapaport, Elizabeth. "The Death Penalty and Gender Discrimination," *Law and Society Review* 25 (1991).

Scott, Phillip B. "Jury Nullification in the American System: A Skeptical View," *Texas Law Review* 54 (1975-6).

Shaffer, Martha, "R v. Lavallee: a Review Essay," *Ottawa Law Review* 22 (1990).

Strange, Carolyn. "The Lottery of Death: Capital Punishment, 1867-1976," *Manitoba Law Journal* 23 (1996).

_____. "Wounded Womanhood and Dead Men: Chivalry and the Trials of Clara Ford and Carrie Davis," in Franca Iacovetta and Mariana Valverde, eds. *Gender Conflicts: New Essays in Women's History*. Toronto: University of Toronto Press 1992.

____. "Discretionary Justice: Political Culture and the Death Penalty in New South Wales and Ontario, 1890-1920," in her *Qualities of Mercy*.

Stuesser, Lee. "The 'Defence' of 'Battered Woman Syndrome' in Canada," *Manitoba Law Journal* 19 (1990).

Swainger, Jonathan. "A Distant Edge of Authority: Capital Punishment and the Prerogative of Mercy in British Columbia, 1872-1880," in Hamar Foster & John McLaren, *Essays in the History of Canadian Law: VI - British Columbia and the Yukon*. Toronto: The Osgoode Society/University of Toronto Press 1995.

Thompson, E.P. "Subduing the Jury," *The London Review of Books*, 4 Dec. 1986.

Tomes, Nancy. "A 'Torrent of Abuse': Crimes of Violence between Working-class Men and Women in London, 1840-1875," *Journal of Social History* 11 (1977-8).

Van Herk, Aritha. "Driving Towards Death," in Elspeth Cameron & Janice Dickin, eds., *Great Dames*. Toronto: University of Toronto Press 1997.

Wharam, Alan. "Casement and Joyce," *Modern Law Review* 41 (1978).

Williams, Glanville L. "The Correlation of Allegiance and Protection," *Cambridge Law Journal* 10 (1948).

Wright, Barry. "'Harshness and Forbearance': The Politics of Pardons and the Upper Canadian Rebellion," in Carolyn Strange's *Qualities of Mercy*.

UNPUBLISHED MATERIAL, THESES ETC.

Gadoury, Lorraine and Antonio LeChasseur. eds. "Persons Sentenced to Death in Canada, 1867-1976: An Inventory of Case Files in the Records of the Department of Justice." Ottawa: National Archives of Canada 1992 [ICF].

Paterson, Janet. "The History of Newfoundland 1713-1763," M.A. thesis. University of London 1931.

Stairs, H. Gerald. "The Stairs of Halifax." Typescript held by Public Archives of Nova Scotia, 1962.

Stoddard, Edward. "Conflicting Images: the Murderess and the English Canadian Mind, 1870-1915," M.A. thesis. Dalhousie University 1991.

Index